Turkey and the Post-Pandemic World Order

Turkey and the Post-Pandemic World Order

Edited by
Ahmet Salih Ikiz

LEXINGTON BOOKS
Lanham • Boulder • New York • London

Published by Lexington Books
An imprint of The Rowman & Littlefield Publishing Group, Inc.
4501 Forbes Boulevard, Suite 200, Lanham, Maryland 20706
www.rowman.com

86-90 Paul Street, London EC2A 4NE, United Kingdom

British Library Cataloguing in Publication Information Available

Library of Congress Cataloging-in-Publication Data

Names: Salih Ikiz, Ahmet, 1968– editor.
Title: Turkey and the post-pandemic world order / edited by Ahmet Salih Ikiz.
Description: Lanham : Lexington Books, [2022] | Includes bibliographical references. | Summary: "This book explores the post-pandemic era with special emphasis on Turkey. It evaluates the current role of Turkey with respect to economic, security, and foreign policy perspectives"— Provided by publisher.
Identifiers: LCCN 2021045357 (print) | LCCN 2021045358 (ebook) | ISBN 9781793638502 (cloth) | ISBN 9781793638519 (epub)
Subjects: LCSH: Turkey—Economic policy—21st century. | Turkey—Foreign relations—21st century. | COVID-19 (Disease)—Turkey—Economic aspects. | World politics—21st century.
Classification: LCC HC492 .T867 2022 (print) | LCC HC492 (ebook) | DDC 338.9561—dc23/eng/20211104
LC record available at https://lccn.loc.gov/2021045357
LC ebook record available at https://lccn.loc.gov/2021045358

This book is dedicated to the healthcare workers who have fought valiantly and those who passed away so that many others could live during the COVID-19 pandemic in Turkey.

Contents

Preface

There are extraordinary times that have created historical breaking points with certain impacts in the following decades. Those times are the future indicators of certain alterations in the globe. The Great Plague in Europe had radically changed countries. Giovanni Boccaccio in his famous *Decameron* gave enlightening new world by reconnoitering the role of religion in daily life, which is the early signs of renaissance. Today, during the pandemic, humanity isolated themselves not behind strong citadel walls but rather in their houses; but the amazing thing is people are surrounded by the ocean of knowledge via the global network of the internet. Meantime doubts are lingering that the vastness of information creates much more confusion and cacophony in daily life. Many of us are under isolation and living with the lower levels of necessities in Maslow hierarch of needs. Even though there are some optimistic scenarios for the post-pandemic period, some argue that we are at the edge of new world order with changing hegemonic powers as in the case of the Spanish flu where, in the following decades, US hegemon initiated. One cannot easily elucidate this process with simple short termism; we have an absolute diverse zeitgeist. Perchance, new winds of change in global context would be elicited. Humanity today has extreme communication and travel abilities compared to our ancestors; therefore, controlling pandemics would be far beyond our capabilities.

Land of Anatolia with Mesopotamia and Levant region nested many civilizations, even those empires which were the hegemons of their ages. Turkish Republic's reign has been less than an age in those lands *ex oriente lux*. In geostrategic terminology, Turkey is defined as a cross-country passage for different cultures or a bridge among continents. In recent years, it has been transforming on issues such as energy hub, security, and stability force for not only in his soils but also in neighbor countries. Besides new emerging hegemons in the Atlantic-Pacific axis, pandemic may be simultaneously laying new stepping stones for global order.

If there were a new world system with its own dynamics, Turkey would be one of the dominators of the new world. That is the main aim of the book with interdisciplinary studies and having a new possible new mindset from different perspectives both for Turkey and globe. Unquestionably, we are, I think, still in the beginning stage of the process, and there are many pessimistic and optimistic views for the future evolution of the pandemic in the globe. In addition, it is not an easy task to verdict for the new world system since we are still experiencing status at the verge of a new historical breakdown. In an epistemological context, the new information generation is based upon the lightening of former experiences. But in this new normal, we humanity are not certain about new formats and how to evolve them. For sure, Homo-Sapiens will standstill or even start to evolve as Homo-Deus as Hariri mentioned but we do not know what and how it will happen in long term since there is a possibility of new pandemic waves in the near future.

Turkey has not entirely disinterested its roots with imperial legacies with former Ottoman lands. In the last two decades, there has been complete political stability with the same ruling party, but it has had crises in its borders with the ongoing problems in the Middle East. From the Berlin conference where the West initiated the disintegration of the Ottoman Empire, both the Western world and Russia have had their own agendas and plans for deserted lands of the decadent empire. Today, after 2013, there is a new player in the globe with the Belt and Road initiative, which is China. Stability in Turkey meshed with the stability of its sphere of influence in the region. Its economic fragilities and other international factors will derive the layers of a new power block. Thus, the international political economy as with most other countries will affect Turkey, which is experiencing a harsh economic crisis as well.

This book contains chapters from academicians from both economics and international relations. Well-known Turkish economists shared their future expectations for both globe and Turkey. In addition, experts from international relations will discuss how the new world will shape Turkey.

EDITORIAL NOTE

I hereby confirm that Dr. Emre Alkin's paper on Capitalism solely depends upon the author's own academic foundations. Thus there was no reference to any academic source with his own will.

Introduction

COVID-19: The Last Wake-Up Call

Hasan Kazdağli

Dr. Paul Caulford was the chief of family medicine and community services director at Scarborough Hospital, Toronto. When the severe acute respiratory syndrome (SARS) epidemic devastated some cities in Canada, he was on the front lines. In December 2003, after the emergency had passed, he raised the matter concisely and concretely as if he had seen the novel coronavirus crisis we are currently suffering:

> SARS must change us, the way we treat our planet, and how we deliver health care, forever. Will we be ready when it returns? SARS brought one of the finest publicly-funded health systems in the world to its knees in a matter of weeks. . . . Without substantive changes to the way we manage the delivery of health care, both locally and on a worldwide scale, we risk the otherwise preventable destruction of millions of people, either by this Virus or the next. (Caulford 2003)

The SARS pandemic of 2002–2003, the first major emerging disease threat of the twenty-first century, was the first test of the new structures created nationally and worldwide to combat infectious diseases. After appearing in China in November 2002, SARS erupted as an international health threat in March 2003. The epidemics affected 8,098 people, caused 774 deaths, brought international travel to a halt in entire regions, and cost more than US$40 billion in gross expenditure and business losses to Asian countries alone (Lee, McKibbin, and Jong-Wha 2004).

Although the world had managed to control its spread, Dr. Caulford's troubling question remains. Are the lessons we learned from that epidemic instructive enough to keep us awake and alert? Have we changed forever? Unfortunately, what is happening in the current pandemic does not allow us to give an affirmative answer to these questions. Regrettably, people are notorious for predicting the future, and countries are not much better. Cognitive biases, emotional responses, and mental shortcuts lead to bad decisions and bad policies. With the onset of a pandemic, the scale of what's happening is hard to understand, and it's logical to ask whether the COVID-19 pandemic is the so-called black swan that society and business have been scared of. The answer is, undoubtedly, it is. However, it also could be the kind of challenge we now will encounter all the time—a new normal (Winston 2020).

Epidemics are remembered as horrible events in specific periods of history, and until recently, they were assumed to pose a risk only to geographically and economically distant communities. The novel coronavirus, which emerged in Wuhan, China, shattered this illusion in December 2019 and once again showed that the new pathogens are serial killers that affect everyone and every society equally.

In many ways, the current outbreak is very similar to its predecessors. Past experiences provide us that predictable or not disease outbreaks have always caught the authorities off guard, and the agencies often failed to respond quickly and decisively. Albert Camus portrays this trend in his well-known novel *The Plague*.

We were not too surprised as we observed a similar behavior pattern when the Chinese government initially hid information about the outbreak. US president Donald Trump did the same, downplaying the threat and comparing COVID-19 to seasonal flu. As one official in Camus' novel put it, the plague is nothing more than a "*special fever*" seen in humans.

Sadly, the plain truth is even though we live in the richest or most developed economies, we are vulnerable to new biological risks, particularly the diseases spread by nonhuman animals that result from natural evolution and are facilitated by social activities. The spread of a virus, bacteria, or parasitic organism from nonhuman mammal species is always a highly probable event.

With the outbreak of a highly contagious novel coronavirus, 2020 had been a tough year, leaving the wrecked world behind, still struggling to avoid the epidemic. The World Health Organization (WHO) declared the outbreak a pandemic in March, and it has spread to more than 200 countries, with dreadful public health and economic consequences. The governments' response to COVID-19 created a different world with lockdowns and social distance measures. The worldwide economy has almost come to a standstill, and the vibrant social life has disappeared. Most of the activities have shifted to the virtual world.

According to data compiled by Johns Hopkins University, more than 3 million people have died and at least 150 million infected of the novel coronavirus as of April 2021. It took only a few months for the novel coronavirus to spread to the far corners of the globe. The actual case and death counts are probably far higher than the confirmed tally due to widespread testing limitations and under-reporting.

The outbreak has dire economic and social consequences, both in the short and long term. World Economic Forum founder Klaus Schwab states that nothing since World War II has had such a profound global impact as COVID-19. The pandemic triggered a public health and economic crisis on a scale not seen for generations and worsened systemic problems such as inequality and great power stance (Schwab 2020). Although COVID-19 is a relatively mild pandemic by long-term historical standards, it ranks first in terms of damage.

In a recent paper, David Cutler and Lawrence Summers of Harvard University laid out shocking figures that the total cost of COVID-19 for the United States has reached US$16 trillion (Cutler and Summers 2020). It would be sufficient for comparison to state that it is around 75 percent of the United States' gross domestic product (GDP). These distinguished economists explain that almost half of the said loss comes from the cumulative value of GDP losses due to forgone production of goods and services at the face of the epidemic. The remaining losses are based on premature deaths and deterioration of physical and mental health. Their total cost is four times the recession after the 2008 financial crisis. If we apply the same loss coefficients to the rest of the world, the figure we would get could be exaggerated. However, even if we take half or even a third of the number we found according to this calculation, we encounter a vast cost.

Moreover, as António Guterres, the secretary-general of the United Nations (UN), puts it,

> This novel coronavirus pandemic has laid bare severe and systemic inequalities both within and between countries and communities. More broadly, it has underscored the world's fragilities—not just in the face of another health emergency, but in our faltering response to the climate crisis, lawlessness in cyberspace, and the risks of nuclear proliferation. People everywhere are losing trust in political establishments and institutions. (Guterres 2020)

Besides, COVID-19 is further accelerating technological movements that are already widely advancing. The most critical problem that will affect humanity here is that these big technology companies are in uncontrolled growth. The growing concentration of power and wealth at the hands of a few big tech giants will profoundly affect politics nationally and worldwide when the pandemic ends. These global digital firms derive their revenues from intangible sources like data, algorithms, and intellectual property instead of just physical labor or tangible assets such as goods and services. Worse, they have been taking advantage of weak digital governance to avoid paying taxes and social security contributions. The rising disparity between the winners and losers of the digital economy is manifested in the rapidly increasing inequality and middle-class erosion. Unfortunately, the ongoing pandemic contributes to large digital firms' growth in the short term, making the problems worse (Jonsson and Taylor 2020).

When we look at the human development aspect of the issue, we also face a dismal outlook. The United Nations Development Program (UNDP) Administrator, Achim Steiner, gives a critical warning:

> The World has seen many crises over the past 30 years, including the Global Financial Crisis of 2007-09. Each has hit human development hard, but overall, development gains accrued globally year-on-year. COVID-19—with its triple hit to health, education, and income—may change this trend. (UNDP 2020)

With school closures, the UNDP estimates of the "effective out-of-school rate"—the ratio of primary-school-age kids, adjusted to reflect those without internet access—reveal that 60 percent of children are not receiving an education, leading to large-scale levels not seen since the 1980s.

When discussing the pandemic and its effects, it is of great benefit to recall our most critical global challenges: population, resource use, and greenhouse gas emissions. The problems have been a cumulative result of releasing a significant amount of greenhouse gas emissions into the atmosphere since the 1770s, when the Industrial Revolution started.

We all do our businesses in the illusion that the planet we live in will never reach its carrying capacity limit. We operate as if there is unlimited arable land, endless forest, ocean, and atmosphere that can absorb the excess CO_2 we produce due to our consumption and production activities. However, as we push these limits, either knowingly or unknowingly, we run the risk of changing the Earth beyond recognition.

The emergence of viruses such as the one that causes COVID-19 is probably closely related to pushing nature's limits so much. People who changed ecosystems and encroached on natural boundaries have left themselves vulnerable over time. Therefore, they were exposed to constantly emerging microbes, viruses, and bacteria. The pressure created by population growth and economic development efforts underlies this trend. Thus, more opportunities and environments for humans and animals to encounter began to emerge. Advances in global trade and the worldwide expansion of tourism have created new ways to help spread diseases.

Nearly 8 billion people are excessively exploiting nature's resources in order to survive on a single planet. Consequently, when we see nature as something to be used only, we tend to overuse it. In the subsequent decade or two, the economic destruction triggered by climate change will likely be as awful as having a COVID-size pandemic every decade. If we continue to produce emissions at the current level, there will be no world left for future generations to live on at the end of the century.

Failures in planning and operating those plans ineffectively without governments and society's full participation extensively provide disastrous and unrepairable outcomes for us. History displays numerous events that infectious diseases and pandemics exerted substantial transformative changes in nature, social cohesion, and humankind's fate. Therefore, justifications such as negligence, abstention, ignorance, and incompetence against these risks and threats are not something we can afford because they may result in existential consequences for humanity.

All over history, there have been those who claim that they can see the future. The majority remained charlatans, and some were justified. Today, many experts from various specialities make data-driven predictions for what the future will look like. Experts repeatedly try to warn us and get our attention, and unfortunately, they are often ignored. Undoubtedly, we are right to ignore most of those who proclaim themselves prophets. However, as the new coronavirus epidemic has shown, failure to pay attention to the correct warnings about certain disasters will cost us a heavy price. People die if we fail to distinguish the prophet from the charlatan.

For the moment, the world's attention is focused on surviving the immediate health crisis, not on preventing the coming climate crisis or the next financial crisis. As we recover from the current situation, we can do more than just stimulate economic growth. We can focus on building a better and livable world instead of returning to the troubled world full of risks that we create. The coronavirus pandemic should not lead to myopic decisions' risk, focused on only visible, imminent problems captured by short termism. Due to the severe dangers it faces, our world no longer has the chance to repeat the mistakes of history.

This new coronavirus outbreak should be a wake-up call for us. Remembering Dr. Paul Caulford's bold question after the SARS epidemic, all political leaders, administrators, and nongovernmental organizations need to understand that our assumptions and approaches to how we work and live must change entirely in the face of significant risks, a severe threat to all humanity.

EMERGENCE AND SPREAD OF COVID-19

In March 2020, after coronavirus first emerged in Wuhan, China, the WHO declared the novel coronavirus pandemic. The outbreak spread to the farthest corners of the world in just a few months. On the other hand, new variants of the virus have alerted researchers and policymakers.

Accurate numbers of cases and deaths are said to be much higher than confirmed numbers, possibly due to widespread limitations in testing and governments' concealment of numbers. The *Financial Times* newspaper collected and analyzed data on the worldwide death rate, defined as extreme as above and beyond the historical average, and found that death numbers in some countries were more than 50 percent above average (*Financial Times* Latest Figures 2020).

The average number of coronavirus deaths in Europe surpassed Asia in early March. Since mid-April 2020, the focus has shifted to the United States, the country where the number of fatalities remains consistently high. Latin America became the epicenter of the pandemic in the summer of 2020, and nearly half of the deaths every day come from this region. But the emergence of the new wave in Europe since autumn and explosion in Indian case and death numbers in April 2021 means that COVID-19 remains a global epidemic.

The United States, with the highest number of confirmed cases and deaths worldwide, reached over 573,000 deaths and nearly 35 million cases in late April 2021. President Trump has repeatedly voiced belittling rhetoric about the virus and disputed the numbers. In turn, public health experts, including Anthony S. Fauci, director of the National Institute of Allergy and Infectious Diseases, stated the figures were correct and worrying. "Those are real numbers, real people and real deaths," Fauci replied during an appearance on *NBC News'* "*Meet the Press*" on January 3, 2021 (Todd 2021).

In terms of the number of cases, the United States is followed by India, Brazil, and Russia. In some European countries, infection cases have increased significantly during the winter. In Britain, for example, infections have increased despite targeted restrictions, and Prime Minister B. Johnson was forced to declare a third national lockdown on January 4 (Prime Minister's Office 2021).

As the new coronavirus pandemic has surged globally once again, cases have increased for the first time in some countries that avoided the worst in the first wave. Recent increases are primarily seen in some parts of Central and Eastern Europe. Highly praised for low case numbers over the summer, these countries are being hammered at the world's highest infection rates. Some countries in Latin America, the Middle East, and South Asia have seen the same. Significant worries are still raised as these setbacks may be temporary or, in some cases, just being lucky. The fact that some countries avoiding the first wave see large daily case numbers justifies these concerns. For example, the Czech Republic, where residents held a street party to bid farewell to coronavirus in June 2020, suffered one of the worst outbreaks in the world just a few months later (Meredith 2021).

There is consensus among experts that the most effective way to eradicate the virus is through *mass vaccination programs*. After the UK, the first country in Europe to introduce large-scale vaccination in December, several countries started vaccination programs. China and Russia had begun distributing their own vaccines globally before completing the testing standards that many governments were subject to. Having experienced several waves in a row, Israel got ahead of other countries. The United States has accelerated in vaccination after President Biden took office. It looks like the country will achieve at least 70 percent of the population, in vaccination, by the mid-summer of 2021.

By looking at the current pace and inequalities, it seems clear that there is still a long way to go for success in vaccination. Many poor countries have not yet been able to purchase a sufficient dose of vaccine. Experts warn that inequality in vaccine distribution can delay pandemic prevention and have lasting effects on global development (Schumaker 2020). The WHO director-general Dr. Tedros Adhanom Ghebreyesus expressed deep concern that the world is on the brink of a devastating moral failure in vaccines' fair distribution among all countries. He warns that the price of this failure will be paid with lives and lost livelihoods in the world's most impoverished countries (WHO 2021).

Because none of us will be safe from COVID-19 until everyone is vaccinated, we must admit that the only way to defeat the pandemic is to attack it globally. As long as there are countries or people infected with the virus, there will be new cases and even more frightening new variants. What's more, some of these may be more deadly and develop resistance to vaccines that are our only hope.

Invisible Killers: Infectious Diseases

Scientists and experts have been telling for years that there will be an epidemic like COVID-19 and point to the increase of zoonotic pathogens jumping from animals to humans to indicate the burdens people put on planet Earth.

Yuen Kwok-Yung, a sixty-three-year-old professor in infectious diseases at the University of Hong Kong, had been waiting for over a decade to emerge for a virus like this novel coronavirus. China created an animal surveillance database showing that 39 percent of horseshoe bats harbor the coronavirus associated with SARS. The Hong Kong professor wrote in 2007 in the journal *Clinical Microbiology Reviews* that the findings he obtained virtually describe the "time bomb" (Hotz and Khan 2020).

After Chinese officials posted the new coronavirus gene sequence to share with scientists around the world on January 12, he and others became increasingly confident about the source of the killer. Dr. Yuen was convinced that it was very similar to the known coronaviruses related to bat SARS, and therefore, it was one of them.

The Chinese authorities have tried to stir confusion about the virus' origin. With little proof, they have staged theories that the outbreak might have started with imports of tainted seafood, which international scientists and agencies rejected.

In Wuhan, a WHO team launched its investigation into the origins of the virus on January 14, 2021. The WHO team includes virus and other experts from the United States, Australia, Germany, Britain, Japan, the Netherlands, Russia, Vietnam, and Qatar. The WHO researchers began their investigations at the Wuhan Institute of Virology in the city where the outbreak first occurred. The institute is one of China's best virus research laboratories. Genetic information archive about bat coronaviruses was created in the laboratory after the 2003 SARS epidemic. According to the WHO statement on the investigation of the origins of the virus, there was no plan on the research team's agenda to assess whether the coronavirus was released accidentally in the Wuhan lab, as claimed by some American politicians such as President Donald Trump (McNeil and Wu 2021).

Milton Leitenberg, a senior research associate at the Center for International and Security Studies, the University of Maryland, an expert on biological weapons, proposes a theory suggesting a laboratory accident or leak. The lab leak could include a virus that was improperly destroyed or perhaps infected a lab worker and then passed on to others. Wuhan is a virus studies center in China with six facilities with BSL-3 laboratories for processing infectious agents. Published articles show that some of these labs are especially active in coronavirus studies. The most active is the Wuhan Institute of Virology, which has comprehensively studied bat coronaviruses very similar to Shi Zhengli's, who leads a research team, bat coronaviruses that initiated the pandemic. Dr. Shi said that when news of the outbreak first appeared, she checked her lab records to see if experimental materials were misused. She also explained that the novel coronavirus' genetic sequence did not match the viruses her team sampled from China's bat caves (Leitenberg 2020).

The editorial opinion published by *The Washington Post* suggested that the WHO researchers need to find out if there was a leak or a lab accident at the Wuhan Institute of Virology or another lab. For this, the Post notes, researchers must examine archived lab notes, experimental and data records, bat samples, viral strains, and all sequences in the institute collection to compare them with known genetic blueprints of the pandemic virus. And it states that this requires transparency and validation of data and sample sourcing (*The Washington Post* 2021).

Apart from these contentions, infectious diseases all have in common that they inflict severe suffering on people and cause far-reaching dissolution in all societies. Communicable diseases have a unique capacity for anxiety, fear, mass hysteria, and bursts of religiosity, especially in the past. They directly challenge social cohesion and solidarity and, therefore, a society's ability to manage collective crises.

Because every contagious disease is unique, there has been a constant struggle. While some microbes' main feature was transmission speed, the prominent degree of lethality in others was high. Some were bacterial, others viral or parasitic. Some microbes are transmitted by air, others by contaminated water or vectors such as fleas, mosquitoes, and lice (Quinlan 2020).

For understanding the development of societies, it is essential to look at the course of infectious diseases and economic crises, wars, revolutions, and demographic change. This requires considering the medical aspect of epidemics and the impact of outbreaks on individual men and women's lives, religion, art, the rise of modern medicine, and public health and intellectual history (F. M. Snowden 2020). For instance, in his poem "*Piers Plowman*," William Langland wrote, "*God is deaf nowadays and will not hear us. And for our guilt, he grinds good men to dust.*" Langland was one of the lucky few who survived the Black Death, but it is debatable how correct it is to use the adjective "lucky" for such a situation. Because when the Black Death disappeared, what remained was a devastated land and drove people mad with grief and confusion (Woodville 2015).

Where did this plague come from? Why did God allow this to happen? Will it come back again? These are all questions we are still asking today in one form or another.

As author Heather E. Quinlan points out in her new book *Plague, Pandemics and Viruses*, traditional historical research has not focused on diseases in part because it is too mysterious and partly not suitable for writing. However, bacteria or viruses appear destructively and make history (Quinlan 2020). "*I had no idea of the destructive potential of something that is not even considered alive*," Quinlan said. "*It's the closest thing we have to the undead on Earth. It destroys whole civilizations*" (Westhoven 2020).

In recorded history, the war between humans and microbes was a fight between reason and superstition. For centuries, human societies felt powerless in the face of a major epidemic that they could not understand. In desperation, they thought that the disaster that happened to them was because they angered God, and they turned to religious rituals to appease God by asking for forgiveness. Science eventually triumphed over such superstitious spiritual understanding, and research increased on the real cause of the disaster.

There have been many cases of infection epidemics throughout human history. These epidemics tend to follow a cyclical pattern since they often produce immunity in survivors, and the microbes need to wait for a new generation of hosts to infect. Alternatively, disease-causing microbes may migrate geographically to Western countries and immunologically vulnerable populations, producing a pandemic or global epidemic. In this sense, AIDS, a very deadly disease, should be seen as a new disease that adds to a long line of devastating infectious diseases. By the early twentieth century, plague, smallpox, influenza, and other infections wiped out a significant percentage of the world's population. By the second part of the century, many people in the West had come to believe that technological advancement had stopped the spread of these diseases and were replaced by second-generation diseases such as heart disease, diabetes, and cancer, called well-being diseases. However, infectious diseases remain a significant and growing threat. In this context, we can list third waves, emerging threats such as AIDS, as well as re-emerging threats such as plague, cholera, and tuberculosis (Epstein and Chen 2002).

Despite unprecedented progress in disease control, infectious diseases remain a major killer. By the end of the twentieth century, 13.3 of a total of 53.9 million deaths, or 25 percent of all deaths, were caused by infectious diseases. If we take Southeast Asia and Africa alone, we see that infectious diseases cause 45 percent of all deaths. As the twenty-first century was about to enter, more than 1,500 people worldwide were dying from an infectious disease within an hour, with at least half of the deaths being children under five. To understand the magnitude of these numbers, the WHO calculated that since 1945, only three diseases AIDS, tuberculosis, and malaria have claimed 150 million lives. This worrying figure is many times greater than the number of approximately 23 million people lost in wars. The 1918 Spanish Influenza epidemic killed at least 25 million people, including 500,000 Americans. Considering that this pandemic hit 294,000 allied troops in the autumn of 1918 alone, we understand that it is more effective than war. The disease caused short-term problems on both the Allied and German sides (Crosby 2003). As this comparison clearly shows, a handful of diseases pose the greatest threat to human health. According to WHO statistics, about 90 percent of all deaths from infectious diseases and half of all premature deaths are caused by six diseases—AIDS, tuberculosis, pneumonia, diarrheal diseases, malaria, and measles (World Health Organization, Communicable Diseases Cluster 1999).

In the developed West, mortality and morbidity rates from infectious diseases began to fall during the second part of the nineteenth century because of dramatic improvements in wages, housing, diet, and education. On the other hand, advanced countries' governments have developed necessary protective measures regarding public health and hygiene. In this regard, we can list drains, sewers, filtration, and chlorination of water as shields counter to cholera and typhoid; sanitary cordons, quarantine, and isolation against bubonic plague; vaccination against smallpox; and the first effective "magic bullet"—quinine—against malaria (F. Snowden 2008).

The application of science soon added new and powerful weapons against contagious diseases. Antibiotics, vaccines, and widespread advances in sanitation were making the world healthier than ever. During the start of the third quarter of the twentieth century, a general opinion in advanced countries such as the United States was that they could easily overcome all infectious diseases. By that time, polio, typhoid, cholera, and even measles had been eradicated. In 1973, Frank Macfarlane Burnet, Nobel Prize-winning professor of virology, declared confidently that infectious diseases, one of the ancient dangers of humanity, had been eliminated, at least in the affluent West (Burnet and White 1972).

In his book *Epidemic and Society*, Yale University historian Frank M. Snowden shows why the West's peace of mind about viruses is not justified. People who changed ecosystems and eliminated natural boundaries left themselves vulnerable without realizing it. Therefore, they were exposed continuously to developing microbes, viruses, and bacteria. Efforts for economic development have created more opportunities for humans and animals to get closer to each other, and trade worldwide has created new pathways that help spread the disease.

Those who defended the idea that infectious diseases were overcome thought that the microbial world was largely stationary or a slow-growing structure. Therefore, there was little concern that the fight against them would be won if new diseases emerged for which humanity was unprepared and immunologically vulnerable. Victims of this delusion ignored the fact that in the past five hundred years, catastrophic new diseases have repeatedly appeared in the West, such as the bubonic plague in 1347, syphilis in the 1490s, cholera in 1830, and the Spanish flu in 1918–1919. Even though medical professionals in Europe and North America announced success against infectious epidemics, these diseases remained the leading cause of death, especially in the poorest and most vulnerable countries in Africa, Asia, and Latin America. In this regard, looking at the spread of tuberculosis disease will give enough idea. In his 2001 book *Infections and Inequalities: Modern Plagues,* Paul Farmer states that tuberculosis has not disappeared at all. For Farmer, the illusion persisted because the bodies it affected were either in distant lands or out of sight. In addition to its widespread havoc in the South, tuberculosis continued to have a lethal impact among marginalized sections of the North, such as homeless people, prisoners, injecting drug users, immigrants, and racial minorities (Today 2020).

When there are no infectious diseases globally, it would be the biggest mistake to be relaxed. We should not forget that as our body's natural defense power decreases, we are preparing more hospitable conditions for the next pandemic.

It is difficult to develop treatments for these diseases rapidly, and incentives are not always ready to find them. It is also essential to remember that even if a cure is available, the targeted ability to fight the disease will decrease over time as infections develop. Therefore, more diseases emerging increase the chances of future outbreaks. The structure of the modern world will turn many of these outbreaks into pandemics.

Undeniably, when the HIV/AIDS deadly epidemic broke out in the United States in the early 1980s, leaving a death toll of 25 million people and never disappeared, the world had to learn, at a high cost, that infectious diseases had not diminished from the West at all.

Many new and developing infectious diseases come from developing countries. Countries in this category are often poorly equipped for early detection and responding to them appropriately. Therefore, these countries' capacity to prevent the international spread of diseases is relatively low. From the 1990s onward, we have seen outbreaks such as SARS, MERS, Ebola, Zika, and avian and swine flu. Many of these new diseases have primarily affected the poorest parts of the world. These outbreaks were apparent signs that the war against microbes was not yet over.

Governments' Handling of Coronavirus

The COVID-19 pandemic poses a significant challenge for governments worldwide in solving problems ranging from providing citizens with income support and helping companies struggling to survive to strengthen frontline healthcare. It also requires unprecedented levels of cooperation between nations, from the vaccination race to learning how to test and monitor the epidemic. One of the greatest lessons to be learned in this process is that the state's capacity to manage a crisis at this rate depends on the state's cumulative investments in its ability to manage and operate. In a sense, the crisis is often a challenge for countries that ignore the needed investment in what we might call *the public sector's dynamic capabilities (Mazzucato, From Moonshots to Earthshots 2021).*

The WHO director-general, Dr. Tedros Adhanom Ghebreyesus, in opening remarks at the 148th session of the Executive Board of WHO, on January 18, 2021, spoke on the lessons pandemic taught us:

> All of us must have the humility to learn, to change, to innovate, and to grow. COVID-19 surprised even some of the world's richest and most powerful nations. It caught them unprepared and revealed a collective failure to invest in emergency preparedness.

Before the pandemic emerged, a coalition of large foundations had published a Global Health Safety Index (GHSI), which ranks countries' capacity to prevent, detect, and report infection, and respond quickly to disease outbreaks. Accordingly, as expected, high-income countries had higher scores in the index. The United States and the United Kingdom were at the top of countries best prepared to deal with a pandemic. A year later, these rankings seem to have been reversed. "*The ten worst-affected countries by COVID-19 in terms of deaths per million are among the top 20 countries in terms of overall GHSI scores,*" according to a study published in September (*News* 2019).

In the United States, the president first denied the possibility that what started first in China could reach his country. After he finally acknowledged this and realized that the virus was spreading rapidly, he set up a special task force to solve the problem. But he has repeatedly demonstrated a profile of president that contradicts his statements about everything from social distancing to wearing masks, testing, and closing—and when and how to reopen. The epidemic soon became a political as well as a medical issue, with infection rates continuing to rise and severe problems with personal protective equipment and devices such as ventilators needed to deal with the epidemic.

It caused harsh criticism from the medical world in the face of this leadership vacuum in the United States. One of the best medical publications in the world, *the New England Journal of Medicine* (*NEJM*), has made an exception for the first time in more than two centuries of publishing. In a lengthy editorial titled "Dying in a Leadership Vacuum," the journal outlined the terrible failures of the US government on COVID-19. They declared that the pandemic's mismanagement resulted in at least tens of thousands of preventable deaths, saying the US administration had turned a health crisis into a tragedy. The editors of the magazine expressed, in a detailed statement, their deep concerns about the issue, and they did not hesitate to attack the country's political leadership:

> When it comes to the response to the largest public health crisis of our time, our current political leaders have demonstrated that they are dangerously incompetent. (Chow 2020)

As *Washington Post* reports, Donald Trump was the most unpopular president of modern times: a divisive and alienating discourse, an attitude that rarely comes to the middle. Most Americans vehemently opposed his erratic behavior and harsher policies. With this behavior, even before the pandemic, it would be difficult for him to be reelected. However, his aides and allies said the president finally lost because he mismanaged the virus (Post 2020).

Of course, it's too early to declare a "successful model" to deal with the pandemic. There are new waves of epidemics, even in countries that think they have the virus under control. However, we can see that some governments are using their resources, skills, and institutions much more effectively than others. The three lowest-ranked countries in the GHSI rankings stand out as particularly interesting examples (Woods 2021).

Senegal is a developing country with about 15 million people and a per capita GDP of $1,500. The country was ranked ninety-fifth with a modest 37.9 points in the GHSI ranking, where the United States occupied first place with 83.5 points. Senegal was swift to respond to the pandemic. It was already prepared in January 2020, when the WHO first declared an international public health emergency. When Senegal detected its first outbreak case on March 2, it deployed mobile test units that yielded results within 24 hours, established a well-functioning contact tracking system, and set up isolation units in clinics, hospitals, and hotels. The government also banned public gatherings, imposed night lockdowns, restricted domestic travel, and suspended international business flights. By April, face masks were mandatory in all public places. As of October, the country has registered approximately 15,000 cases and 300 deaths.

Another country that surprises the world is Sri Lanka. With a population of 21.5 million, the country, which could rank 120th in the GHSI, quickly responded to the virus' first cases. The government directed the military to help, initiating rapid tests and random PCR tests, developed locally in densely populated areas. It set up a strict contact tracing system, provided support to those in quarantine, enforced face masks in public places, restrained and monitored travelers, and imposed a nationwide shutdown. And as in Senegal, Sri Lanka's government has launched a vast and influential public communication campaign. As of November 2020, the country had only reported thirteen coronavirus deaths.

Vietnam, with a 95 million population and a weak healthcare system, ranked fiftieth in the GHSI. Still, it has shown an impressive performance after the news of the first virus in neighboring China. The government prepared laboratories and tests shortly after the first case and imposed restrictions on entry from China. It has swiftly implemented rapid tests, contact tracing, hospitalization for all infected persons, and isolation systems for all contacts of suspected cases. Until October, only thirty-five people died from the epidemic in the country.

Why did the United States and the United Kingdom fail when these poor countries performed so well? We can say that recent experiences with communicable diseases have positively affected countries in terms of preparedness. In addition to the Ebola experience in Senegal 2013–2016, Vietnam and Sri Lanka also experienced outbreaks of SARS (2003) and MERS (2012). Past epidemics have taught these countries the necessary lessons in return for the high price they paid. For this reason, all three countries created an infrastructure to manage outbreaks. However, we cannot explain why these three countries are much better than the United States and the United Kingdom by referring to their past experiences alone. This explanation alone does not help us understand why rich countries do not implement rapid result testing, contact tracing, and isolation procedures for suspected cases. Why didn't these countries mandate face masks and do more to avoid travel and face-to-face meetings, although they had a large number of experts who knew the consequences? The United States and Britain were still under the siege of the pandemic long after data showed that these measures were effective (Woods 2021).

There are more in-depth lessons about governance that need to be learned from this epidemic. In Senegal, Sri Lanka, and Vietnam, the government united behind a well-defined strategy, adopted an open public communication policy, and partnered with community networks. On the contrary, countries like the United States and the United Kingdom had ambiguities about formulating a coherent national strategy and could not effectively mobilize their world-leading institutions. Instead, both countries' governments succumbed to unproductive arguments between the elite, which turned into a feud.

As far as strategy is concerned, they gave an example of how the US Republican Party and the UK Conservative Party's divisions have caused their leaders to diverge from one approach to another. Experts who advised politicians competed for attention and influence. Experts have consistently defended their models and research, showing no humbleness to seek advice from frontline workers and other countries with relevant experience. The US Centers for Disease Control and the UK Public Health insisted on developing and controlling the testing program alone. While this approach has failed in both the countries, a more collaborative approach has worked in others.

Aside from these impressive examples, we observe that some countries have also shown success in controlling the virus. In New Zealand, which closed its borders in the first wave in the spring of 2020 and ordered people to stay at home, infections were confirmed to have dropped to zero for a while. Taiwan and Singapore have managed to contain their outbreaks much more than in other parts of the world. Some experts point out early response and enhanced monitoring as the main reasons for these success stories. In China, the first epicenter of the crisis, much of the daily life seems to have returned to normal. There were more cases in China in the early months of the outbreak than in any other country. Leaving aside questions about data accuracy, the number of new infections in this country peaked in mid-February and approached zero in mid-March. The virus has declined in China, and most of the population has returned to normal daily life. But concerns about the return of the virus have not subsided: In October, Chinese authorities began conducting mass tests in Kashgar, Xinjiang, following a suspected outbreak (Schumaker 2020).

ECONOMIC IMPACT OF COVID-19

Among the many economic problems faced by the pandemic, perhaps not the most important but a significant problem, is the shortage of paper towels, especially in the United States. This is a striking example to show affluent Western countries' preparedness for a disaster like COVID-19 outbreaks. In these countries, toilet paper and other paper towel products disappeared from the shelves of retail stores, which continued for a long time.

The root cause of the shortage is based on a decades-old quest to run businesses with virtually no additional stocks in such products to make more profits. According to this approach, only enough supplies are ordered to keep the production lines going. It is desirable to have enough wagons for only one day of output, only enough products to stock on one shelf until the next batch arrives. The concept, known as lean manufacturing or just-in-time inventory, was emerged in the efficiency-seeking Japanese automotive industry in the 1970s and turn into a belief for many American CEOs. It reached first to Detroit, then to other manufacturers, and finally to other businesses, from distribution to retail.

In a current emergency, the risk of a shortage in some products has shown how prepared we are for a disaster. The novel coronavirus outbreak highlighted how dependent the affluent Western countries to China, the manufacturing powerhouse of the world. The pandemic showed the world that the lean system should also be questioned in a highly connected world, among many other issues. Suppose one wanted to evaluate how prepared and potent the United States was to the epidemic; I think it would not be an exaggeration to say that it was as strong as "*toilet paper*."

Undoubtedly, the pandemic has the potential to create devastating social, economic, and political effects that will leave deep and long-standing scars. The IMF, the World Bank, and the OECD have all expressed severe worry that the COVID-19 outbreak will drive up inequality all over the world, with deeply harmful effects. This view is supported by Oxfam's survey of 295 economists from 79 countries (Revollo 2021).

People lose their jobs and income every day, not knowing when to return to their everyday lives. For small island states heavily dependent on tourism economically, empty hotels and deserted beaches are sorrowful images that reflect the desperation of unemployed and poor people. The International Labor Organization (ILO) projects that up to 400 million jobs could be lost due to pandemics. Evaluating that the impact of COVID-19 on the labor market may be more significant than its initial estimates, the ILO revealed the number of hours worked for the second half of 2020 with an estimate based on three scenarios. According to the baseline scenario, the number of hours worked will decrease by 4.9 percent, with 140 million full-time jobs lost compared to 2019. In the pessimistic scenario, job loss increases to 340 million and a decrease by 11.9 percent. If the pandemic started to diminish in the second half of 2020, the cost of job loss would be limited to 34 million (Patterson 2020).

The World Bank estimates a US$110 billion decrease in remittances in 2020, which means 800 million people will not be able to meet their basic requirements. As the World Bank Group president David Malpass expressed with deep concern,

> Remittances are a vital source of income for developing countries. The ongoing economic recession caused by COVID-19 is taking a severe toll on the ability to send money home and makes it all the more vital that we shorten the time to recovery for advanced economies. (The World Bank 2020)

If no action is taken, the severe long-term effects of the COVID-19 pandemic could push an additional 207 million people into life-threatening poverty, bringing the total of those affected by extreme poverty to over 1 billion by 2030, according to the findings published by the UNDP.

In the joint study of UNDP and the University of Denver's Pardee Center for International Futures, the outbreak's multidimensional impacts over the next decade were evaluated. The impact of different COVID-19 recovery scenarios on Sustainable Development Goals (SDG) was addressed (Global SDG Integration 2020).

The IMF made a very depressing forecast in October, showing that the 2025 prospects are now, perhaps not catastrophically disastrous, but significantly worse for all regions of the world than they were a year ago. IMF managing director announced that they anticipate a total production loss of $28 trillion by 2025. Accordingly, we would be globally poorer than we would have had if such a crisis had not happened (Wolf 2021). Naturally, we expect that the bill will not be evenly distributed across regions and countries.

Outputs were prevented from being too weak, thanks to large, swift, and unprecedented fiscal, monetary, and regulatory responses that preserve disposable income for households, maintain cash flow for firms, and support loan provision. These policies implemented by governments have prevented the repetition of the financial disaster experienced in 2008–2009 so far. Even though some signs point out that the global economy seems to be coming back, many expect that the ascent will likely be extended, uneven, and uncertain. According to the IMF's forecasts, the global economy is projected to grow by around minus 4.4 percent in 2020. As the pandemic continues to spread, recovery cannot be expected. Reopenings have been paused, and targeted shutdowns have been resumed due to new spikes in COVID-19 infections in areas that reduced local transmission to low levels. The IMF foresees a deep recession in 2020, extending to 2022 (International Monetary Fund 2020) even though China's return to growth was more substantial than expected. Economies everywhere face serious challenges to return to pre-pandemic activity levels. The year 2020 will be recalled as the worst recession since the Great Depression of 1930. The pandemic has hit hard low-income countries most economically. In an interview with the *Financial Times* in January 2021, IMF managing director Kristalina Georgieva said that the world is entering 2021 with a weaker recovery momentum. She expresses this view hoping that intensive vaccinations will bring an economic recovery, although uneven, for 2021. Therefore, the IMF Chief repeatedly underlines that it is essential that governments do not withdraw their policy support prematurely to avoid further disruptions (Wolf 2021).

The situation is naturally a problem for countries with weak financial conditions. As the IMF highlights in the October 2020 *Global Financial Stability Report*, sustaining the recovery will also require intense international cooperation on health and financial support for countries coping with liquidity shortages. According to the same report, most economies will experience permanent damage to supply potential, reflecting the traces of this year's deep recession and the need for structural change. Permanent production losses mean a significant reduction in living standards compared to what was before the pandemic. That is the first time in more than twenty years that such an extreme case of poverty will be encountered. Severe increases are expected in inequalities other than poverty.

Worse, the recession triggered by the COVID-19 pandemic is very different from previous recessions. In previous downturns, service sectors had smaller growth declines than manufacturing. In the current crisis, restrictive public health measures are needed to slow transmission along with behavioral changes. Therefore, service sectors that rely on face-to-face interactions—mainly wholesale and retail trade, hospitality, and arts and entertainment—fall under more significant contractions than manufacturing.

The pandemic's adverse effects are particularly severe for economically more vulnerable people, including young workers and women. The burden of the crisis is unevenly distributed across sectors. Workers most affected by the pandemic are employed in accommodation and catering, transportation, retail, and wholesale (Brussevich, Dabla-Norris, and Khalid 2020). Unfortunately, younger workers, those in less secure work arrangements, and those in small and medium-sized businesses are more vulnerable to keeping their jobs. Overall, low-wage workers have a significantly higher risk of losing their jobs. Similar results are seen in both emerging markets and emerging economies, where workers are more likely to be unemployed than informally employed workers.

In the absence of efforts to regain lost human capital accumulation, closures will have long-term consequences for future social and economic impacts. Shorter and inadequate lifelong education is associated with lower lifetime income.

Such developments exacerbate preexisting inequalities. As the IMF reports in October 2020 Financial Monitoring Annex 1.1, with the financial crisis of 2008–2009, income inequality in many developed economies and some fast-growing emerging markets and emerging economies increased significantly compared to the early 1990s. It reflects the effects of many factors, including a skill-based technological change in favor of higher education levels. As monopolization trends in significant markets increased, the bargaining power of trade unions decreased. Lower marginal tax rates for those who earn the highest income due to lower corporate taxes have become another distorting factor in the last few years.

Extensive school closures due to pandemic lockdown measures have labor market consequences for the children of parents and potential clients. UNESCO states that more than 1.6 billion students worldwide are affected by school and university closures (UNESCO 2020). The epidemic highlighted worrying inequalities within and between countries that need to be addressed urgently to guarantee everyone's right to education—parents' ability to take care of children limits, especially mothers' ability to work. Long school cuts for children limit learning opportunities. Evidence shows that learning loss increases in proportion to downtime (Quinn and Polikoff 2017). Even if online and distance education is implemented as a temporary solution, it is not a sufficient substitute (Baytiyeh 2018).

Many countries had entered the epidemic with a high amount of debt. These countries are mostly those who fail to use their borrowed money due to inadequate project selection and implementation, ineffective targeting of social spending, wasteful subsidies, or outright corruption. The World Bank and IMF, from which these countries borrowed, have developed practical tools to measure the quality of public expenditures of the countries to which they extend loans. The World Bank and IMF have many indices that evaluate a country's performance to which it lends. In other words, assessing countries for these organizations is a fairly standard task. Hence, borrowing and spending more may not be the best course of action for governments with poor performance history due to the pandemic's pressing needs.

As a result, the more the country's governments spend recklessly, the more the citizens of those countries suffer. It is clear for such countries that borrowing in hard currencies will make future debt rescheduling more likely as their exports decline and their exchange rates are under pressure. For international financial institutions such as the IMF, which are now calling for unconditional additional expenditures, this situation will turn into a problem that cannot be solved by usual means.

As distinguished economists Michael Spence and Danny Leipziger point out, there are more effective approaches to dealing with the financial dilemmas facing emerging and developing economies. We can list the combined IMF and World Bank programs, including increasing the amount of aid targeted for vulnerable populations, extending the duration of IMF loans that can be linked to guarantees that resources will be used well, and financial performance measures (Spence and Leipziger 2020).

Path to Recovery

The question on everyone's minds is to what extent the destruction in the economy has reached and how easily we can return to normal. Those who view the issue optimistically believe that the rapid increase in cases and deaths we have seen recently will be brought under control. According to optimists, major economies may follow China relatively quickly and return to work by the summer of 2021.

However, on the contrary, there may be a situation in which we cannot control the disease until 2022. If we got into such trouble, there would be unprecedented increases in our public debt, reaching 20 or 30 percent of GDP. We would have many companies that went bankrupt. There would be many workers who had been out of work for a year and a half or more. Our social unrest would deepen, with serious negative consequences. The trading system would not be able to keep its normal functioning, and it would probably come to the point of collapse. Moreover, there could be a more significant drop in output in the near term than in the Great Depression of the 1930s.

As the IMF often emphasizes, we are now on the edge of an economic rift. According to their projections, GDP in developed countries is expected to decline by about 12 percent between the end of last year and the second quarter of this year. It is thought that recovery will occur after that. Unfortunately, it will take quite a long time to get back to the starting point, but a steady recovery is expected. However, it is not unlikely to say that even this expectation is too optimistic.

Developing countries do not have the developed world's safety nets, so their destiny seems more like it was in the 1930s. Probably, a radical transformation will occur in all societies in this process. Governments will have to borrow enormous amounts. Therefore, they will print a massive amount of money. As a result, it seems inevitable to enter periods of severe inflation in one way or another.

According to Branko Milanovic, a Senior Researcher at the Stone Center on Socio-Economic Inequality at the CUNY Graduate Center and Professor at the LSE, the more gloomy forecasts seem more plausible (Milanovic 2020). He emphasizes that the trade and technology war between China and the United States, while perhaps understandable from a narrow US strategic perspective, is fundamentally harmful from a global perspective. Such a confrontation will prevent the spread of technology and avoid the improvement of living standards in large areas of the world. Slowing growth will make it difficult to eradicate poverty and possibly maintain current levels of global inequality. Gains in real income will be sacrificed to freeze the pecking pattern of the global income distribution. Net real income for all concerned will be zero.

While the widespread COVID-19 vaccination promises a possible return to normal life, the United States is moving toward an unconventional experiment that could create a good or bad economy that many Americans will not recognize. Goldman Sachs expects the economy to grow at an annual rate of 7 percent this year, the fastest since 1984. The question of interest and debate is whether this rapid recovery will be permanent. More precisely, the question is whether the US economy will survive the wave of low growth that has persisted for most of the last twenty years or will instead enter inflation that has not been seen since. Skeptics warn too much spending could ignite long-dormant inflation. Leading economists such as former Treasury Secretary Larry Summers are already warning that potential overheating could result in a new recession. The Biden administration plans to spend $1.9 trillion on top of the $3.7 trillion federal funds that have flowed since March 2020, helping to ensure years of massive government borrowing to boost the economy.

On the other hand, the FED says that even if inflation exceeds its annual target of 2 percent, it will keep interest rates close to zero, making it easier for businesses and consumers to borrow. Since World War II, the economy has been backed by so much deficit spending and so easy money at the same time. According to Bank of America's estimates, thanks to last year's incentive checks, the economy will benefit from the increased spending of consumers who have saved more than $1.6 trillion this year as they return to normal. While President Biden seeks congressional approval to mitigate the effects of the pandemic, he also plans further steps to increase the long-term prospects of the economy. In this context, it is preparing an ambitious spending package that will rise to $3 trillion for a range of Democratic priorities, including infrastructure, clean energy, domestic production, child and elderly care. Republican congressmen are warning against excessive government spending. But, Republicans' complaints do not seem to have much weight after they agreed to add more than $5 trillion in national debt during the Trump administration (Lynch 2021).

The overall GDP of the European Union is expected to remain significantly below pre-pandemic levels. The current bleak outlook suggests that some economies such as Spain and Italy will still not be able to reach their national income levels in 2019 until late 2022. This means that the European Union (EU) will continue to suffer economically from the pandemic longer after it frees itself from the health threat and deadlocks are lifted. The issue comes to the fore whether the political leaders in the EU will allow such a trend or aim to outperform their predictions with more aggressive policy actions than envisaged. If a more aggressive policy is chosen, it will be necessary to continue to fund recovery as much as possible. Governments have so far enacted unprecedented programs primarily to support their economies. Growth will start to increase significantly when the restrictions in economies are lifted from the middle of the year when vaccination programs are sufficiently completed. This is where the probability of reaching a danger point is relatively high. At this point, governments will rightfully abolish income support packages that keep businesses and households going, thinking that the economy is returning to normal. The risk is that such a policy withdrawal would cause the economy to drop too much demand and jeopardize recovery (Sandbu 2021).

CLIMATE CHANGE

Humanity's accomplishments, particularly over the last century, have been extraordinary. People, goods, and news travel faster than we think. An incredible amount of information became accessible, immediate, and cheap. Improved sanitation and rising urban living standards contribute to longer lives almost anywhere in the world. New triumphs are added to the rapidly growing technological, scientific, and cultural achievements every day.

Parallel to this remarkable achievement of industrialization, we are faced with the fact that since the Industrial Revolution, the ecological crisis has paved the way for its development. Human interests have pushed us across many global boundaries that define the biophysical safe space within which society can flourish. Farming, transportation, and industrial production, especially the use of fossil fuels, helped human-induced climate change reach today's proportions. Ultimately, we are faced with the problems of mass destruction of biodiversity and the terrible pollution of the air, soil, freshwater, and oceans. In addition to climate change, several challenges have emerged, including the size of the world's population, age structure, distribution by region, and the world's share in urban areas compared to rural areas (PIK 2015).

According to a Global Footprint Network and Schneider Electric report, *Strategies for one-planet prosperity*, we demand more than the Earth can renew. Human demands on nature have been rising steadily. Humanity's Ecological Footprint is now 60 percent higher than what the world's ecosystems can renew. These demands include food, timber, fiber, land for urban use, and the capacity to absorb excess CO_2 from fossil fuel burning.

Experts are making dire warnings. When global warming climbs above a particular limit (about 2°C above pre-industrial revolution levels), the poles' melting will accelerate and cause natural feedback processes, creating an irreversible chain of effects. The meaning of encountering such a situation is that humanity will lose its ability to control the warming process for various centuries and even thousands of years. There will be an irreversible rise in sea levels until a new balance is established. According to scientists, if we cannot stop global warming in the next twenty to thirty years, the rise of sea levels will destroy all the coastal cities of the planet, the frequency and intensity of extreme climatic events will increase, biodiversity will decrease, and ultimately a catastrophe in the form of destruction will set in (Sato and Hansen 2020).

There are close connections between climate change and transmissible diseases. Overlaps and dependencies between these two most fundamental problems exist inexorably. As our planet warms, the seasons are getting longer, and the ranges of many dangerous infections such as dengue fever, malaria, chikungunya, and West Nile virus expand. We need to review our health policies and system by taking all these trends into account. On the other hand, when the seas rise due to global warming and some areas become uninhabitable, such disasters will increase immigrants' numbers. For the increasing number of refugees in desperate situations, little economic and health support is likely available (Winston 2020).

That brings us to the SDGs, also known as the Sustainable Development Goals, seventeen Global Goals set by the UN in 2015 for the year 2030. As the goal for our world in 2030, the SDGs are a unique opportunity for all sectors to rally around a shared global agenda to end poverty, protect the planet, and ensure that all people enjoy shared and durable prosperity.

There is a growing global effort of people using business as a force for good. This movement seems to be spreading everywhere and has many leaders all over the world. It is encouraging to see both small businesses and multinationals in this new movement. Some companies use the business to reduce poverty, and others go into restoring the environment. Undoubtedly, they all create meaningful work with dignity and purpose. It is understood that investors are increasingly focusing on environmental, social, and governance (ESG) risks, which will pose a tremendous financial risk to companies that do not act appropriately on a range of climate and social matters. As investors and insurance companies took proactive steps to respond to the coronavirus outbreak, ESG bond issuance increased by 272 percent annually in some periods of 2020. However, as Edward Vaughan Dixon, ESG head of Aviva Investors Real Assets, emphasized, we cannot immediately conclude that the economy is heading for a low-carbon and socially resilient future (Mace 2021).

Investing in low-carbon businesses continues to be a more complex issue for investors. Investors such as BlackRock and Aviva have begun to warn that they will give up companies that refuse to adapt to climate change. However, one must not forget that what is sustainable in the corporate world is more complicated than decarbonization alone. A key obstacle to investors and institutional engagement is the ambiguity about what is sustainable and therefore investable. A survey of 650 institutional investors with assets of more than $25.9 trillion globally shows that investor-corporate involvement in environmental issues is increasing. Still, disappointment is also high about greenwashing, which means exploiting environmental issues for commercial purposes (Mace 2021).

Believing that the Sustainability Revolution is no longer just an idea, *Lombard Odier,* a company that collaborates on sustainability issues with *Financial Times*, explains that it is taking action to radically redesign the current unsustainable economic model (Odier 2019). For this purpose, the company has prepared applicable sustainability documents.

However, the world economy is already transitioning toward a paradigm where growth decouples from its harmful social and environmental footprint employing a series of value-seeking strategies to attain this goal. They describe this as the transition from the WILD *(Wasteful, Idle, Lopsided, and Dirty)* model to *CLIC (Circular, Lean, Inclusive, and Clean)* model. In the linear WILD model, we operate in a *wasteful, idle, lopsided, and dirty* manner. Since the arguments they use in explaining the WILD and CLIC naming are attractive and functional, I find it helpful to quote them briefly (Lombardodier 2020).

We are far from compensating for our high *wastefulness* with low recycling rates. We often forget the fact that nature's resources are limited. For example, 79 percent of plastic produced was dumped in landfills. Overall, only 43 percent of all materials are re-entering the economy through water treatment, land application, composting, recycling, and other recovery forms. Consequently, the regenerative ability of our ecosystem has exceeded its limit.

In general, our economy is very *Idle.* We consume and accumulate excessive amounts of goods. Take passenger cars and office spaces as examples. It is striking that passenger cars' usage rate is approximately 8 percent, and for office spaces, this figure is 35–50 percent. Therefore, no one expects this linear "Take, Make, Waste" model to be sustainable (Ellen MacArthur Foundation 2015).

The world is *Lopsided.* Prosperity is not shared fairly; a significant portion of the global population is increasingly disenfranchised and unable to access healthcare at reasonable prices. This situation leads to increased inequality and social tensions. Moreover, the middle classes are beginning to melt away, and race and gender inequality is spreading.

A carbon-intensive, *Dirty* economy is seriously disrupting the world ecosystem. Climate change and increasing food demand are putting extreme pressure on arable land. The complex system of supply chains increases business profitability at the company level. But this system creates extra social costs with additional transportation and energy requirements. Overuse of chemicals, especially fertilizers and pesticides, threatens human health, biodiversity, and the planet's food chain. The world cannot continue in this way.

The transition from the current *WILD* structure into a better future, the *CLIC* model, will only be possible by creating a *Circular* economy. In the circular economy, the demand for goods will decrease, the valuable life of products will increase, and waste will decrease. In contrast to the linear model, the circular system means redesigning business models and products to enable product reduction, repair, reuse, redistribution, and recycling. This move, actually, means that our production and consumption system is changing from beginning to end. For example, we can mention implementing strategies such as cleaning projects to reduce, reuse, and manage plastic waste, improve inventory management, introduce innovative packaging, and use technology to treat waste.

Learning to be *Lean* is essential in this new economy. Being lean means focusing on efficient production and consumption and extracting only natural resources that can be sustained or reproduced. If we work with this understanding, it will be possible for us to produce higher-quality products with fewer resources. Lean will take us into the future away from personal ownership toward a sharing-based economy, including travel, home, and office sharing. Sharing economy is a significant step toward more rational consumption and production forms, mobilizing idle assets.

Creating an *Inclusive* economy means not excluding anyone and being able to provide affordable solutions to everyone. In such a world, businesses will no longer simply be actors pursuing commercial profits but organizations that consider the triad of people, nature, and profit together. Therefore, a new social order will be introduced where productivity gains are shared with employees through fair wages and advancement opportunities. Governments' primary role is to invest in education, provide health and public services, and help create green urban systems. In this context, technologies such as Artificial Intelligence (AI) will be used to develop smart solutions.

Transition to a *Clean* economy is crucial. Cost reductions, renewable energy becoming competitive without government support, and the shifting to electric vehicles in mobility are significant first steps. If we want to move to a net-zero emission world, we need to take decisive steps in high energy efficiency, pollution control, and carbon pricing. We must also make necessary policy alignment and market design revisions for a clean economy, eliminating wasteful and inefficient subsidies, sustainable food and land-use systems, and negative emission technologies. Achieving a clean economy requires a more sustainable relationship with nature and a transition to lower emissions.

Path to Net-Zero with Growth

Time is running out rapidly to reduce emissions that tend to climb to dangerous levels and minimize climate change risks. With the right approach and planning, it can be ensured that the road to net-zero also brings essential investment opportunities. While moving toward reducing carbon emissions, the importance of focusing on net-zero with methods and technologies to remove the same amount of carbon dioxide from the atmosphere equal to the emissions that cannot be avoided from being released has recently increased. In this context, the coronavirus' emergence has pushed it to an even sharper relief in the face of the collapse of traditional energy markets such as coal and oil. Net-zero emissions require an overhaul of existing behavioral patterns at the social and industrial levels and improved waste and emission management (*Financial Times* 2020).

Emissions continue to increase despite the stringent measures agreed in the 2015 Paris Agreement. In this regard, the imperative to make meaningful progress is more important given the limited time left to mitigate climate change's harmful effects, such as temperature increases. If no significant action is taken, temperatures are expected to rise to 3° C within this century, which will create disastrous consequences for the environment (Kaminker and Church 2020). Therefore, to keep the global temperature rise below 2° C, it is essential to reduce carbon emissions by 50 percent until 2030.

With the impact of the coronavirus crisis, global energy companies such as B.P., Total, and Shell also make statements to acknowledge the need for a more substantial commitment to sustainability, which should be considered a positive development with some caution (Raval 2020).

The main driving force behind the move toward net-zero is undoubtedly the increasing voice calls primarily from consumers and stakeholders. We should also consider the development of technology that can facilitate such a dramatic transformation as an essential factor. The intervention of governments with a regulator's role, especially in manufacturing and heavy industry sectors, is also very critical. In the UK, for example, the government reported spending more than £800 million on infrastructure to capture and bury millions of tons of carbon dioxide (Thomas 2021).

Public policies, especially at the EU level, have been a critical factor in decarbonization. The EU demonstrates its determination with directives such as the Green Deal, aiming to make its region the first climate-neutral continent by 2050 (*Financial Times* 2020). Market forces and the public's commitment to reducing emissions are also in line with consumer trends steadily moving toward a more sustainable lifestyle.

Suppose we want to maintain the ambitious temperature targets foreseen under the Paris Agreement and reduce global warming to 1.5° C by the end of the century. In that case, we need to be aware that we have as little as seven years to consume the world's remaining carbon budget.

But linked to this challenge, there are attractive opportunities for companies prepared to modify business models pursuing net-zero dramatically. Increased efficiency, process improvements, investment potential in a range of sectors, and shareholder satisfaction will go hand in hand with the move toward decarbonization.

Waste and emission management areas offer significant potential for investors who want to turn to profitable areas. Besides, investments to increase efficiency in the transport and construction markets, food and land use, and digitization of industries are also promising. There are government incentives for companies to make net-zero commitments, and the benefits are becoming more and more apparent.

A substantial amount of capital is required to address the risks posed by carbon emissions. Undoubtedly, the amount of funding and how it is deployed can significantly affect growth, with the possibility to boost global GDP by up to 5 percent by 2050.

The decision of the new US president, Mr. Biden, to rejoin the Paris climate agreement a few hours after taking office has been welcomed around the world. Joe Biden pledged to take concrete steps to address the climate change problem. *"It is very clear that we will be successful globally if we only have big players,"* said Markus Beyrer, managing director of BusinessEurope, an umbrella organization for EU national chambers of commerce. The US return *"can get us back on track"* considering the recent increase in China and other countries' commitment to do more to tackle climate change, it is hopeful that the world's leading countries have a positive attitude in this regard. As we mentioned earlier, companies invest heavily in technologies that reduce greenhouse gas emissions (Gold and Bender ve Landers 2021).

Despite all these commitments, global emissions continue to increase. Groups that have been watching progress in this area are cautiously optimistic. They question how sincere most of the countries that signed the Paris Agreement are in achieving the targets they have set to reduce emissions.

Fortunately, today, there are plenty of opportunities for significant technological changes to lower the human impact of technology per unit of GDP. These opportunities include the transition from fossil fuels to renewable energy (wind, solar, hydro, geothermal, and others), which will provide more power with lower greenhouse gas emissions. Another opportunity is to shift the diet of humans from overeating meat, especially beef, to using more plant protein that is more beneficial to human health and reduces animal feed and pasture pressure. A third opportunity is improved building designs that significantly reduce the need for heating and cooling and, therefore, energy demand. The fourth opportunity is precision agriculture: more precise water and fertilizer applications, such as drip irrigation and fertilizing (direct injection through a fertilizer irrigation system). Recent advances in technology such as significant cost reductions in photovoltaics, the development of biodegradable plastics, the development of plant-based substitutes for meat, and the improvement of agricultural methods to reduce pesticides, water, and chemical fertilizers increase the chance of success. Our goal is to plan carefully and soundly, and methodically regulate businesses, reducing or banning technologies that exacerbate ecological crises.

THE RISE AND DOMINANCE OF BIG TECH

As new technologies create winners and losers in the market, technological advances contain the seeds of growing inequality within them. The spinning machine's advent and the steam-powered loom have displaced and impoverished many spinners and weavers in India. The mechanization of agriculture has impoverished countless small farmers worldwide who fled to cities desperate to find a livelihood. The addition of robots to the assembly lines of auto factories created unemployment, resulting in falling wage levels for workers fired by factories. Moreover, the digital economy is now coming, with smarter machines and systems to fulfill the tasks workers are currently performing. Who will win and who will lose?

In general, the winners of the future labor market will be those with higher skills that machines cannot replace or those who have the skills to work with new smart devices, such as the technical skills required to program new machines. The losers will be workers whose tasks are left to more robots and AI. In the last four decades, job losses have concentrated in the goods-producing sectors, particularly agriculture, mining, and manufacturing. These job losses will continue in the future. Both agriculture and mining are increasingly being automated with driverless vehicles such as multipurpose tractors in combination and extensive digging and transport equipment at mine sites. Robots continue to replace workers on factory floors in various manufacturing industries.

Moreover, it seems clear that other jobs in the service sector will also disappear in the future. Trucks and taxis can drive on their own, thus firing millions of professional drivers. Warehouses are increasingly operated with robots that transport, stack, and pack goods. Besides, retail stores lead to e-commerce and direct delivery of purchases, with expert systems and potentially self-driving delivery vehicles.

In recent years, less-skilled workers displaced by machines have seen their earnings stagnate or decline, while more skilled workers have been made more productive by the same machines and have seen their incomes rise. These trends have been a critical cause of growing income inequality in many countries, particularly the United States. However, the ultimate impact of this trend depends on two additional factors. To the extent that low-skilled workers can acquire higher skills through increased education and training, the workforce's proportion suffering from stagnant or declining earnings can be reduced. Furthermore, even if market wages are pulled down, governments can compensate for these opposing market forces through increased taxation of those with high and growing incomes and increased transfers to those with low and falling incomes so that all segments of society share the gains from technological progress.

Development challenges will be compounded for the world's poorest countries, as they often depend on labor-intensive export earnings and tourism to finance their future economic growth. On the other hand, the digital revolution continues to replace low-cost labor with smart machines. For example, rapid advances in robotics resulted in the automation of jobs in the textile and apparel industries, which were the stepping stone industries for low-wage countries that climbed the economic development ladder in the past. While the digital revolution will undoubtedly help the poorest countries in specific areas such as low-cost healthcare, expanded education opportunities, and infrastructure improvements, likely, this revolution may also close traditional pathways for economic development. In this situation, global solidarity with rich countries to provide additional development assistance to support the most impoverished nations to invest in new digital technologies and accompanying skills may become vital.

Digital technologies have become more lifeline than ever before. When the new coronavirus swept the world after its discovery in China, most routine works came to a halt. All industries were shut down, millions of workers were laid off, and nearly everyone was forced to self-isolate and work from home. As a result, the use of services offered by major technology platforms increased rapidly, while other industries were in a rapid decline. Video conferencing tools like Zoom have evolved into mundane office devices often used by your grandparents or your kids for hours on end. Netflix, Amazon Prime, and other video streaming media services have exploded. This shift to the virtual world has also begun to affect people's attention from the gloomy news outside. Bandwidth consumption has risen to such high levels that telecommunication carriers have limited streams and reduced video quality to avoid overloading the internet.

These developments have increasingly begun to be evaluated in striking contrast with the rise of social media and the widespread positive perception of the past. Until very recently, it was a very accepted approach to say that digital technologies will provide more access to information, facilitate collective organization, and strengthen civil society. The Arab Spring, the so-called *color revolutions*, and other digitally fed social movements like them seemed to demonstrate the unstoppable popular power unleashed by our always online, interconnected world. Indeed, during most of the 2000s, tech enthusiasts praised every new innovation as a way to bring people together and develop democracy (Diamond 2010).

Regulating the Big Tech

In the brief history of the internet, which has swept wildly from the naive libertarian utopism of the cyberspace forerunners of the 1990s to the desperate dystopianism of the upsurge of surveillance capitalism and techno-authoritarianism in recent years, we may perhaps be entering the new era of realism in which civil society fights against the use of the internet for the sovereign state and corporation's interests.

Regulators around the world have finally started to focus on major technology platforms. Innovative entrepreneurs and digital activists, empowered by cheap and accessible new technologies, aim to tame the immense power that major tech firms have accumulated by challenging the established online order. Even technology platforms acknowledge that they cannot operate without a public license anymore and call for limited regulation to clarify rules about privacy and freedom of expression.

As the leading digital platforms have practically become essential service providers, there is a growing consensus that platforms abuse their power, make profits using consumer privacy, destroy competition, and buy potential competitors. With Twitter's decision to close the US president's account for inciting the violence, a debate began on whether these platforms had too much political power. However, the extreme economic power that big tech has achieved is unquestionable. The year 2020 has been an excellent year for tech's leading companies. The seven most valuable US technology companies (Apple, Microsoft, Amazon, Alphabet, Facebook, Tesla, and Nvidia) increased their market value by $3.4 trillion in 2020, thanks to a global epidemic and a broader economic crisis (Levy 2020). Apple, Facebook, Amazon, Microsoft, Google owner Alphabet, and Tesla are now collectively worth more than $8.1 trillion, accounting for nearly 25 percent of the total $33.3 trillion market value of all the companies in the S&P 500 (La Monica 2021).

Increasingly, many are in consensus that the Gilded Age of the early twentieth century has emerged in the United States today in a different form. It has become frequently called the New Gilded Age. In his book *Liberty From All Masters*, journalist Barry Lynn highlights the similarities between today's high-tech monopolists and the robber barons of the early twentieth century. Lynn argues that they share a similar strategy claiming the enormous inequality that emerged is a tragic but inevitable consequence of capitalism and technological change. But as Lynn writes, one of the main differences between then and now is that fewer people believed in such rationalizations in the Gilded Age. Most Americans today see the excessive accumulation of wealth and power as normal. Nearly a century ago, a significant number of Americans rejected such inequality and fought decades of struggle for a just and democratic society. On the other hand, today's anti-monopoly movements are deliberately interracial. Thus, it paves the way for failure when populists and progressives leave Black Americans alone, who played a crucial role in promoting both the movements (Teachout 2021).

Since the 1970s, the best way to evaluate the proper functioning of a market has been considered to be identifying practices that put consumers at a disadvantage. Built on this assumption, the principle of consumer welfare became dominant in competition law. However, this assumption has started to lose its validity as big technology companies such as Google, Amazon, and Facebook offer "*free*" services to their users. Even if the leading digital platforms pay their users, they can still be advantageous because one of the primary sources of value in these markets is to collect user-generated data to sell or drive targeted ads.

Therefore, regulators should look at other aspects of the market, particularly the supplier market. Even if consumers are buying products cheaper, there are questions about how Google treats creators, Amazon treats sellers, Uber treats drivers, and Facebook treats merchants.

Google, which has a monopoly position in internet search, can direct the search traffic as it wishes in order to receive the advertising revenue that went to an ecosystem of web content providers. Similarly, e-commerce monopoly Amazon creates unfair competition by using rich data such as buyer preferences and search queries related to shopping transactions on its platform. This way, it can replace existing merchants by offering their own comparable products and forcing suppliers to buy (or increase price) Amazon ads for visibility. In addition to the fact that monopoly-powered platforms extract so much data and offer little to users, the ability to strengthen their position to weaken and exploit traders and content providers in their ecosystems will lead to the destruction of competition in the future.

Mariana Mazzucato and her colleagues argue that as digital platforms tend to move beyond the existing competitive structure, there is a need for a new toolkit with new metrics of market power and, in particular, a clear definition of platform power. She says outdated theories can only explain part of the story can be explained. When changed to account for new realities, market power arguments tend to conclude that major platforms should break down and key mergers should be undone (Mazzucato et al. 2021). If we take these new theories further, it follows that some digital services should be considered as social infrastructure. It is clear that the economies of the platforms differ from the economies of traditional offline and unilateral markets. Therefore, it is necessary for policymakers to reexamine some of the most fundamental assumptions about markets and make sure they focus on the correct issues.

CAPITALISM NEEDS RENEWAL

Especially in the period following World War II, with converging growth and diminishing poverty, the world economy might appear out of the forest. Technological advances have made the end of poverty accessible, with the rebalancing of the much fairer international order for countries outside the North Atlantic region. However, there was no way of confidently saying that the system was functioning correctly. The increasing levels of anxiety seen around the world were indicative of the deeper causes behind the problem.

In his latest book, Jeffrey D. Sachs makes convincing arguments that implementing the concept of sustainable development should be the core mission of today, arguing that for more than a decade, we have increasingly faced at least three significant global risks (Sachs 2020). The first global risk is a dramatic and destabilizing increase in economic inequality when technology is adequately operated and promises to end poverty. The benefits of economic growth are not shared equally. In many countries, including both the United States and China, inequality has risen with economic growth. While some workers' earnings, especially those with advanced training, are rising, the earnings of workers who are replacing their jobs with robots and AI are stagnant or declining. While those who benefit from the increase in income can, in principle, compensate for those left behind, in fact, there is little redistribution of income in the United States and many other countries.

The second global risk is a devastating global environmental crisis which we explored at length in the climate change section. Two hundred years of rapid economic growth has created several interrelated global ecological shocks. The first is human-induced global warming caused by the massive emission of heat-absorbing greenhouse gases into the atmosphere. The biggest culprit is carbon dioxide (CO_2) released by burning fossil fuels. Second, we must count the massive loss of biodiversity, with an estimated 1 million species threatened with extinction, according to numerous experts. The main culprit of biodiversity loss is the enormous transformation of land pushed to the brink of extinction, with countless habitats taken from other species for agricultural production. Third, mega pollution of air, soil, freshwater, and oceans. We attack the environment with industrial chemicals, plastics, and other waste streams that are not properly recycled or reduced in production and consumption.

The third global risk is the rising prospect of war in a world armed to the teeth. The war between essential countries at the moment may seem unthinkable, as the consequences will be so dire and devastating. Let us not forget that the same was said about the possibility of a great war in 1910, on the eve of World War I. Likewise, it is assumed today that the absence of war between the great powers will continue forever in the future, as was believed in 1910. However, history proves otherwise. Warfare has typically accompanied each new era of globalization, accompanied by profound changes in geopolitical power. Extraordinary peacebuilding efforts are needed in the coming years to avoid the self-defeating patterns of conflict that have been prevalent throughout history.

These challenges—inequality, environmental crisis, and the fragility of peace—are the main reasons many scientists, moral leaders, and politicians encourage the world to adopt sustainable development principles. The concept itself represents a holistic approach to globalization that combines economic growth with social inclusion, environmental sustainability, and peaceful societies. Sustainable development theory and globalization's history suggest that growth based on *the market economy* will never be enough. Since the 1500s, which can be regarded as the beginning of capitalist globalization, the global economic system has been a ruthless and violent structure where inequality and war are fundamentally unresolved. What is more, we now have additional environmental challenges that are complex, global, and unprecedented for our species. Without a guide on moving forward, we endanger the planet in ways we have never done before.

In his book, *Capitalism: The Future of an Illusion*, Fred L. Block, a research professor of sociology at the University of California, Davis, says that the widespread confidence that we live in a capitalist society is an acknowledgment that has severe consequences for our lives. According to Block, when we look thoroughly at the subject, we realize that most of the stories people tell us about capitalism's nature consist of legends similar to the Garden of Eden's biblical story. In the book, he aims to refute the view of capitalism that has become hegemonic. The author has argued that removing this illusion would open up the possibilities for political and economic reform that currently exists only at the limits of contemporary political debate (Block 2018).

The political crises in both the United States and Europe, which have deepened after the first decade of the twenty-first century, point to the need for essential reforms to improve the functioning of the system. The unexpected election of Trump is an indication of how badly the US political system is breaking. Despite being an outsider, Trump won the Republican Party presidential nomination because most Republican voters were in open rebellion against the party establishment. Trump's populist style against immigrants and free-trade agreements and his promise to "*make America great again*" echoed with voters. Similarly, Bernie Sanders' populist challenge to Hillary Clinton was far more successful in the Democratic Party candidacy race than most observers expected. Ultimately, Clinton won the Democratic presidential nomination, but the echo of Sanders' attacks on the millionaire and billionaire class also showed deep streams of discontent among voters.

John Judis, an author and American journalist, linked the populist rebellions led by Trump and Sanders with similar patterns in European politics. Due to differences in electoral systems, European rivals tend to come from outliers parties. Still, Judis shows that while support for traditional mainstream ruling parties has been eroding, right- and left-populist parties are gaining support in many European countries. Right-wing populist parties include the UK Independence Party, the French National Front, the Danish People's Party, and the Alternative Party in Germany. In contrast, left-wing populist parties have Syriza in Greece and Podemos in Spain (Judis 2016).

Judis and other analysts say that these populist revolts' success stemmed from the United States and Europe's economic difficulties since the 2008 global financial crisis. Mainstream parties have been claiming for years that a global economy based on free-trade and free-capital mobility will grow the economy and ensure ever-rising living standards. On the other hand, large masses see the increasing unemployment and underemployment levels and the stagnation in income much more significant economic problems. In this sense, directing the popular vote to various populist riots means a severe warning to current political leaders that something is extremely wrong and something needs to be done.

However, the messages of these protest voters were not fully perceived. In 2015, angry voters in Greece brought Syriza, a newly formed leftist populist party, to power. However, in negotiating a new financial aid package for Greece, European Community leaders told the new government that they had to ignore the voters. The European leadership insisted that Greece must continue the same massive austerity measures that drove voters to revolt in the first place.

You could say that the example of Greece is an extreme case. But for years, highly respected economists have been saying that governments in Europe and the United States should invest heavily in spending on new infrastructure and take advantage of historically low long-term interest rates to boost weak economies. Large government investments in infrastructure will create additional employment opportunities, encourage more significant private investment, and contribute to the fight to mitigate climate change damage. However, the expected infrastructure spending did not materialize. The centrist, center-right, and far-right political leaders all in a coalition tried to prevent the increase in infrastructure investments.

How can we explain this contradictory political structure? In the face of voters everywhere turning to populist candidates in protest of established policies, mainstream politicians are expected to do something to reduce voter discontent. A similar situation was happening in the United States in the 1930s. Faced with the threat of socialist and communist movements on the left and populist politicians on the right, Franklin Roosevelt carried out the ambitious legal reforms of the New Deal (Katznelson 2014).

In the period right after World War II, under the threat of powerful left movements, centrist politicians in Europe also carried out comprehensive reforms, which included significantly expanding the role of the state in managing the economy and providing various forms of social insurance (Esping-Andersen 1990). One would think that this last populist agitation period that we are currently in will lead to creating a wave comparable to the bold reforms of the 1930s.

We expected at least a comprehensive discussion on crucial reform measures that could restore economic prosperity after the 2008 Financial Recession. The only thing we've seen is that, along with some debates about more spending on infrastructure, few bold ideas have been put forward to revitalize the European Community and accelerate growth in the US economy. And despite the election rhetoric, Trump had only followed the plan of high tax cuts familiar to corporations and the wealthy when they took office. At the very least, the ruling parties can be expected to discuss such reform ideas hoping that voters will return to them rather than the protest parties in the next election. Still, such a new idea is primarily absent on both sides of the Atlantic.

In order to explain this policy inertia, it is often said that mainstream politicians in all these countries are intertwined with too many business interests to take any action that could threaten these powerful economic elites. This generalization is not always correct because business interests are not highly compatible. Many business leaders state that they are not satisfied with the global economy's low performance in recent years. For example, many large firms will benefit enormously from new public infrastructure investments.

Indeed, even in the United States, there are signs of business interests lobbying for such spending (Swanek 2021). In earlier reform times, when populist revolts put pressure on political leaders, they discovered ways to shape a reform agenda that business leaders could also accept.

Financial Times published an Editorial Board (The Editorial Board 2020) view on the economic crises when the early mounts of the pandemic. In their view, crises create credibility for some and discredit others. One of the lasting consequences of the 2008 financial crisis was to portray the world's bankers as bad guys for their role in the banking system's collapse. Today's health epidemic is of different sizes and is not the fault of large businesses. However, what matters here is the response of capitalism to the crisis. We can divide companies into two groups in terms of their response to the crisis: those who treat their employees and others well and those who try to take advantage of it.

Before the coronavirus brought economies to a halt, business leaders had pledged to adopt a new, more caring type of capitalism, the *Financial Times* mentioned in the editorial view. The Business Roundtable, a body representing senior executives of some of the largest American companies, announced last year that it would release the "shareholder first" belief that has driven capitalism for the past fifty years. Instead, companies stated that they would choose an approach that takes other stakeholders into account. At that time, no one predicted today's devastating health and financial emergency. Now is the moment for business executives to step up. Will, they really do this, or will they take advantage of this crisis as well?

Mariana Mazzucato, one of the world's most influential economists on a mission to save capitalism from itself, strives to change the way society thinks about economic value fundamentally. Unfortunately, contrary to expectations, digitalization and the expansion of globalization have helped capitalism produce more significant inequalities and divisions. It would not be an overstatement to say that capitalism does not contribute to human well-being in its current form. We need to reimagine capitalism to include a socially sustainable, livable environment and the well-being of people.

While many economists have criticized capitalism's shortcomings and failures lately, Dr. Mazzucato is focused on redesigning the basic premises of capitalism. She is looking for answers to some of the basic questions. Where does the growth come from? How do we trace the source of innovation? How can the state and private sector collaborate to create the dynamic economies we want? Her questions about capitalism are the ones which we have stopped asking for nearly forty years.

Dr. Mazzucato, in three books of modern political-economic theory, *The Entrepreneurial State* (2013), *The Value of Everything* (2018), and *Mission Economy (2021)*, opposes the long-acknowledged agile private sector and a cumbersome, inefficient state distinction. She convincingly demonstrates that the state is an under-appreciated driver for growth and innovation. Citing markets and technologies such as the internet, iPhone, and clean energy, she says that all of them are financed by public funds at crucial stages. To forget the significant public support provided by the taxes of the people behind the success achieved in these areas means not understanding the dynamics of the system sufficiently. If we overlook this point, we cannot correctly operate the mechanism behind creating wealth or value.

We see that her ideas are increasingly spreading around the world. Her messages draw attention among politicians in the United States, such as Senator Elizabeth Warren, Representative Alexandria Ocasio-Cortez, Democrat of New York, and even Republican Senator Marco Rubio of Florida. Her work has influenced then Labor leader Jeremy Corbyn and former prime minister Theresa May in the UK. Scottish leader Nicola Sturgeon has consulted her to design and implement a national investment bank. She also advises government agencies in Germany, South Africa, and elsewhere.

She reveals the fallacy of the mainstream neoliberal agenda that slashing public budgets and reducing the state's role in the economy promotes economic growth. According to Dr. Mazzucato, there is a kind of strange symbiosis between mainstream economic thought and stupid politics. She objects to many neoclassical economic theory principles taught in universities around the world: the basic assumption that supply and demand forces lead to a market equilibrium in which price equals value, and perhaps most importantly, seeing the State as a last resort investor tasked with correcting market failure. The state's role should not be a "*last resort investor*" but a "*first resort investor*" to create inclusive and sustainable wealth. Viewing the state as an entrepreneur and thus treating it as one of the main drivers of long-term economic growth made Mazzucato popular. As Mariana Mazzucato expressed correctly, if we continue to portray the state as just a facilitator and ruler and tell it to stop dreaming, all we got will be this corrupt order.

Columbia University economist and Nobel laureate Joseph Stiglitz have also been unfolding inconsistencies and failures of current operations of capitalism for some time. According to him, there is an urgent need to design a new comprehensive program to reduce income inequality. To start with, he advocates, we need to recognize that the competitive equilibrium model that has dominated the thinking of economists for more than a century does not provide a good picture of today's economy. This model is, in particular, no longer adequate to explain the growth of inequality. Evidently, we have a different view of the economy compared to 40 years or so. Big firms with massive market power now reduce competition and sustain an economy that operates based on exploitation rather than value creation. Unfortunately, the rules of the game are in favor of the powerful.

State regulations to control corporate power have rapidly weakened since the 1980s (Stiglitz 2020).

Therefore, we need an open-minded reassessment of the absurdities of the global economic system. We can start by reviewing the neoliberal ideology. It is clear that the doctrine of free-market fundamentalism has gone too far. It eroded workers' rights and economic security, triggered a deregulation race to the bottom and devastating tax competition, and enabled the emergence of gigantic new global monopolies. In this context, we will need new benchmarks applied to human and planetary progress. We now have to move forward with metrics that reflect the actual cost, risk, and opportunities of human activities, evaluating the well-being in an innovative way beyond GDP metrics.

Above all, we will need to reconsider our collective commitment to "*capitalism*" as we know it. Obviously, we shouldn't give up the essential engines of growth. Klaus Schwab, the founder of the World Economic Forum, proposes that the fundamental answer to be given in the crisis environment brought about by the pandemic is the "*Great Reset*," where the entire social and economic system will be redesigned (Schwab 2020).

Suppose we are sincere about "*the Great Reset*." In that case, the new system should start by re-setting the rules of the game in recognition of workers as stakeholders, not as a party with weak bargaining power, but as the essential elements of production. And this must be based on the understanding that eliminates all the distorted rules governing the exploitation of consumers, borrowers, students, and workers. When we establish a democratic governance model sensitive to environmental and social issues, instead of a poorly performing system that rests on rent-seeking and exacerbates inequalities, we may be optimistic about the post-pandemic future that will emerge.

CONCLUSION

As I have highlighted in previous sections, we are at an unprecedented moment in the history of humanity and our planet. Almost all of the warning lights for the world and our populations have turned red. In fact, we have been living in a world full of risks for a while. The COVID-19 outbreak is primarily the latest upsetting consequence of these deep problems. As we discussed in detail in the sections on climate change and viruses, scientists have long warned that unknown pathogens will emerge more frequently due to humans' interactions with livestock and wildlife. These interactions have steadily increased in scale and intensity over time, and as a result, they strained local ecosystems so much that deadly viruses spread. The novel coronavirus may be the most living threat we have faced in this sense, but it will not be the last unless we relax our pressure on nature.

The recent pandemic has shown how the effects of large-scale shocks emerge out of ecological systems under pressure from social and economic activities. These shocks affect the main components of human development with unprecedented magnitude, synchronization, and global reach. Simulations of the pandemic's real-time impact suggest that during 2020, all the capabilities accounted for in the Human Development Index were severely affected (Report 2020).

It would not be exaggerated to say that the times of globalization we have experienced since the past have broadened our perspective and interdependence. Indeed, we have learned to think globally on a large scale during these periods. By looking at the problems above and understanding our collective history and common vulnerability, we see that we will be able to grasp our common interests and values. When we approach challenges this way, it will be possible to find a path to shared prosperity and peace.

I guess this isn't the first time you read about how COVID-19 will profoundly change our world. Many opposing views are exhibited almost every day after the epidemic. We are faced with significant uncertainty and a broad spectrum of possibilities that leave everyone astonished. It is not easy to get a clear idea of what will happen next in such a wide range of predictions. Indeed, the future seems to be primarily determined by who moves where, how, and when. In short, we are in a rare period when humanity can truly shape our future.

With these in mind, I want to underline three critical questions for our time. First, is it possible to choose a shared path of prosperity, social inclusion, and environmental sustainability in the current era of globalization the world has reached? An affirmative answer to this question means we are to enter the course of sustainable development globally. Second, if the Anglo-American age, as it seems likely, is over and we are now in a truly multipolar world, how should our global governance form be organized? In other words, we must be able to find practical ways to solve the multilateral governance problem on a global scale. Third, is it possible to achieve international peace, and if so, by what human understanding and ethical model can this be achieved?

Lee Drutman, a senior fellow in the Political Reform program at New America, puts it well that one of the critical lessons history has taught us is that those moments of crisis force individuals and societies to reckon with and rethink. When things go terribly wrong, we all ask if there is a better way to survive in the world we live in, from people on the street to intellectuals to experts to decision-makers. Undoubtedly, such inquiries have been made before. Still, in a crisis that affects the whole world, the old order's mistakes and distortions attract much more attention and become subject to intense criticism. Past experiences show that new ideas and structures emerge and begin to gain acceptance when the old ones lose their validity and are cleared (Drutman 2020).

In disasters such as the ongoing epidemic or the previous economic crisis, governments intervene to protect the lives and livelihoods of their citizens. We witnessed massive bailout efforts by governments in the aftermath of the 2008 financial crisis. Due to the Great Financial crisis, governments have transferred more than $3 trillion to the financial system globally, mainly in the United States and EU. The aim was to support the credit markets and get the global economy working again. Eventually, most government aids went to the financial sector rather than to support the real economy. In other words, governments have done nothing but save the big investment banks that directly contributed to the crisis in the name of stimulating the economy. As the economy revived, taxpayers were left with a global economy that was as corrupt, unequal, and carbon-intensive as before.

As expected, to cope with the new health and economic crises caused by the pandemic, governments stepped in to implement stimulus packages to protect jobs, draft rules to slow the spread of the disease, and invest in treatment and vaccine research and development. There is no doubt that these rescue efforts are necessary. At this point, if a lesson is to be learned from the past, the most important thing is that countries experiencing severe health and economic problems due to the coronavirus epidemic should not repeat the same mistake.

Governments' missions are not limited to intervening in the economy as a last resort when markets collapse or crises occur. Governments, with full force, should also focus on implementing policies that generate enduring solutions for the post-crisis period. If this critical point is missed, facing repeated crises will be inevitable in the future. It will also not serve businesses dealing with long-term growth opportunities. The corporate bailout interventions burdened by taxpayers will be wasted, and the missed opportunity will only prepare for the dawn of a new crisis. Hence, it is crucial that the interventions, from the very beginning, are designed in a way that eliminates the root cause of the problems and prevents the recurrence of similar issues.

Therefore, it is fair to say that as countries emerge from the current crisis, governments can do more than stimulate economic growth. They can drive economic growth toward the goal of building a better economy. Instead of distributing unconditional aid to companies, governments can pursue their rescue operations dependent on policies that protect the public interest and solve societal problems. For example, government support to companies that develop the COVID-19 vaccine could be tied to the condition that the vaccine is accessible to all social segments. By the same logic, governments may refuse to bail out companies that do not limit their carbon emissions or keep their profits in tax havens.

We also face the lack and insufficiency of government capacity. But after an apparent market failure, governments often step in, and their policies are too small and too late. When the state is seen as a repairer and not a partner in creating value, publicly funded resources become insufficient for other areas deemed necessary by society. Therefore, social programs, education, and health services are often under-financed.

For nearly forty years, we have observed that governments in the Western world, especially in the United States, have followed a policy that protects large companies rather than prioritizing society and people against risks. To put it more clearly, they privatize the rewards while trying to make society pay for the risks they face. When in trouble, many businesses rush to ask governments for help, but when their business is good, they want governments to get out of their way. Joseph Stiglitz rejects such economic policies and makes strong criticism as follows:

> We're not in the business of giving gifts. They put themselves in that position of having too little capital buffers, and they paid out huge amounts in share buybacks and dividends. Why should we bail them out? The answer is that we worry about jobs and we worry about the macro effects, but we can effectively claw back that money from the shareholders by providing it as loans. The free money is basically going to the rich shareholders. (Stewart 2020)

I believe that the COVID-19 crisis offers a tremendous opportunity to fix this unfair relationship. The situation may improve if companies rescued by the government are forced to act more in the public interest. A new form of agreement emerges that allows taxpayers to share the benefits of recovery traditionally only going to the private sector.

Thanks to the development of a range of vaccines, many countries are looking forward to returning life to normal. I don't believe the majority of people want to go back to the old normal they suffered a lot. As I mentioned earlier, advanced economies suffered from major structural flaws long before the COVID-19 hit, in the "*old normal.*" For example, the financial sector was mainly devoting its resources to itself. As a result of this policy, the economy's long-term growth trend has begun to erode seriously. Much of the financial sector's profits were reinvested in finance (banks, insurance companies, and real estate) rather than productive uses such as infrastructure or innovation. The current financial structure feeds a debt-driven system and speculative bubbles, and when these burst, banks and others plead with the government to bail them out.

Another point is that companies generally operate with a short-term, in a sense, myopic approach. Indeed, we observe that many large businesses neglect long-term investments for short-term gains. First of all, CEOs and corporate boards, constantly looking at quarterly returns and stock prices, reward shareholders by taking back stock, increasing the value of the remaining shares and stock options that are part of most executive pay packages. The fact that Fortune 500 companies have repurchased more than $3 trillion of their own shares annually since 2010 is clear evidence of this. These repurchases are made at the cost of investment in wages, worker training, and research and development.

The world we live in now faces urgent and severe social, technological, and economic problems. What will the future of the welfare state most of us aim for? How can digital platforms, which have become typical environments of today, be managed democratically and inclusively? What is the best way to deal with the climate change problem that profoundly affects our lives and our future? What new forms of investment, regulation, and cooperation do we need for this purpose?

The answers to these questions necessitate public and private organizations to collaborate in new ways and become more purpose-driven. In this context, governments need different tools and capabilities to co-create and co-shape markets, not just fix market failures.

The crisis today reveals the limits of the overmarketed economy. The consequences of a patchwork, a costly market-driven healthcare system, and a large uninsured population have never been more evident. The interconnectedness of the global economy with fragile "just in time" supply chains creates a fundamental need for a fundamental reassessment of an industrial model that has long placed efficiency and profit ahead of flexibility and stability. And of course, in a big crisis, most of those who advocate a small government disappear. Keynesianism is revived, and its supporters grow in numbers.

Just as the stagflation seen in the economies in the 1970s eliminated the old economic doctrines of that time and made the economic policy more market-oriented, now we have the chance to reconsider the current deficient system. We have the great opportunity of rebuilding the economic bargains of the market economy and the social safety net in the post-pandemic world.

The same is true for cities, towns, and villages as well as land-use policies in general. We could design and build our cities in a way that allows people to develop in harmony with nature and achieve sustainable development. For this, instead of wild capitalism principles based on rent generating and excessive commercialization, all we need is to work with an insight based on human-oriented, eco-city development and ecological principles. Cities, towns, and villages could be designed to improve their residents' health and quality of life and maintain the ecosystems they depend on. The vision of developing new cities or transforming old ones includes citizen initiative, public administration, ecologically efficient industry, people's needs and desires, harmonious culture, and landscapes in which nature, agriculture, and the built environment are functionally well integrated.

Furthermore, we need to reinvigorate ambition and vision in our day-to-day policy-making process. We should not just be content with bold statements but take action. First of all, we must believe in the indispensable role of the public sector in the economy. The next step focuses on developing the public's core capabilities, such as the ability to interact with other value creators in society and design public benefit contracts. At this point, it is critical that it creates more effective interfaces with innovations in the whole society. It will also be necessary to rethink how public policies will be designed around the new goals in the way of restoring the public purpose in economic policies where the public interest comes to the forefront rather than making profits. The main goal should be to create tangible benefits for citizens. On the other hand, it would be a significant change to put a purpose at the center of corporate governance and ensure that the needs of not only shareholders but also all stakeholders, including employees and community organizations, are taken into account.

To solve the world's current vast problems, we need not only technological but also social, organizational, and political innovation. Problems are gigantic, complex, and resistant to simple solutions. This leads us to politics. Political scientists have long stated that high levels of economic inequality are a fundamental threat to democracy. The survival of democracy depends to a large extent on believing that the system benefits everyone. This belief has been weakening for a long time. The need to rethink and redesign the foundations of our political system has never been greater, as is the immediate issue of correcting our corrupt and distorted economic system. Conflicts are even more complex as they become a seemingly inevitable part of any policy choice, as costs and benefits are not equally distributed along with stakeholders. There is no doubt that those who benefit from the current system's functioning try to block the necessary action by using their money to influence decision-makers and the media.

As António Guterres, UN secretary-general boldly, puts it:

> COVID-19 has been likened to an x-ray, revealing fractures in the fragile skeleton of the societies we have built. It is exposing fallacies and falsehoods everywhere: The lie that free markets can deliver healthcare for all; The fiction that unpaid care work is not work; The delusion that we live in a post-racist world; The myth that we are all in the same boat. While we are all floating on the same sea, it's clear that some are in super yachts, while others are clinging to the drifting debris. (United Nations 2020)

The old slogans of Western democracy and free global trade leading humanity to a shared prosperity increase have continually faded and lost credibility with the past two decades' events. Suddenly such a pandemic engulfed the world, shaking these old ideas intensely and even destroying them for some.

At such moments, as Lee Durtman puts it, it's natural for our instinct to focus on immediate needs first. However, we know that we do not have the chance to ignore what kind of future awaits us. Uncertainty creates an opportunity for a broader range of long-term results. Our ultimate path depends on the long- and short-term assets we invest, the conversations we have, and the political and economic preferences we make.

The world is facing a radical challenge to norms it had come to take for granted. The pandemic has revealed that postwar institutions, though still functioning, are fatigued and need reviving. It has uncovered the costs of systemic weaknesses that enabled populists and extremists to gain power in many places. Above all, it has demonstrated that we are all in this together regardless of where we live.

Maybe, we cannot predict the future with precision, but if we act now with reason and compassion, we can shape it in a way that encourages joint development. We cannot afford to repeat historical mistakes because we no longer have time to waste.

The clock is ticking fast for the doomsday of our planet. This pandemic could be the last wake-up call for all humanity and the survival of our world.

REFERENCES

Baytiyeh, Hoda. "Online Learning During Post-earthquake School Closures." *Disaster Prevention and Management* 27, no. 2 (2018): 215–227.

Block, Fred L. *Capitalism: The Future of an Illusion.* University of Colombia Press, 2018.

Brussevich, Mariya, Era Dabla-Norris, and Salma Khalid. "Who will Bear the Brunt of Lockdown Policies? Evidence from Tele-workability Measures Across Countries." *International Monetary Fund.* June 12, 2020. https://www.imf.org/en/Publications/WP/Issues/2020/06/12/Who-will-Bear-the-Brunt-of-Lockdown-Policies-Evidence-from-Tele-workability-Measures-Across-49479.

Burnet, Frank Macfarlane, and David O. White. *Natural History of Infectious Disease.* Cambridge University Press, 1972.

Caulford, Paul. "SARSR: Aftermath of an Outbreak." *The Lancet* 362, no. Special Issue (2003): 2–3.

Chow, Denise. "New England Journal of Medicine: 'Dangerously Incompetent' Politicians Must Go." *NBC News.* October 8, 2020. https://www.nbcnews.com/science/science-news/leading-medical-journal-americans-must-vote-out-current-leaders-n1242487.

Crosby, Alfred W. *America's Forgotten Pandemic: The Influenza of 1918.* UK: The Press Syndicate of The University of Cambridge, 2003.

Cutler, David M., and Lawrence H. Summers. "The COVID-19 Pandemic and the $16 Trillion Virus." *JAMA* 324, no. 15 (2020): 1495–1496.

Diamond, Larry. "Liberation Technology." *Journal of Democracy* 21, no. 3 (2010): 69–83. https://www.journalofdemocracy.org/articles/liberation-technology/.

Drutman, Lee. "What Comes After the Pandemic?" *New America*. April 21, 2020. https://www.newamerica.org/weekly/what-comes-after-pandemic/.

Ellen MacArthur Foundation. *Towards a Circular Economy: Business Rationale for an Accelerated Transition*. 2015. https://www.ellenmacarthurfoundation.org/publications/towards-a-circular-economy-business-rationale-for-an-accelerated-transition.

Epstein, Helen, and Lincoln Chen. "Can AIDS Be Stopped?" *The New York Review*. March 14, 2002. https://www.nybooks.com/articles/2002/03/14/can-aids-be-stopped/.

Esping-Andersen, Gøsta. *The Three Worlds of Welfare Capitalism*. Princeton University Press, 1990.

Financial Times. *Decarbonisation: Plotting the Path to Net Zero*. June 25, 2020. https://channels.ft.com/rethink/decarbonisation-net-zero/.

Financial Times Latest Figures. May 11, 2020. https://www.covidmapp.com/blog/financial-times-latest-figures.

Global SDG Integration. *Impact of COVID-19 on the Sustainable Development Goals*. December 2020. https://sdgintegration.undp.org/accelerating-development-progressduring-covid-19.

Gold, Russell, Ruth Bender, ve Peter Landers. "President Biden Quickly Rejoined Paris Climate Accord. Meeting the Emissions Goals Will Be Harder." *The Wall Street Journal*. January 21, 2021. https://www.wsj.com/articles/president-biden-quickly-rejoined-paris-climate-accord-leading-again-will-be-harder-11611257931.

Guterres, António. "Global Wake-up Call—The Manila Times." July 2, 2020. https://www.manilatimes.net/2020/07/02/opinion/analysis/global-wake-up-call/736917/.

Hotz, Robert Lee, and Natasha Khan. "'Really Diabolical': Inside the Coronavirus That Outsmarted Science." *The Wall Street Journal*. September 7, 2020. https://www.wsj.com/articles/really-diabolical-inside-the-coronavirus-that-outsmarted-science-11599498840.

International Monetary Fund. "World Economic Outlook: A Long and Difficult Ascent." Washington, DC, 2020.

Jonsson, Oscar, and Owen Taylor. "How to Govern the New Digital Domain." *Project Syndicate*. October 20, 2020. https://www.project-syndicate.org/commentary/three-priorities-for-governing-digital-economy-by-oscar-jonsson-and-taylor-owen-2020-10?barrier=accesspaylog.

Judis, John B. *The Populist Explosion: How the Great Recession Transformed American and European Politics*. Columbia Global Reports, 2016.

Kaminker, Christopher, and Kristina Church. "Building Back Better - A Sustainable Post-covid Recovery." *Lombard Odier*. May 20, 2020. https://www.lombardodier.com/contents/corporate-news/responsible-capital/2020/may/building-back-better---a-sustain.html.

Katznelson, Ira. *Fear Itself: The New Deal and the Origins of Our Time*. Liveright, 2014.

La Monica, Paul R. . "Proof Big Tech is Way Too Big: It's a Quarter of Your Portfolio." *CNN.* January 6, 2021. https://edition.cnn.com/2021/01/06/investing/stocks-sp-500-tech/index.html.

Lee, Jong-Wha, Warwick J. McKibbin, and Lee Jong-Wha. "Estimating the Global Economic Costs of SARS." In *Learning from SARS: Preparing for the Next Disease Outbreak: Workshop Summary*, by Institute of Medicine. Washington DC: The National Academies Press, 2004.

Leitenberg, Milton. "Did the SARS-CoV-2 Virus Arise from a Bat Coronavirus Research Program in a Chinese Laboratory? Very Possibly." *Bulletin of the Atomic Scientists*, June 4, 2020.

Levy, Ari. "Tech's Top Seven Companies added $3.4 Trillion in Value in 2020." *CNBC.* December 31, 2020. https://www.cnbc.com/2020/12/31/techs-top-seven-companies-added-3point4-trillion-in-value-in-2020.html.

Lombardodier. *From WILD to CLIC.* 2020. https://www.lombardodier.com/clic.

Lynch, David J. "U.S. Economy May Have its Best Chance in Years to Break from Era of Subpar Growth." *The Washington Post.* February 20, 2021. https://www.washingtonpost.com/business/2021/02/20/economy-growth-pandemic/.

Mace, Matt. *Finance and Policy: The External Drivers Forcing Businesses to Take Climate Action.* February 3, 2021. https://www.edie.net/library/Finance-and-policy--The-external-drivers-making-businesses-take-note-of-climate-action/7031.

Mazzucato, Mariana, Rainer Kattel, Tim O'reilly, and Josh Entsminger. "Reimagining the Platform Economy." *Project Syndicate.* February 5, 2021. project-syndicate.org/onpoint/platform-economy-data-generation-and-value-extraction-by-mariana-mazzucato-etal-.

Mazzucato, Mariana. "From Moonshots to Earthshots." *Project Syndicate.* February 3, 2021. https://www.project-syndicate.org/commentary/moonshots-earthshots-state-investment-in-the-public-interest-by-mariana-mazzucato-2021-02?barrier=accesspaylog.

McNeil, Sam, and Huizhong Wu. "WHO Team Arrives in Wuhan to Investigate Pandemic Origins." *AP News.* January 14, 2021. https://apnews.com/article/who-team-arrives-wuhan-virus-origins-db3e9adcbfa801d3e8274c1976ea5fcd.

Meredith, Sam. *CNBC.* July 1, 2021. https://www.cnbc.com/2020/07/01/coronavirus-thousands-attend-farewell-pandemic-party-in-prague.html.

Milanovic, Branko. "The World Is Becoming More Equal Even as Globalization Hurts Middle-Class Westerners." *Foreign Affairs.* August 28, 2020. https://www.foreignaffairs.com/articles/world/2020-08-28/world-economic-inequality.

News, US. *U.S. News Staff.* July 9, 2019. https://www.usnews.com/news/best-countries/slideshows/the-10-most-economically-influential-countries-ranked-by-perception.

Odier, Patrick. *Patrick Odier on Lombard Odier's long term sustainable thinking.* May 10, 2019. https://www.lombardodier.com/contents/corporate-news/in-the-news/2019/may/patrick-odier-on-lombard-odiers.html.

Patterson, Jennifer A. "As Jobs Crisis Deepens, ILO Warns of Uncertain and Incomplete Labour Market Recovery." *ILO.* June 30, 2020. https://www.ilo.org/global/about-the-ilo/newsroom/news/WCMS_749398/lang--en/index.htm.

PIK. *Four of Nine Planetary Boundaries Now Crossed* . January 16, 2015. https://www.pik-potsdam.de/en/news/latest-news/four-of-nine-planetary-boundaries-now-crossed.

Post, The Washington. *How Trump's Erratic Behavior and Failure on Coronavirus Doomed His Reelection.* November 7, 2020. https://www.washingtonpost.com/elections/interactive/2020/trump-pandemic-coronavirus-election/?tid=ss_tw.

Prime Minister's Office. *gov.uk.* January 4, 2021. https://www.gov.uk/government/speeches/prime-ministers-address-to-the-nation-4-january-2021.

Quinlan, Heather E. *Plagues, Pandemics and Viruses: From the Plague of Athens to Covid 19.* Visible Ink, 2020.

Quinn, David, and Morgan Polikoff. *Summer Learning Loss: What is it, and What Can We do about it?* https://www.brookings.edu/research/summer-learning-loss-what-is-it-and-what-can-we-do-about-it/, 2017.

Raval, Anjli. "Big Fossil Fuel Groups All Failing Climate Goals, Study Shows." *Financial Times.* October 7, 2020. https://www.ft.com/content/16091645-98b3-4041-9ca2-053fb60181ba.

Report, The 2020 Human Development. *The Next Frontier: Human Development and the Anthropocene.* United Nations Development Programme, 2020.

Revollo, R. Espinoza. *The Inequality Virus: Methodology Note.* UK: Oxfam International, 2021.

Sachs, Jeffrey D. *The Ages of Globalization: Geography, Technology, and Institutions.* Columbia University Press, 2020.

Sandbu, Martin. "The Moment of Danger for Europe Will be when the Recovery Starts." *Financial Times.* February 14, 2021. https://www.ft.com/content/1d8e4012-1593-46ed-a96d-a6764e74af9e.

Sato, Makiko, and James Hansen. *Updating the Climate Science: What Path is the Real World Following?* December 17, 2020. http://www.columbia.edu/~mhs119/SeaLevel/.

Schumaker, Erin. "Coronavirus Map: Tracking the Spread in the US and Around the World." August 7, 2020. https://abcnews.go.com/Health/coronavirus-map-tracking-spread-us-world/story?id=69415591.

Schwab, Klaus. *Post-Covid Capitalism.* USA. October 12, 2020. https://www.project-syndicate.org/commentary/post-covid-capitalism-great-reset-by-klaus-schwab-2020-10?barrier=accesspaylog.

Snowden, Frank M. "Emerging and Reemerging Diseases: A Historical Perspective." *Immunological Reviews* 225, no. 1 (2008): 9–26.

Snowden, Frank M. *Epidemics and Society: From the Black Death to the Present.* Yale University Press, 2020.

Spence , Michael, and Danny Leipziger. "The Pandemic Public-Debt Dilemma." *Project Syndicate.* December 8, 2020. https://www.project-syndicate.org/commentary/pandemic-spending-debt-dilemma-by-michael-spence-and-danny-leipziger-2020-12?barrier=accesspaylog.

Stewart, Emily. *Nobel Laureate Joseph Stiglitz on How to Fix the Economy During and After the Pandemic.* October 28, 2020. https://www.vox.com/covid-19-coronavirus-economy-recession-stock-market/21536710/joseph-stiglitz-interview-covid-19-recovery (accessed 2021).

Stiglitz, Joseph. "The Pandemic Has Laid Bare Deep Divisions, but it's Not Too Late to Change Course." *IMF*. Fall 2020. https://www.imf.org/external/pubs/ft/fandd/2020/09/COVID19-and-global-inequality-joseph-stiglitz.htm.

Swanek, Thaddeus. "Infrastructure and Workforce Development Are Key to Rebuilding America." *The U.S. Chamber of Commerce*. January 15, 2021. https://www.uschamber.com/series/above-the-fold/infrastructure-and-workforce-development-are-key-rebuilding-america.

Teachout, Zephyr. "Monopoly Versus Democracy: How to End a Gilded Age." *Foreign Affairs*. January/February 2021. https://www.foreignaffairs.com/articles/united-states/2020-12-08/monopoly-versus-democracy.

The Editorial Board. "Virus Puts Responsible Capitalism to the Test." *Financial Times*. March 29, 2020. https://www.ft.com/content/a47c734a-702e-11ea-89df-41bea055720b.

The Washington Post. *We're Still Missing the Origin Story of This Pandemic: China is Sitting on the Answers to the Pandemic*. February 5, 2021. https://www.washingtonpost.com/opinions/2021/02/05/coronavirus-origins-mystery-china/.

The World Bank. *World Bank Predicts Sharpest Decline of Remittances in Recent History*. April 22, 2020. https://www.worldbank.org/en/news/press-release/2020/04/22/world-bank-predicts-sharpest-decline-of-remittances-in-recent-history.

Thomas, Nathalie. "Environment Groups Question UK's Carbon Capture Push." *Financial Times*. January 11, 2021. https://www.ft.com/content/c92f62ce-451b-4727-8bf9-6ce5429d38d7.

Today, Decentralize. *6 Warnings and 1 Myth From Epidemics and Society*. August 8, 2020. https://dt.gl/6-warnings-and-1-myth-from-epidemics-and-society/.

Todd, Chuck. *Meet the Press*. January 3, 2021. https://www.nbcnews.com/meet-the-press/meet-press-january-3-2021-n1252689 (2021 tarihinde erişilmiştir).

UNDP. "COVID-19: Human Development on Course to Decline This Year for the First Time since 1990." *UNDP*. May 20, 2020. https://www.undp.org/content/undp/en/home/news-centre/news/2020/COVID19_Human_development_on_course_to_decline_for_the_first_time_since_1990.html.

UNESCO. *From COVID-19 Learning Disruption to Recovery: A Snapshot of UNESCO's Work in Education in 2020*. December 16, 2020. https://en.unesco.org/news/covid-19-learning-disruption-recovery-snapshot-unescos-work-education-2020.

United Nations. *Secretary-General's Nelson Mandela Lecture: "Tackling the Inequality Pandemic: A New Social Contract for a New Era."* July 7, 2020. https://www.un.org/sg/en/content/sg/statement/2020-07-18/secretary-generals-nelson-mandela-lecture-%E2%80%9Ctackling-the-inequality-pandemic-new-social-contract-for-new-era%E2%80%9D-delivered (accessed 2021).

Westhoven, William. "Hired to Write Pandemic Book in 2018, Parsippany Author Adds Dr. Fauci on Deadline." *Daily Record*. October 18, 2020. https://www.dailyrecord.com/story/news/2020/10/16/parsippany-author-adds-dr-anthony-fauci-pandemic-book/3649392001/.

WHO. *WHO Director-General's Opening Remarks at 148th Session of the Executive Board*. January 18, 2021. https://www.who.int/director-general/speeches/detail/who-director-general-s-opening-remarks-at-148th-session-of-the-executive-board.

Winston, Andrew. *Is the COVID-19 Outbreak a Black Swan or the New Normal.* Massachusetts. March 16, 2020. https://sloanreview.mit.edu/article/is-the-covid-19-outbreak-a-black-swan-or-the-new-normal/.

Wolf, Martin. *Economists Exchange.* January 18, 2021. https://www.ft.com/content/74cdb0f1-02ed-408f-ad19-6a6c7408d637.

Woods, Ngaire. "The Brutal Governance Lessons of 2020." *MyRepublica.* April 25, 2021. https://myrepublica.nagariknetwork.com/news/the-brutal-governance-lessons-of-2020/.

Woodville, Louisa. "The Black Death." *Smarthistory.* December 30, 2015. https://smarthistory.org/the-black-death/ (accessed April 24, 2021).

World Health Organization. Communicable Diseases Cluster. *Removing Obstacles to Healthy Development : Report on Infectious Diseases.* World Health Organization. 1999. https://apps.who.int/iris/handle/10665/65847.

Chapter 1

The World after Corona

A Multilevel Approach

Emre Erdoğan

The pandemic has already affected the globe in a very negative way. As of October 1, 2020, nearly 31,900,000 people have been infected, and the number of deaths is about 1 million. A wide range of restrictions have been imposed in many countries to prevent contagion or to flatten the curve (Lolla et al. 2020). According to the IMF, the pandemic has caused the "worst economic downturn since the Great Depression" (Gopinath 2020). Different sources have calculated an economic decline of up to 35 percent in the first quarter of the year, and it was estimated that the globe will experience a negative growth rate of about 5 percent in 2020. In some developing countries, this rate is about 10 percent (IMF 2020a). The World Bank estimates that COVID-19 will push 71–100 million people into extreme poverty by wiping out the progress made in the fight against poverty over the last ten years (World Bank 2020). The most vulnerable segments of society, children, and women living in the worst conditions will be hurt by the pandemic, and the income gap within societies will increase (Azcona et al. 2020; UNICEF 2020). To prevent such economic devastation, governments are implementing economic stimulus packages reaching up to 20 percent of their GDP; the extent to which this effort will ease the damage, however, is uncertain (Elgin et al. 2020; IMF 2020b).

Turkey experienced a negative growth rate of 10 percent in the second quarter of the year. Despite the ban on laying off employees, 2.7 million people left the job market, and the labor force participation rate declined by 4 percent; this decline is 7 percent among young people (TURKSTAT 2020). It is clear that those working in the informal sector, seasonal agricultural workers, and, most importantly, Syrian immigrants are also going to be affected by all aspects of this pandemic (DİSK-AR 2020; Kalkınma Atölyesi 2020).

Unsurprisingly, this kind of devastation will have a massive effect on the world we live in, and the world after COVID-19 will be very different.

There is much speculation about our global future, and the consensus is far from being reached. It is possible to classify these speculators as optimists and pessimists. While there are people from both ends of the political spectrum in the optimist wing, left-leaning optimists believe that the pandemic and future crises are the product of capitalism, which has shown its weaknesses. Although the developed world holds only 15 percent of the world population, 79 percent of deaths related to the pandemic occurred in these countries, especially in the United States, the United Kingdom, Italy, and Spain. Empirical studies show that the number of COVID-19 deaths per million is higher in relatively wealthier countries. Several studies confirmed this relationship after controlling for other variables such as the proportion of elderly, the density of the population, and obesity rates (Schellekens and Sourrouille 2020; Chodcik and Weil 2020; Chaudhry et al. 2020).

This failure of the dominant mode of production, that is, capitalism, is related to several factors, especially the death rate of people in the welfare states because of the attack of neoliberal governance. Commercialization of health services and the reduction of funds channeled to public services created a very unsuitable environment for vulnerable people. This contributed to the increase in the number of deaths (Navarro 2020; Saad-Filho 2020). For the optimists, the market forces poisoned by neoliberal ideology failed to deal with the pandemic and suggest it will fail to fight against the economic consequences. Hence, they believe that the pandemic created a good opportunity to revise this style of governance and establish a new and more equal societal system (Maylam 2020; Sen 2020). As the famous economist, Daron Acemoğlu (2020), states: "Many advanced economies need a stronger social safety net, better coordination, smarter regulation, more effective government, a significantly improved public-health system, and, in the US case, more reliable and equitable forms of health insurance."

The pessimists and optimists agree on the simple fact that the current system failed to respond to the challenge of the COVID-19 pandemic as well as the challenge of previous pandemics or global warming. However, for the pessimist wing, this failure will lead to the rise of a hostile environment filled with political-economic crises, other pandemics, and wars (Allen et al. 2020; Krastev 2020). Like the rise of fascism after World War I, political scientists such as Stephen Walt foresee the rise of "corona-nationalism" and authoritarianism: "The pandemic will strengthen the state and reinforce nationalism. Governments of all types will adopt emergency measures to manage the crisis, and many will be loath to relinquish these new powers when the crisis is over" (Walt 2020).

Besides a simple, binary, negative, or positive approach to the world after the coronavirus, I believe that changes at three different levels will occur and all of them will interact with each other. Such complex interactions will present many diverse paths to our future. These changes will arise in the relations between (a) states, (b) states and society, and (c) individuals.

CHANGE AT THE INTERNATIONAL LEVEL

Like other pandemics, the COVID-19 contagion is going global. It started in a province of China, and in less than five months, almost every country has been infected by this virus. Several studies suggest that more globalized countries are among the more infected due to a greater openness to immigration, international travel, and trade (Zimmermann et al. 2020). Even within countries, more connected regions have been heavily affected compared to the more isolated areas (Allain-Dupré et al. 2020).

Although the contagion was global, the response was not. The experience of the last year has demonstrated that the international and supranational organizations failed to deal with the virus and its consequences rapidly and effectively. The WHO is the scapegoat for the failure of global cooperation against the pandemic. Many countries, including the United States, criticized the WHO for accepting the official statements of China and causing a delay in a declaration of emergency at the global level (Tufekci 2020). The WHO also has been accused of giving contradictory information about the virus in critical issues such as wearing masks or using specific medications for treatment (Schumaker 2020; Blouin-Genest et al. 2020). The WHO seems to have lost its international reputation and some of its financial resources even though it is the only institution that could act as a platform for coordination and solidarity (Peel 2020).

The WHO is not the only supranational institution that has failed to satisfy the expectations of the global community. The EU, which has already triggered a massive wave of skepticism because of its weak performance following the financial crisis of 2018 and the refugee crisis of 2015, acted very slowly to stimulate a collective effort against the pandemic. Although it has the necessary tools, the EU delayed in providing medical equipment, such as masks, to Italy and Spain and failed to prevent the ban on the export of these goods by member countries such as Germany and the Netherlands. This gap has been filled by other countries, such as China and Turkey, which have provided medical assistance. Similarly, the EU failed to organize a common border policy; member countries preferred to apply individual travel bans and border restrictions. Finally, the EU also delayed creating a financial package to ease the fight against the economic damage of the pandemic

(Gostyńska-Jakubowska and Scazzieri 2020; Krastev 2020). Although the EU eventually took steps to help the old continent to deal with the first wave of the pandemic, its slow response damaged its reputation in the eye of the public (Janse and Tsanova 2020).

In addition to the WHO and the EU, other international and supranational institutions also failed. The Bretton Woods Institutions—the World Bank and the IMF—and the UNCTAD have been threatened by increased economic nationalism and the focus of national governments on stimulating economic growth to prevent collateral damage of measures taken against the pandemic. The UNHCR is facing the worst crisis in its history. The pandemic threatens 26 million refugees, three-quarters of whom live in developing countries. The UNHCR must continue to cover their basic needs, such as housing, education, food, and health services, with its resources in a milieu where national governments are unwilling to channel their funds to foreigners (Blanco and Rosales 2020; Global Compact 2020; Krastev 2020). This failure of the international and supranational institutions to deal with the pandemic has led to an erosion of trust. A recent survey conducted by the European Council of Foreign Relations (ECFR) found that the majority of the European public (with up to two-thirds of respondents in Italy and France) thinks that the EU responded to the pandemic poorly. According to the same survey, about half of the voters in the surveyed countries believe that the EU was "irrelevant" during the crisis (Krastev and Leonard 2020).

The recent rise of populist movements in the world will not ease the job of international and supranational institutions. Populist leaders always become critical toward international institutions and use them as the scapegoats in the failure of the national governments, even though they were in power. The UK, Hungary, Poland, Germany, and France are countries where Euroscepticism has become the central issue of everyday politics (Balfour 2020). The pandemic created an opportunity for populist leaders to voice their criticisms against these international institutions and enhance their voter base (Meyer 2020; Stavrakakis and Katsampekis 2020). Although some studies have shown the presence of the "rally around the flag" effect, namely increased support for governing parties and mainstream leaders (Bol et al. 2020; Henley 2020), and created optimism about the death of the populist movements because of their "incompetence" to deal with the crisis (Kendall-Taylor and Nietsche 2020), the populist leaders have mastered exploiting the negative consequences of the crisis and the hope for a return to mainstream politics was short-lived (De Vries and Hobolt 2020).

Under these conditions, the multilateralism in the global order and the empowerment of international and supranational institutions seem almost impossible. The fight against the pandemic and its social and economic consequences requires cooperation at the global level. Without the cooperation of nations, the cost of the pandemic will be greater. There are demands for "a global Marshall Plan" (Goldin and Muggah 2020), "international solidarity," "a Hamiltonian moment" (Calhoun 2015), and "a left-populist strategy" (Mouffe 2020). However, in the age of rising "corona-nationalism," and in the presence of populist leaders ready to exploit the failure of international bodies, such an effort to rebuild international cooperation will be very difficult.

Changing State-Society Relations

The second level of change will be observed in the state-society relations. The reaction of governments to the pandemic and their performances have been discussed in detail, especially in the early days of the pandemic. Some governments were faster in taking extreme strict measures, such as school closures, and others focused on economic support; there was a significant variation across governments. China, South Korea, Hong Kong, Sweden, and the UK were relatively slow (Lolla et al. 2020). Another group of researchers shows that governments were quick in adopting easy-to-implement policies, such as external border restrictions, the forming of task forces, public awareness campaigns, and efforts to increase health resources, and they were unwilling to implement difficult policies, such as curfews, closures of schools, restrictions of nonessential businesses, and restrictions of mass gatherings. Although there has been some convergence on government policies over time, New Zealand and Latvia were very active in implementing these policies, and the United States was among the slowest (Cheng et al. 2020). Reasons for this variation between countries attracted the attention of scholars; some empirical work suggests that the exposure to the risk—number of deaths, closeness to China—was the most crucial determinant of the rigidity of measures, whereas the government effectiveness and the quality of the health system are negatively correlated (Porcher 2020).

The most important discussion on the determinants of the government responses to the pandemic was related to the regime type. It is generally accepted that authoritarian governments have more opportunities to take extreme measures as they are not dependent on societal approval, but democratic regimes need to have the support of society. The cost of extreme measures is high for elected governments if they fail, but the authoritarian governments have the luxury of hiding the facts by restricting information flow (Kavanagh and Singh 2020; Greer et al. 2020).

However, some explanations suggest that the failure of some democracies should not hide the overall supremacy of democracies over authoritarian regimes. According to Alon, Farrell, and Li (2020), democracies performed better because of the responsibility of elected officials to the people; the failure of some democracies, such as the United States, was related to its partisan polarization, which locked the reaction of the independent institutions. Carothers and Wong (2020) argue that authoritarian regimes have innate weaknesses, such as the lack of civil society and independent institutions, the paranoia of leaders of presenting their failures, a personalistic style of governance that prevents the development of coherent policies, and their vulnerability against the economic consequences of the pandemic as their legitimacy is highly based on their economic performance. From this perspective, it is easy to explain the failure of some democracies, such as the United States and Brazil, with their authoritarian tendencies (Carothers and Wong 2020). Acemoğlu (2020) also explains the failure of the United States with the rise of authoritarian politics in the country and the decline of independent institutions as a result of hyper-politicization.

Given that the COVID-19 pandemic is not the last global threat toward humanity—there will likely be other pandemics and we are already facing global climate change and the exhaustion of natural resources—societies are seeking an answer to a simple question: What kind of government do we need to fight against these threats? The unfinished COVID-19 experience will provide some clues about the nature of the successful government of the future.

Despite the lack of evidence about the success of authoritarian regimes (Frey et al. 2020), the pandemic seems to have threatened liberal democracies. First, the pandemic illustrated the need for a quick reaction from governments to take extreme measures against the will of the people. A fragile government seeking the approval of the parliament or its coalition partners cannot act in that way, and citizens may support a more decisive government style. Second, our experience showed that the surveillance of society played a vital role in the success of countries such as South Korea and Singapore. These new instruments of surveillance, including the active regulation of the internet, may be abused by authoritarian leaders to restrict human liberties (Cooper and Aitchison 2020). Third, authoritarian leaders exploited the pandemic to increase their control over society by imposing extra measures to restrict liberties and received extraordinary powers from their parliaments (Fukuyama 2020). This trend may be contagious in the uninstitutionalized democracies of Eastern Europe, Latin America, and Central Asia, which are already facing a new wave of "autocratization" (Rapeli and Saikkonen 2020). The V-Dem Institute already estimated that forty-eight countries have a risk of democratic decline as a result of pandemic-related government policies (Lührmann, Edgell, and Maerz 2020).

The choice between democratic or authoritarian regimes will certainly depend on the performance of governments during the next phase of the pandemic. Current global statistics signal a very strong possibility of a second wave, which will hit most countries, and many countries have started to implement preemptive measures to reduce its negative effects (Graham-Harrison 2020). Experts are almost sure that a second wave will have devastating costs on the economy and governments will be unwilling to use the same harsh measures (OECD 2020a). These circumstances will create a suitable environment for authoritarian, rightist, and populist movements which will exploit the climate of fear dominating the globe.

Change in Relations between Individuals

The third radical change in the world after COVID-19 will be observed in interpersonal relations, mainly because of the psychological consequences of the pandemic. The COVID-19 pandemic coincided with the highest level of globalization regarding the movement of goods, investments, and people, despite the negative effects of the financial crisis of 2008 (Czaika and de Haas 2014). The uniqueness of this wave of globalization is the globalization of consumption, tastes, and culture, leading to the illusion of "sameness" around the globe (Pagel 2014). The rise of the internet and the information society led to the emergence of the Millennial generation (those born between 1981 and 1996), assumed to be the children of the digital age (Western Union 2017) and accepted as the first global citizens (Maiers 2012; Dimock 2020). It is possible to add the newer generation Z (those born between 1997 and 2011) as the more globalized juniors. Both generations are accepted as strictly different from their elders due to their flexibility and openness to change, in addition to their mastery of information technologies (Varkey Foundation 2020). Unfortunately, the pandemic ended this hope of the rise of a golden generation which would replace their conservative and xenophobic parents.

The psychological climate created by the pandemic will be a central determinant of changing interpersonal relations. The coronavirus pandemic resurrected a very important emotional state that society fell into after the 2000s, the "fear climate" (Mythen and Walklate 2006). Terrorist attacks, especially triggered by the September 11 attacks, trigger the most important feeling to which humanity owes its existence, fear. So much so that the children of Ares, the God of War in ancient Greek mythology, are known as the twin brothers Fear and Terror walking hand in hand, aiming to reach the goal of terror by way of concern. In this respect, we can characterize the coronavirus pandemic as a kind of terrorist attack because it targets those closest to us like terror and proceeds almost randomly, and we feel helpless against it. We know the effect of fear very well: When we are afraid, it directs our energy to survive, the person who is afraid has an "attention economy," focusing on the threat to their existence. Perceptions of risk change; the more frequently there are risks, the consequences of risks appear greater, and non-risks are perceived as risks (Lerner and Keltner 2001). Terror also causes people to face their mortality, which is intolerable. When one remembers that they are mortal, they cling to their values and cultural norms. Religion and ideologies function as frames that provide a "delusion of immortality" (Pyszczynski, Solomon, and Greenberg 2003). Faced with terrorism, people who do not share the same delusion with others raise their walls and "distance themselves" (Menzies and Menzies 2020).

In that kind of environment of uncertainty, leaders and ideologies that promise certainty become more attractive, and identities that give a sense of *us* become stronger. Media and politicians skillfully exploit this environment created by fear. The media not only portrays the world as more fearful than it is but also commercializes fear; it not only multiplies fear but also constructs the object of fear. In an environment of fear, politicians use this feeling to consolidate their power. Not only do they describe the causes of fear in line with their own interests, they also point out the cause of fear, they find *scapegoats*. Faced with terrorism under these conditions, a person falls into a passive situation with the contributions of the media and politicians and seems to have no other choice but to be afraid.

The COVID-19 pandemic created this culture of fear. The virus itself is invisible but created a type of terrorism that affects everyday life. The victims of the virus have been random. Our neighbors, families, and loved ones were among the targets of the pandemic; like terrorism, the virus does not discriminate. Both terrorism and the virus led to "social distancing," a kind of xenophobia and a tendency for further isolations (Marone 2020). There are many candidates for the role of scapegoats, from Chinese workers to those violating the rules, from immigrants to ethnic minorities (Cole 2020). The helplessness of individuals against the pandemic pushed people to seek any kind of information that provides a minimum feeling of certainty. Thus, the infodemic became more harmful than the COVID-19 pandemic itself. The WHO (2020) defines infodemic as

> an overabundance of information—some accurate and some not—occurring during an epidemic. It makes it hard for people to find trustworthy sources and reliable guidance when they need it. Even when people have access to high-quality information, there are still barriers they must overcome to take the recommended action.

Fake news, misinformation, and conspiracy theories have become prevalent in the age of social media and have skyrocketed since the beginning of the COVID-19 pandemic (Depoux et al. 2020). Similar to the metaphor of "war on terror" (Lakoff 2001), politicians preferred to use the war metaphor to label their efforts against the pandemic (Chenoy 2020; Widmann 2020).

The human brain is wired for forgetting and fear will be replaced with hope, an essential emotion for survival. However, the economic and social consequences of the pandemic will shape the collective memory of a generation, and it will give its name: "Coronavirus Generation." What we have learned from the sociology of generations is that the members of a given cohort experiencing the same historical events (moments or locations) during their formative years have similar worldviews and values. Inglehart (1985, 103) explains this phenomenon with two competing hypotheses: the scarcity hypothesis states that "an individual's priorities reflect one's socio-economic environment" and the socialization hypothesis means that "to a large extent, one's basic values reflect the conditions that prevailed during one's preadult years." According to this approach, the scarcity hypothesis implies short-term effects (period), and the socialization hypothesis brings long-term (cohort) effects to one's life. Traumatic events, such as recessions, economic crises, and famines, push the cohort to be more conservative, emphasizing survival values over self-expression and aesthetic values. Periods characterized by economic stability, growth, and an abundance of resources and opportunities create a fertile environment for the rise of generations prioritizing self-expression in life, instead of fighting for survival (Inglehart and Abramson 1994).

From this perspective, the new generation—young people between sixteen and twenty-six years old—is facing a scarcity climate as the estimates of economists indicate that the global economy will shrink at least for two years and many countries will experience a period of recession (OECD 2020b). Unemployment will continue to increase (UN 2020; Thompson 2020) and will especially hit young people (ILO 2020). The post-corona world will be characterized by declining education opportunities with competition for a limited number of seats in good institutions. The closure of schools and enhanced online education already discriminates against vulnerable people and disadvantaged groups, and there is no reason for the reversal of this trend (ReliefWeb 2020). Rising borders during the pandemic are still alive, leading human mobility to be significantly reduced and the segregation of nations and communities within nations to continue; hence, only a small portion of this new generation will be capable of becoming global citizens (Bonaccorsi et al. 2020). These scarcities will create a feeling of insecurity coupled with the anxieties of the memories of the lockdown period. The coronavirus generation will be characterized by their virtual merits, which are also a source of inequality, but they will be oriented toward their survival.

Divergent Roads in the Wood

Not all roads in the wood provide the same destiny to us. Some roads seem very familiar and comfortable. The negative scenarios of change at the three different levels of relations presented above are very familiar because there are many examples in the history of societal collapse following enormous historical moments (Stasavage 2020; Blickle 2020). The collapse of multilateralism, the failure of international organizations, the demand of citizens for a more effective and perhaps despotic state, consequences of the emotion of fear triggered by the pandemic, and the demand for a more secure world by younger generations may lead to the rise of a dystopia seen in Hollywood movies. The basic premise of Hobbes may come true: "Man, to man, is a wolf."

Meanwhile, the god of social sciences is Janus-faced. On the one hand, social scientists can construct the world we live in by interpreting our experiences. The rise of the Cold War and the Clash of Civilizations are two good examples of how social sciences acted as self-proving prophets and how Mr. X and Samuel Huntington shaped our worldview by their very powerful paradigms. On the other hand, social scientists can falsify their predictions, by prompting humanity to act against the next crisis. In such situations, they will be accused of being "the Pied Piper of Hamelin"; however, measures taken as a result of their pessimistic expectations may prevent the emergence of a worse alternative.

Here, we are the point of the decision. Under normal conditions, as we learned from history, the worst and pessimistic scenario is more realistic. However, as the citizens of the world, we have a chance to intervene and alter the reality in which our children will live. It is possible to discuss the weaknesses of international institutions and consider remedies to empower them for another pandemic or the global climate crisis, such as the possibility of creating a global New Deal and pushing for a new version of the welfare state that will strengthen citizens without restricting their liberties. The declining interpersonal trust may be rehabilitated by investing in a safety net that will guarantee a minimum level of security for younger generations, in terms of employment, education, and mobility. Lastly, we can continue to fight against our demons, without losing our angels.

REFERENCES

Acemoglu, Daron. 2020. "The Post-COVID State." *Project Syndicate*, June 5, 2020. https://www.project-syndicate.org/onpoint/four-possible-trajectories-after-covid19-daron-acemoglu-2020-06.

Allain-Dupré, Dorothée, Isabelle Chatry, Varinia Michalun, and Antti Moisio. 2020. "The Territorial Impact of COVID-19: Managing the Crisis across Levels of Government." *OECD*, June 16, 2020. http://www.oecd.org/coronavirus/policy-responses/the-territorial-impact-of-covid-19-managing-the-crisis-across-levels-of-government-d3e314e1/.

Allen, John. 2020. "How the World Will Look After the Coronavirus Pandemic." *Foreign From Insights to Action: Gender Equality in the Wake of COVID-19 | Digital Library: Publications*coroanvirus-pandemic/.

Alon, Ilan, Matthew Farrell, and Shaomin Li. 2020. "Regime Type and COVID-19 Response." *FIIB Business Review*, 9, no. 3: 152–60 https://doi.org/10.1177/2319714520928884.

Azcona, Ginette, Antra Bhatt, Jessamyn Encarnacion, Juncal Plazaola-Castaño, Papa Seck, Silke Staab, and Laura Turquet. 2020. "From İnsights to Action: Gender Equality in the Wake of COVID-19." UN Women Digital Library: Publications; https://www.unwomen.org/digital-library/publications/2020/09/gender-equality-in-the-wake-of-covid-19.

Balfour, Rosa. 2020. "Why Populism Can Survive the Pandemic." *Carnegie Europe*. Accessed September 26, 2020. https://carnegieeurope.eu/2020/07/15/why-populism-can-survive-pandemic-pub-82293.

Blanco, Masaya Llavaneras, and Antulio Rosales. 2020. "Global Governance and COVID-19: The Implications of Fragmentation and Inequality." *E-International Relations*, May 6, 2020. https://www.e-ir.info/2020/05/06/global-governance-and-covid-19-the-implications-of-fragmentation-and-inequality/.

Blickle, Kristian. 2020. "Pandemics Change Cities: Municipal Spending and Voter Extremism in Germany, 1918-1933." Federal Reserve Bank of New York Staff Reports, August 11, 2020. https://www.newyorkfed.org/medialibrary/media/research/staff_reports/sr921.pdf.

Blouin-Genest Gabriel, Anna Bogic, Natalia Torres Orozco, Nathalie Burlone, and Éric Champagne. 2020. "The WHO's Risky Communication Strategy Created Confusion around COVID-19." *The Conversation*. Accessed September 26, 2020. http://theconversation.com/the-whos-risky-communication-strategy-created-confusion-around-covid-19-140043.

Bol, Damien, Marco Giani, André Blais, and Peter John Loewen. "The Effect of COVID-19 Lockdowns on Political Support: Some Good News for Democracy?" *European Journal of Political Research* 60, no. 2: 497–505. https://doi.org/10.1111/1475-6765.12401.

Bonaccorsi, Giovanni, Francesco Pierri, Matteo Cinelli, Andrea Flori, Alessandro Galeazzi, Francesco Porcelli, Ana Lucia Schmidt, et al. 2020. "Economic and Social Consequences of Human Mobility Restrictions under COVID-19." *Proceedings of the National Academy of Sciences* 117, no. 27: 15530–35. https://doi.org/10.1073/pnas.2007658117.

Calhoun, George. 2020. "Europe's Hamiltonian Moment – What Is It Really?" *Forbes*. Accessed September 26, 2020. https://www.forbes.com/sites/georgecalhoun/2020/05/26/europes-hamiltonian-moment--what-is-it-really/.

Carothers, Thomas, and David Wong. 2020. "Authoritarian Weaknesses and the Pandemic." *Carnegie Endowment for International Peace*, August 11, 2020. https://carnegieendowment.org/2020/08/11/authoritarian-weaknesses-and-pandemic-pub-82452.

Centre for European Reform. 2020. "The EU Needs to Step up Its Response to the COVID-19 Outbreak." Accessed September 26, 2020. https://www.cer.eu/insights/eu-needs-step-its-response-covid-19-outbreak.

Chaudhry, Rabail, George Dranitsaris, Talha Mubashir, Justyna Bartoszko, and Sheila Riazi. 2020. "A Country Level Analysis Measuring the İmpact of Government Actions, Country Preparedness and Socioeconomic Factors on COVID-19 Mortality and Related Health Outcomes." *EClinical Medicine* 25: 100464. https://doi.org/10.1016/j.eclinm.2020.100464.

Cheng, Cindy, Joan Barceló, Allison Spencer Hartnett, Robert Kubinec, and Luca Messerschmidt. 2020. "COVID-19 Government Response Event Dataset (CoronaNet V.1.0)." *Nature Human Behaviour* 4, no. 7: 756–68. https://doi.org/10.1038/s41562-020-0909-7.

Chenoy, Anuradha. 2020. "Why Populist Leaders Use War Rhetoric for All Things Related to the COVID-19 Pandemic." *The Wire*, August 19, 2020. https://thewire.in/politics/covid-19-war-militarism-public-health-populist-leaders.

Chodcik, Gabriel, and Clara Weil. 2020. "Covid-19 Death Toll: The Role of the Nation's Economic Development." *medRxiv* https://doi.org/10.1101/2020.07.18.20156778.

Cole, Diane. "Why Scapegoating is a Typical Human Response to a Pandemic." *NPR*, August 29, 2020. https://www.npr.org/sections/goatsandsoda/2020/08/29/906225199/why-scapegoating-is-a-typical-human-response-to-a-pandemic.

Cooper, Luke, and Guy Aitchison. 2020. "The Dangers Ahead: Covid-19, Authoritarianism and Democracy." Monograph, http://www.lse.ac.uk/international-development/Assets/Documents/ccs-research-unit/OSF/the-dangers-ahead-Covid-19-authoritarianism-democracy.pdf.

Czaika, Mathias, and Hein De Haas. 2014. "The Globalization of Migration: Has the World Become More Migratory?" *International Migration Review* 48, no. 2: 283–323. https://doi.org/10.1111/imre.12095.

Depoux, Anneliese, Sam Martin, Emilie Karafillakis, Raman Preet, Annelies Wilder-Smith, and Heidi Larson. 2020. "The Pandemic of Social Media Panic Travels Faster than the COVID-19 Outbreak." *Journal of Travel Medicine* 27, no. 3. https://doi.org/10.1093/jtm/taaa031.

De Vries, Catherine E., and Sara B. Hobolt. 2020. "Does the Pandemic Spell the End of Populism? Most Likely Not—Here's Why." *Washington Post*, July 23, 2020. https://www.washingtonpost.com/politics/2020/07/23/does-pandemic-spell-end-populism-most-likely-not-heres-why/.

Dimock, Michael. 2020. "Defining Generations: Where Millennials End and Generation Z Begins." Pew Research Center, July 28, 2020. https://www.pewresearch.org/fact-tank/2019/01/17/where-millennials-end-and-generation-z-begins/.

DİSK-AR. 2020. "DİSK-AR Raporu Yayınlandı: COVID-19 İşçileri Nasıl Etkiledi? [DISK-AR Report Published: How Did COVID-19 Affect Workers?]." July 8, 2020, http://disk.org.tr/2020/07/disk-ar-raporu-yayinlandi-covid-19-iscileri-nasil-etkiledi/.

Elgin, Ceyhun, Gokce Basbug, and Abdullah Yalaman. 2020. "Economic Policy Responses to a Pandemic: Developing the COVID-19 Economic Stimulus İndex." *Covid Economics* 1, no. 3: 40–53.

Frey, Carl Benedikt, Chinchih Chen, and Giorgio Presidente. 2020. "Democracy, Culture, and Contagion: Political Regimes and Countries Responsiveness to Covid-19." *Covid Economics* 18: 1–20.

Fukuyama, Francis. 2020. "The Pandemic and Political Order." *Foreign Affairs* 99: 26.

The Global Compact on Refugees | Digital Platform. "Refugees in the COVID-19 Crisis." Erişim 26 Eylül 2020. https://globalcompactrefugees.org/refugees-covid-19-crisis.

Goldin, Ian, and Robert Muggah. 2020. "The World Before This Coronavirus and After Cannot be the Same." *The Conversation*. Accessed October 02, 2020. http://theconversation.com/the-world-before-this-coronavirus-and-after-cannot-be-the-same-134905.

Gopinath, Gita. 2020. "The Great Lockdown: Worst Economic Downturn Since the Great Depression." *IMF Blog*, April 21, 2020. https://blogs.imf.org/2020/04/14/the-great-lockdown-worst-economic-downturn-since-the-great-depression/.

Gostyńska-Jakubowska, Agata, and Luigi Scazzieri. 2020. "The EU Needs to Step up Its Response to the COVID-19 Outbreak." Centre for European Reform. https://www.cer.eu/insights/eu-needs-step-its-response-covid-19-outbreak.

Graham-Harrison, Emma. 2020. "Global Preparation: How Different Countries Planned for the Second Wave of Covid-19." *The Guardian*, September 20, 2020. https://www.theguardian.com/world/2020/sep/20/global-preparation-how-different-countries-planned-for-the-second-wave-of-covid-19.

Greer, Scott L., Elizabeth J. King, Elize Massard da Fonseca, and Andre Peralta-Santos. 2020. "The Comparative Politics of COVID-19: The Need to Understand Government Responses." *Global Public Health* 15, no. 9: 1413–16.

Henley, Jon. "Democratic Leaders Win Surge of Approval during Covid-19 Crisis." *The Guardian*, April 2, 2020, https://www.theguardian.com/world/2020/apr/02/democratic-leaders-win-surge-of-approval-during-covid-19-crisis.

ILO. 2020. "Youth & COVID-19: Impacts on Jobs, Education, Rights and Mental Well-Being." August 11, 2020. http://www.ilo.org/global/topics/youth-employment/publications/WCMS_753026/lang--en/index.htm.

IMF. 2020a. "World Economic Outlook Update, June 2020: A Crisis Like No Other, An Uncertain Recovery." June 1, 2020. https://www.imf.org/en/Publications/WEO/Issues/2020/06/24/WEOUpdateJune2020.

IMF. 2020b. "Policy Responses to COVID19." September 11, 2020. https://www.imf.org/en/Topics/imf-and-covid19/Policy-Responses-to-COVID-19.

Inglehart, Ronald. 1985. "Aggregate Stability and İndividual-Level Flux in Mass Belief Systems: The Level of Analysis Paradox." *American Political Science Review* 79, no. 1: 97–116.

Inglehart, Ronald, and Paul R. Abramson. 1994. "Economic Security and Value Change." *American Political Science Review* 88, no. 2: 336–54.

Janse, Kalin Anev, and Iliyana Tsanova. 2020. "What We Can Learn from Europe's Response to the COVID-19 Crisis." World Economic Forum, August 10, 2020. https://www.weforum.org/agenda/2020/08/europe-response-covid-19-coronavirus-economic-crisis-euro-fiscal-monetary-policy-green-deal/.

Kalkınma Atölyesi (Development Workshop). 2020. "Virus or Poverty: Impact of Coronavirus Outbreak on Seasonal Migrant Agricultural Workers and their Children and on Crop Farming A Rapid Assessment." http://www.ka.org.tr/dosyalar/file/virus percent20or percent20poverty.pdf.

Kavanagh, Matthew M., and Renu Singh. 2020. "Democracy, Capacity, and Coercion in Pandemic Response—COVID 19 in Comparative Political Perspective." *Journal of Health Politics, Policy and Law* 45, no. 6: 997–1012. https://doi.org/10.1215/03616878-8641530.

Kendall-Taylor, Andrea, and Carisa Nietsche. 2020. "The Coronavirus is Exposing Populists' Hollow Politics." *Foreign Policy.*

Krastev, Ivan. 2020. "The Seven Early Lessons of the Global Coronavirus Crisis." March 20, 2020. https://www.newstatesman.com/world/europe/2020/03/coronavirus-early-lessons-global-crisis.

Krastev, Ivan and Mark Leonard. 2020. "Europe's Pandemic Politics: How the Virus has Changed the Public's Worldview." June 24, 2020. https://www.ecfr.eu/publications/summary/europes_pandemic_politics_how_the_virus_has_changed_the_publics_worldview

Lakoff, George.2001 "Metaphors of Terror by George Lakoff." Accessed September 26, 2020. https://cse.buffalo.edu/~rapaport/575/F01/lakoff.on.terrorism.html.

Lerner, Jennifer S., and Dacher Keltner. 2001. "Fear, Anger, and Risk." *Journal of Personality and Social Psychology* 81, no. 1: 146–59. https://doi.org/10.1037/0022-3514.81.1.146.

Lolla, Aditya, Ahmed Safar, Alan Yang, Alejandrina Cripovich, Alejandro Franco, Aleksander Zagajewski, Alexander Mok, Alfredo Ortega, Ali Arsalan Pasha Siddiqui, and Alice Eddershaw. 2020. "Coronavirus Government Response Tracker." Blavatnik School of Government, September 14, 2020. https://www.bsg.ox.ac.uk/research/research-projects/coronavirus-government-response-tracker.

Lührmann, Anna, Amanda B. Edgell, and Seraphine F. Maerz. 2020. "Pandemic Backsliding: Does Covid-19 Put Democracy At Risk." University of Gothenburg, Varieties of Democracy Institute: V-Dem Policy Brief 23.

Maiers, Michele. 2017. "Our Future in the Hands of Millennials." *The Journal of the Canadian Chiropractic Association* 61, no. 3: 212.

Marone, Francesco. 2020. "A Tale of Two Fears: Comparing Terrorism and the Coronavirus." *European Eye on Radicalization*, May 29, 2020. https://eeradicalization.com/a-tale-of-two-fears-comparing-terrorism-and-the-coronavirus/.

Maylam, Paul. 2020. "A Post-Pandemic World Is Unlikely to Focus on Meeting Need over Human Greed." *The Conversation*. Accessed September 26, 2020. http://theconversation.com/a-post-pandemic-world-is-unlikely-to-focus-on-meeting-need-over-human-greed-141228.

Menzies, Rachel E., and Ross G. Menzies. 2020. "Death Anxiety in the Time of COVID-19: Theoretical Explanations and Clinical Implications." *The Cognitive Behaviour Therapist* 13. https://doi.org/10.1017/s1754470x20000215.

Meyer, Brett. 2020. "Pandemic Populism: An Analysis of Populist Leaders' Responses to Covid-19." Erişim 26 Eylül 2020. https://institute.global/policy/pandemic-populism-analysis-populist-leaders-responses-covid-19.

Mouffe, Chantal. 2020. "Why a Populist Left Should Rally around a Green Democratic Transformation." *openDemocracy*, September 15, 2020. https://www.opendemocracy.net/en/rethinking-populism/left-populist-strategy-post-covid-19/

Mythen, Gabe, and Sandra Walklate. 2006. "Communicating the Terrorist Risk: Harnessing a Culture of Fear?" *Crime, Media, Culture: An International Journal* 2, no. 2: 123–42. https://doi.org/10.1177/1741659006065399.

Navarro, Vicente. 2020. "The Consequences of Neoliberalism in the Current Pandemic." *International Journal of Health Services* 50, no. 3: 271–75. https://doi.org/10.1177/0020731420925449.

OECD. 2020(a). *OECD Employment Outlook 2020.* https://doi.org/10.1787/1686c758-en.

OECD. 2020(b). *Building Confidence amid an Uncertain Recovery.* http://www.oecd.org/economic-outlook/september-2020.

Pagel, Mark. 2014. "Does Globalization Mean We Will Become One Culture?" *BBC Future.* November 18, 2014. https://www.bbc.com/future/article/20120522-one-world-order.

Peel, Michael. 2020. "WHO Struggles to Prove Itself in the Face of Covid-19." *Financial Times.* July 12, 2020. https://www.ft.com/content/c2809c99-594f-4649-968a-0560966c11e0.

Porcher, Simon. 2020. "'Contagion': The Determinants of Governments' Public Health Responses to COVID-19 All around the World." *SSRN Electronic Journal.* https://doi.org/10.2139/ssrn.3581764.

Pyszczynski, Tom, Sheldon Solomon, and Jeff Greenberg. 2003. *In the Wake of 9/11: The Psychology of Terror.* Washington: American Psychological Association, 2003. https://doi.org/10.1037/10478-000.

Rapeli, Lauri, and Inga Saikkonen. 2020. "How Will the COVID-19 Pandemic Affect Democracy?" *Democratic Theory* 7, no. 2: 25–32. https://doi.org/10.3167/dt.2020.070204.

ReliefWeb. 2020. "Policy Brief: Education during COVID-19 and Beyond (August 2020) – World." Accessed September 26, 2020. https://reliefweb.int/report/world/policy-brief-education-during-covid-19-and-beyond-august-2020.

Saad-Filho, Alfredo. 2020. "From COVID-19 to the End of Neoliberalism." *Critical Sociology* 46: 477–85. https://doi.org/10.1177/0896920520929966.

Schellekens, Philip, and Diego M. Sourrouille. 2020. "COVID-19 Mortality in Rich and Poor Countries: A Tale of Two Pandemics?" World Bank Policy Research Working Paper 9260.

Sen, Amartya. 2020. "A Better Society Can Emerge from the Lockdowns." *Financial Times* 15.

Schumaker, Erin. 2020. "CDC and WHO Offer Conflicting Advice on Masks. An Expert Tells Us Why." May 30, 2020. Video. https://abcnews.go.com/Health/cdc-offer-conflicting-advice-masks-expert-tells-us/story?id=70958380.

Stasavage, David. 2020. "Democracy, Autocracy, and Emergency Threats: Lessons for COVID-19 From the Last Thousand Years." *International Organization* 74, no. S1: E1–17. https://doi.org/10.1017/s0020818320000338.

Stavrakakis, Yannis, and Giorgos Katsampekis. 2020. "Populism and the Pandemic: A Collaborative Report." Loughborough University Report. https://hdl.handle.net/2134/12546284.v1.

Thompson, Jamie. 2020. "Global Risk Survey: Recovery May Be Longer and Slower." *Forward Thinking*. September 15, 2020. http://blog.oxfordeconomics.com/coronavirus/recovery-may-be-longer-and-slower.

Tufekci, Zeynep. 2020. "The WHO Shouldn't Be a Plaything for Great Powers." *The Atlantic*. April 16, 2020. https://www.theatlantic.com/health/archive/2020/04/why-world-health-organization-failed/610063/.

TURKSTAT. 2020. "Türkiye İstatistik Kurumu, İşgücü İstatistikleri, Haziran 2020." (TURKSTAT, Laborforce Statistics, June 2020). Accessed September 20, 2020. http://www.tuik.gov.tr/PreHaberBultenleri.do?id=33790.

UN. "Policy Brief: Education during COVID-19 and Beyond (August 2020) - World." *ReliefWeb*, August 4, 2020. https://reliefweb.int/report/world/policy-brief-education-during-covid-19-and-beyond-august-2020.

UNICEF. 2020. "Impact of COVID-19 on Multidimensional Child Poverty." September 16, 2020. https://data.unicef.org/resources/impact-of-covid-19-on-multidimensional-child-poverty/.

Varkey Foundation. 2020. "Generation Z: Global Citizenship Survey." Accessed September 26, 2020. https://www.varkeyfoundation.org/what-we-do/research/generation-z-global-citizenship-survey/.

Walt, Stephen M. 2020. "The Global Order After Covid-19." İnstitut fuer Sicherheitspolitik. https://www.institutfuersicherheit.at/wp-content/uploads/2020/06/ISP-Working-Paper-Stephen-M.-WALT-The-Global-Order-After-COVID-19.pdf.

Western Union. 2017. "Millennials Stand for Globalism and Want to Shape the Future." The Western Union Company - Investor Relations. November 15, 2017. http://ir.westernunion.com/news/archived-press-releases/press-release-details/2017/Millennials-Stand-for-Globalism-and-Want-to-Shape-the-Future/default.aspx.

Widmann, Tobias. 2020. "Fear, Hope, and COVID-19: Strategic Emotional Rhetoric in Political Communication and Its Impact on the Mass Public." *SSRN Electronic Journal*. https://doi.org/10.2139/ssrn.3679484.

World Bank. 2020. "Projected Poverty Impacts of COVID-19 (Coronavirus)." June 8, 2020. https://www.worldbank.org/en/topic/poverty/brief/projected-poverty-impacts-of-COVID-19.

World Health Organization. 2020. "1st WHO Infodemiology Conference." Accessed September 25, 2020. https://www.who.int/news-room/events/detail/2020/06/30/default-calendar/1st-who-infodemiology-conference.

Zimmermann, Klaus F., Gokhan Karabulut, Mehmet Huseyin Bilgin, and Asli Cansin Doker. 2020. "Inter-Country Distancing, Globalisation and the Coronavirus Pandemic." *The World Economy* 43, no. 6: 1484–98. https://doi.org/10.1111/twec.12969.

Chapter 2

Capitalism, Financial Liberalization, and Monetary Economics

A Criticism of the System

Emre Alkin

LIBERALIZATION DILEMMA

Twenty years ago, financial liberalization seemed like a "must" to me, a set of measures deepening the markets, increasing savings therefore investments, promoting competition and fair trading in favor of society, ultimately enhancing economic growth and development. But today, I witness financial liberalization retrogressing every day, especially through financial institutions, its key intermediaries for the last ten years.

The title of my PhD thesis I wrote in 1996 was "Financial Liberalization and Monetization." The central argument of my thesis stated a set of measures to prevent oligopolistic hegemony from manipulating prices in order to bring inflation under control by integrating certain elements, which have not yet been incorporated into financial markets, into the system and by ensuring financial deepening through monetization. In my thesis, I argued that the number of players would increase as the market deepens. No one, neither individually nor collectively, would have enough power to influence and manipulate the markets when an infinite number of buyers would meet with an infinite number of sellers (a romantic requirement of a perfect competition market). Besides, different groups had different expectations, different interests, and this wide range of expectations would help markets naturally, harmoniously reach a new point of balance where no extreme price movements take place.

Now, I notice that the markets today are neither "competitive" nor "deep," whereas in 1996, the year I wrote my thesis, I violently agreed that they were both of those things. The financial institutions which changed their names too many times due to constant acquisitions and mergers are now dominating the markets, and most of them are owned by the seemingly subsidiaries of centrally controlled financial organizations founded by American financiers. To illustrate, just like a food company diversifies its products so as to appeal to the taste of all consumers, financial institutions as well have established their own subsidiaries of different characters and ownership structures in order to address different capitals in different markets. For instance, while they were offering interest-free banking services in Islamic countries, in the world's other regions, they preserved the regular banking system. However, the impression that these institutions have always been run by the same elite group never faded away.

I think we can argue that interventions by the IMF and the World Bank have been equally used to prepare a favorable environment for these financial institutions. In my 1996 thesis, I highlighted the success that the former Eastern Bloc countries had achieved by putting an end to Soviet dominance in order to start a transition to multibranch commercial banking. I honestly don't know what we should call the West now but back in the day, the West was the great representative of modernism and the things the West said were crucial in terms of transitioning to a New World Order. That is the reason why my thesis strongly emphasized former Eastern Bloc countries' transition to multibranch commercial banking as well as their efforts to establish and develop capital markets. But today I realize that I have been hasty in forming and violently defending my argument. The fact that these countries, who had to introduce IMF and World Bank–forced laws, remove restrictions so as to allow free movement of goods and capital ran large current account deficits and were stuck in huge debt did not go unnoticed, yet I must confess that we did not really care about it back then. Today we are seeing the negative outcomes of what happened in the past.

HOW WAS THE IMMUNITY OF THE FINANCIAL SECTOR BUILT UP?

Indeed, close ties between the IMF, World Bank, and other financial institutions that dominate the world have led to a roadmap defined as "modernization" by countries like ours: Here's how modernization works: First, foreign trade regime and industrial policies of the country are turned into a platform where foreign capital can move freely, immediately followed by the liberalization of exchange rate regime. Serious adjustments in exchange rate are made prior to making inflation more stable, thus making it easier for foreign investors to buy more assets of that country using their own money. In the meantime, maybe on purpose, national investors are made more vulnerable.

Then, the country starts facing impositions to implement legal regulations on social and economic life in order to create the most convenient platform for capital markets.

The financing need becomes more than a need in the face of growing demand, it's rather an obligation. However, raising capital through banks and financial institutions would not be enough, because in traditionally introvert countries, companies do not easily hand over to a new buyer or they are reluctant to welcome new partners. Accordingly, companies are encouraged to go public, emphasizing the "obligation-free fund generation" function of capital markets. This is the best possible way to allow a foreign investor to become a shareholder of those companies. In the meantime, obviously, the country goes under a serious privatization process. The fact that Government Business Enterprises (GBEs), which were initially established to produce high-quality and affordable goods and services for the people, became corrupt over time, has been an important factor in their privatization. Their operation in capital markets makes us think about a so-called "financial deepening"; it even makes us happy, seeing the competition grow.

Unfortunately today, when we say "competitive," we only refer to the fact that there are a large number of companies operating in the market. But, we never question whether their number is enough to induce competition or we cannot figure out if these companies are acting in agreement with each other to serve their own purposes. Although the companies that produce goods and services are often questioned as to whether they genuinely compete with each other, financial institutions have never been the subject of such questioning, because it's considered almost taboo to question them, because they inspire confidence, reliability. But, sadly, today it has become disputable whether they can be genuinely trusted or how much they are reliable.

Similarly, today, the markets too we consider to be deep are not actually that deep. When we use the term "deep" today, we only refer to significant increases in trading volume due to derivative instruments. One wonders, "Since the markets are so deep, why are there buyer or seller-free financial instruments?" The fact that a buyer in a financial market fails to buy or a seller fails to sell the product during a transaction shows that the market is not that deep as thought. In fact, there are millions of account numbers but most of them belong to the same market players again. The hegemony in large-scale markets belongs to large financial institutions whereas in emerging markets, there is the hegemony of large customers. These customers or accounts are actually major financial institutions that opened accounts in emerging countries, and very soon they will be opening their own branches.

In emerging markets, the regulations and taxation policy to which foreign investors are subject to always seem to be confusing. Treasuries in such countries have to offer high real interest rates to keep the investors. This very situation not only does corrupt the financial market of the supposedly modernized country but also starts damaging its local markets: National industry becomes too weak to stand on its own two feet and national investors, rapidly leaving the manufacturing industry; they leave their places to foreign companies with powerful capital. Such companies are known as "global brands."

The financial institutions mentioned above which change their skin according to the "place and culture" have begun to move all the savings in the world in line with a specific plan. "All resources" Turkey has been longing for have been supplied to the monetary economy, in other words, the full monetization of the economy has been achieved unfortunately by the hands of these financial institutions, yet the resources have been quickly bastardized. To illustrate, in the early 2000s, an American bank had sponsored a panel titled "Baking in the Middle East" held as part of the World Economic Forum in Jordan. The then Turkish minister responsible for the economy had attended the panel as a guest speaker. Suddenly, the vibe of the panel changed to an approach that insults Turkish banking while praising the banking sector in the Middle East, particularly in Kuwait. Although some Turkish participants, including myself, had declared our discomfort about those statements, soon after, we had understood the real reason behind this humiliation. The American bank, the sponsor of the panel, had organized the panel with the purpose of achieving something that it has been pursuing for a long time: opening a branch in Kuwait. While getting Turkey out of perspective, it had offered its demand to the speaker who had been representing the State of Kuwait. Well, the outcome of the panel was just inevitable considering that the moderator himself was the vice-chair of that bank's executive board.

The instances such as these show how international financial institutions manipulate the international markets so as to collect others' money and use it to realize their own plans. Besides, rather than Americans, it is the Arabs, Kazakhs, Russians, and Azerbaijanis who lost most money due to the economic crisis we are going through today.

The project of integrating people living in rural areas into the monetary economy, which was another important detail in my thesis, has been accomplished by the so-called competitive and deep markets as well as the IMF and the World Trade Organization. Being highly sensitive about the agricultural products, the developed countries of the world, the United States in particular, have taken control over the movement of agricultural merchandise from less developed countries to developed countries for the last thirty years, and determined the place of these goods in financial markets according to their own plans, therefore leaving the agricultural laborers with no guarantee for the sale of their products. The agricultural producers have never received their well-deserved share of the increasing prices because of hundreds of middlemen. So, it's always been large buyers and people who sit in front of their computer screens in financial markets who set the price for agricultural goods, not the producers.

Apart from a handful of lucky investors who succeeded in selling their products for their market price, the fate of millions of producers, who could not sell their products for the price they see fit and only made enough money to survive, did not change. The primary aim of my 1996 thesis was to provide practical suggestions as to how to help local producers to get their goods and services recognized in financial markets, ensure that this recognition encourages formal economy, therefore, makes it easier to monitor economic activity, and finally induce financial institutions to gather together the suppliers of funds and the users of funds with more competitive prices. I must say that, during a fourteen-year period, I have never seen any progress made about it, except for some well-intentioned, yet fruitless, efforts.

MANAGING RISK IN THE FACE OF MONEY ILLUSION

As a matter of fact, even during the 2001 financial crisis, my opinions weren't as nearly well-shaped as they are now. Nevertheless, I wrote my book titled "Finansal Aracılığın Evrimi" (Evolution of Financial Intermediation), which was a synthesis of the 2001 financial crisis and the "experiences sanctified by the West," which was mentioned in my PhD thesis as well. I felt quite happy when I was writing the closing lines of my thesis with the coauthor of my two previous books, Dr. Tuğrul SAVAŞ, a specialist in Risk Management and Agricultural Economics. However, this feeling of happiness seems kind of a romantic memory now, because, although the Turkish Financial System had learned its lesson from the financial crisis, the rest of the world had not, and all of us together had been heading toward the next big disaster.

During the writing process of the book, we tried to provide as many details as we could about the financial risk measurement and assessment methods, making a special effort to warn against the derivative instruments, which number has been increasingly growing. We even addressed to risk managers, saying, "If you ever face anything you cannot explain by mathematics, use your gut feelings instead; if that doesn't help you either, don't even think about taking that risk."

The English version of the book, "Risk Management," provides numerous layers of information and warnings against risk and economic hazards. It is a known fact that large financial institutions often times use developing countries as an experimental lab. If their attempts in these countries achieve success, they start trying out similar methods on low-income groups in their home countries. However, these supposedly successful trials have been the main reason lying behind the "subprime mortgage" crisis, which is one of the causes of the financial crisis we are going through today. Inspired by the so-called successful attempts made in countries where income per capita is below $2,500, the global financial institutions have unfortunately thought that it was more profitable to provide loans to low-income groups suspected of having money under the mattress rather than people who actually have money, since such people would have low demand for loan funds, making it impossible for the financial institutions to impose the interest rate level they desire. "Low-income groups have higher demand for loans, which can help us earn more satisfactory interest. Besides, they can pay off their debts out of their own pocket in case of any trouble," financial institutions wrongly thought up until now.

From a mathematical point of view, if personal savings constitute the basis for investments, the income must have a function somehow. This applies not only to spot instruments but also to derivative ones. So, how did the volume of derivative instruments alone reach $120 trillion considering that the total average GDP worldwide is $60–65 trillion? Initially created for hedging purposes, these instruments have gradually become the root causes of economic adversities.

During the last five years, we have been wondering where a new possible financial crisis would start. While everyone was enjoying their sweet earnings from stocks and interest, only a handful of people were sensing that a storm was coming since they knew that a market in which "everybody wins" was simply not possible. As real-estate prices, stock prices, even the prices of the most basic goods and services have been drastically increasing, people who have wanted to buy these goods and services were unable to do so since their low income would not let them.

As in the Dubai model, the securities and immovable properties have increased in value through constant trading, where both the buyers and the sellers thought they were doing a profitable business. But in fact, it was a money illusion effect rather than a real gain. Even in Turkey, this factor has played an important role in generating ten times more bank money than the number of printed paper money.

The fact that interest rates dropped to critical levels abroad has forced major financial institutions to act more boldly because the cost of luxury living was increasing due to excessive spending of petrodollars by Russians, Kazakhs, and Arabs, who needed to earn more money to keep their luxurious lifestyles. To do that, they needed to guarantee their returns while growing funds.

It was precisely the reason why hedge funds were created in the first place. As risk grew, the number of hedge funds and other similar collective investment organizations has started to increase. They spread all over the world like an epidemic disease. The markets helped the investors make serious amounts of money until stock and commodity exchanges got used to the high levels of cash inflows. The prices in markets were growing every day. The whole world has almost turned into a construction site, where the prices of immovable properties have been increasing by the minute. Degeneration and corruption were inevitable in a place where huge amounts of money were being traded.

THE YEAR 2001: A MILESTONE

As for how everything got started, although the former chair of the Fed, Greenspan was blamed for it, after the September 11 attacks, the US government had caused even larger black holes by covering up corruption in some US large companies by using a series of so-called sanctions. In 2001, confidence in the Financial System as well as audit organizations and credit rating agencies was badly damaged. As the consecutive military interventions in Afghanistan and Iraq have been diverting the international community's away and the US-led dollar pumping to the world has made the investors richer, a veil has been cast over the confidence erosion. Indifference toward not only small problems but also structural problems has started to emerge as people's income grew further. People chose to react to social and political conflicts only when they sensed a threat to their monetary and financial assets. Taking good advantage of the excessive liquidity period of 2001–2007, governments have succeeded in creating millions of individuals, a large pool of potential voters, becoming even more silent as their wealth grew larger.

THE IMPLICATIONS OF CAPITALISM AND DOLLARIZATION FOR TURKEY

In the meantime, people's habit of denominating their wealth in US dollar terms remained unchanged. Previously tested in the former Eastern Bloc countries, the "reverse currency substitution" process which took place from 2002 to 2013 in Turkey, on the other hand, played an even more detrimental part, causing a rise in dollar-denominated national assets. The fact that dollar's swift depreciation took place simultaneously with the rise in TRY-denominated assets has been wrongly interpreted. Everyone thought Turkey was getting wealthier and more prosperous whereas in fact the result has been artificially increased since the denominator was getting smaller. Before long, the process of going back to the national currency, which is described in Turkey as the "reverse currency substitution," damaged the dynamics of the real market.

As exchange rates kept falling and foreign currency loan interest rates kept remaining at lower levels compared to the Turkish Lira, industrial inputs and a certain part of financial liabilities have started to get denominated in foreign currency. Given the fact that the domestic producers of intermediate and investment goods became much more expensive than their competitors, they started to pull out of the market one by one due to lack of demand. Turkish Manufacturing Industry fell into the trap of contract manufacturing, producing goods under the label or brand of global firms, increasing the Turkish economy's vulnerability to external impacts. Banks and financial institutions created a serious "foreign currency" lobby through foreign currency-indexed loans they took from foreign institutions so as to offer to domestic borrowers. Retailers soon became a part of this lobby, which were obviously followed by the representatives of the freshly emerged real-estate sector. The floating rate combined with high interest rates caused the Turkish Lira to appreciate more and more, thus, from 2002 to 2008, paving the way for the collapse of export sectors and national industry that produces intermediate goods and investment goods.

In the meantime, the fact that those who increased their wealth thanks to high TRY interest rates have gladly watched their USD-denominated wealth grow bigger as exchange rates kept falling helped the foreign currency lobby I mentioned above to find more and more supporters. Thus, a misleading approach of "exchange rates are falling, which means things are going pretty well" has slowly started to influence the public. Those who ignited discussions about exchange rates were warned harshly by the government, banks, and media as well. In order to prevent debates about the "floating exchange rate" during that period, the Turkish Central Bank has set forth its "price stability mission" and often emphasized, in a not very scientific manner, that a "national" monetary policy could not be implemented due to Turkey's integration to the global economy.

Turkish Central Bank was right at some point, which was: Turkish economy has been opening to more outside investment since 1997. Accordingly, Turkey's will to handle an economic program all alone has been weakened. Over time, matters that had been considered "of secondary importance" in the past, such as foreign investors, international markets, the situation in countries similar to Turkey, IMF, World Bank, US policies in the region, negotiations with the EU, have become the fundamental elements of the national economic program which had been claimed to be written but never actually got written.

At this point, Turkey, a country that is integrated into the world, and its counterparts have neither power nor will left to determine GDP growth, their citizens' social and economic level of welfare. In countries like these, as government, economy, and autonomous organizations are separated from each other under the impositions of the IMF and EU, business people do not have the support of the government as opposed to their American colleagues, and their access to global capital can only be possible with the help of a powerful foreign partner. Otherwise, they have to do what they always did despite the high cost of funding in their own countries. Indeed today, hundreds of global enterprises have partners from developing markets, operating in infrastructure, superstructure, motorways, dams, airports, overhead power lines, telecommunication, oil exploration, oil drilling, investments of large amounts of cash such as downstream as well as food, retail, banking and finance, automotive and major appliances, gas stations, even restaurant chains.

Although some actors, who made their wealth back in the times when Turkey had a closed economy, were upset by this situation at first, they too adapted to the new order and grew their businesses through foreign partnerships. The difference was that the state was their partner in the past, but now these unmerciful and relentless giant international institutions have become their new partners. Consequently, national firms had to change their ways of doing business and their organizational structures under the roof of foreign partnerships.

All of these things I mentioned above have revealed the danger of suddenly losing fifty- to sixty-year-old values when exposed to outer shocks. The foreign funds used in project financing could cause financial losses, even the collapse of companies due to the sudden depreciation of national currency. The banks are also to blame for this situation as they always want to grow their assets to keep with the competition.

Focusing on treasury departments in periods of high interest rates has drastically grown their balance sheets through the government domestic debt securities. With a decline in the "crowding-out" effect following interest rate cuts, they started to sell their financial obligations to persons and corporate entities as a line of credit. The rapidly accelerating competition and the ever-degenerating/corruptive styles of management caused banks to go off the rail in 2001. The following argument is from the book I had written that year:

> The banking system must work on the basis of transparent and scientific criteria, forcing every activity and sector it interacts with to adopt and comply with these criteria.

MORAL HAZARD

Obviously, no one can change the circumstances that easily. To create change, one must push the circumstances. The necessity for banks that shoulder the heaviest burden of Financial Intermediation, to place their risk reception on a more mathematical and rational basis, wasn't only my idea. This was the reason the Banking Regulation and Supervision Agency of Turkey (BDDK) was established in the first place, and it has become now clearer that it functions quite well as a regulatory authority. Despite this fact, there were rumors that the loan processes of public banks have been rather flexible for political reasons. Perhaps, Turkey was lucky that the financial crisis emerged before this situation has spread to private banks as well.

Yet quite surprising, it is a fact that the major banks of developed economies have not been as cautious as Turkish banking system has been. During their international expansion, the quality of human resources has declined significantly, not to mention their embellished balance sheets. Due to the chaos in the hierarchy of authority, people who sat in front of their computer screens all day long for financial and trading purposes have been given significant initiatives. The side effects of this delegation of authority, billion-dollar fraud cases, were either quickly forgotten or covered up.

Although the flaws of the system have been surfacing one after another, the system itself continued to be. As I have mentioned earlier, people could not rely on a single income alone to finance their lives. They had to take out loans. Individuals who did not spend their money but used it to take out loans when interest rates were high and repaid their debts with their credit cards have been deprived of an important additional income for the last five years due to decreasing interest rates. People had abandoned their old habit of "spending today's income tomorrow" and developed a new one instead: "spending tomorrow's income today." Mortgage loans, auto loans, consumer loans, and credit cards encouraged individuals to spend more than they earn. In the early 2000s, US household spending exceeded household income for the first time in sixty years. Due to rises in stock exchange prices, more than 20 percent of global consumption growth started to come from American Citizens who had additional income, apart from their regular salaries. So, today, in order to put an end to this crisis, the spending instinct of American Citizens must be brought under control.

Despite all of the facts mentioned above, I am still insisting on my previous argument from my 2001 book: "If it weren't for the Financial Intermediaries, the world could not have achieved economic growth and development." I think it would not be very realistic to blame the instrument itself for being used by irrational persons who are not capable of using that instrument, to begin with. I do believe that banks did not create the "desire for making more money." However, it is undeniable that they have facilitated this desire with numerous means and methods. From this perspective, it must be said that they failed the test of rationality and ethics in terms of showing people that it's possible to make money without producing anything, for the last twenty years.

Having lost its national senses after 1997, banking has kind of an introverted mood. It doesn't think for the whole system, just like its competitors. It sticks to the philosophy of "Après moi, le deluge" while making efforts to keep the ship afloat anytime there's a storm. Traditionally, banks always felt responsible for the money of hundreds of thousands of investors and depositors. However, we should remember that the 2001 Turkish economic crisis happened in the first place because of the fact that the full guarantee on deposits (introduced in the 1990s) had remained in effect for a very long time, weakening the banks' sense of responsibility. The right thing to do here is to create a system where investors, bankers, and account holders are aware of the existing and future risks. It would be more useful to look for the why of this situation both in the banking itself and in outside environments in order to find the root causes.

The fact that a banking system exists in a country doesn't mean that it could help overcome the adversities the country is facing. If the habits and customs in a country, as well as the legal, social, and political structure, remain as obstructions before the development, the presence of banks and nonbank financial institutions won't help deal with the problems, on the contrary, it might even worsen the situation. Accordingly, the Turkish 2000–2001 banking crisis and similar instances in South Korea and Taiwan should always serve as an example for the world. We have all seen that the crisis reached alarming levels with the collapse of even the largest banks and the real sector had been exposed to serious threats due to failure to meet credit needs. Such developments will inevitably cause government changes in many countries. Very soon, the governments in EU countries will change. There are numerous effects of such changes we're already experiencing.

So, the banking system alone is not responsible for the existing problems nor is it the remedy for the structural diseases in the countries. Bearing the responsibility of gathering together fund suppliers and fund users, the financial institutions contribute to the general degeneration and corruption not more or less than other sectors. However, it is certain that, without banks and financial institutions, the wheel of degeneration and moral corruption would not turn as rapidly. After all, these institutions are responsible for the management of money, which, itself, manages everything. It's a risk on its own to manage the very thing that manages everything.

While, from 1960 to 1980, the banking sector was struggling amid negative real interest rates, harsh exchange rate regimes, and lack of financial instruments, it had entered a brand new era with the emergence of financial liberalization in the 1980s. Liberalization of interest rates and quick transition to convertibility necessitated the recruitment of specialized staff with international education background.

Not only regular banks but also Central Banks, Treasuries, and the IMF itself were caught off guard by the sudden and rapid changes in markets. The governments, however, took these changes and turned them into opportunities by inventing the government domestic debt securities. Used to collect people's savings either through public banks or public institutions in the old system, governments started to use banks, which number was rapidly growing thanks to financial liberalization, as intermediaries. Probably, it was the first moment when banking has gone off the rails.

DEGENERATION OF THE FINANCIAL SYSTEM AND GOVERNMENT DOMESTIC DEBT SECURITIES

While the main function of the banks was to collect savings from the depositors and give it to the real sector, in other words, those who wanted to build a business or do business, they suddenly became an entity that finances the state treasury. As the interest rate offered by the government was both satisfactory and guaranteed, the system of "take from the people and give it to the government" has, after a while, pushed the banking's positive creativity to the bottom level. And worse, banks started to spend their capital on government domestic debt securities, which would later lead to the collapse of some of these banks. Enterprises may collapse, but governments do not.

As can be understood from the statements above, the convenient environment for corruption was actually created by governments, not the banks. Those who have paved the way for an environment that favors degeneration and corruption should be to blame for this tiresome competition that corrodes moral values with constant authorizations to establish a bank and the vicious circle of high interest rate-high inflation. Also, certain organizations and their executives who exerted heavy pressure on markets, companies, and the society to solve this twenty-year-old disease of high interest rate and inflation in just a couple of years seem equally to blame as governments.

The danger of the internal debt spiral has increased further with foreign investors entering Turkish markets. In countries which removed their border restrictions in order to facilitate both merchandise and capital traffic following the financial liberalization, the current account deficit became a chronic and structural issue and the portfolio capital, which was flowing into the country due to high interest rates, started to create a bigger addiction, in other words, a crucial mistake was made: trying to finance the current account deficit (caused by the import of goods and services that are essential to production processes) using funds that could leave the country anytime. Although nominal interest rates have declined due to this threat, the real interest rate remained satisfactory as always. Most developing countries were quite worn out by this interest rate competition. Latin American countries, for instance, have faced numerous financial crises while people in Russia and Asia have experienced serious financial bottlenecks.

Typically, when countries borrow money from other countries or institutions, they don't intend to fully pay off their debt one day. Although thirty to forty years ago perhaps, their motive was to repay their debt in full, today no country in the world becomes indebted with the intention of fully paying it off at some point in the future. There are two reasons for that: one, their already enormous pile of debt; second, their creditors have no such demand because the important thing for the creditors is the interest earnings; the principal capital has become so insignificant next to such profitable interest income. The total amount of interest payments made from the past to present have exceeded by far the initial amount of borrowed money.

As the capital markets of developing countries became more organized, the borrowing market too has equally expanded. Today, Brazil and Turkey are among the countries government bonds and bills play a dominant role as an investment class in the market. And the reason for that involves the volume created by buyers and sellers as well as the huge debt pile of both countries. The fact that the debt market is both liquid and deep appeals to investors, it also helps them quickly convert their money into foreign currency and leave the market.

CAPITAL MARKETS AND PRIVATE SAVINGS

Personal savings are the most important key to economic growth and development. The lack of savings has made people pursue more funds, consequently creating the banks and financial institutions, helping the creation of capital markets, and finally rendering the secondary market more functional. However, inadequate national savings has forced the investors to develop a dependency on foreign funds. This is the exact point where the non-equilibrium begins.

As the financing needs of the post-1980s liberal and consumer economy have begun to accumulate, different options have been sought to address these needs. When the poor cash supply and devaluation-inflation spiral has caused higher interest rates, the money created in banks started to exceed the actual money supply. The high number of drawing accounts, term deposit accounts, foreign currency deposit accounts, and repos combined with the rapidly growing supply of bank money has become the main cause of inflation.

The fact that post-1980s governments made all the wrong choices hence caused further growth in bank money supply by dominating the debt market for too long and the fact that they made investment choices without a valid rationale, due to "negative selection," has made the "liberal economy" the target of left-wing criticism. For instance, in Turkey, populist practices like "early retirement" have caused further deterioration in social security's financial outlook. The discomfort from the burden that has arisen out of other wrong practices has prevented the next governments from developing a "National Policy" vis-à-vis the instructions from institutions like the IMF. The fact that people had to pay the price for the nationwide financial distress has resulted in the withdrawal of central political parties from the political scene for a very long time. This political authority gap has caused the emergence of new political figures making "no more poverty" promises. The sad truth was no humanly effort would be enough to repair this structural degeneration. At that point, banks and financial institutions were no different than everyday people were trying to live from day to day.

Obviously, the development of capital markets should be taken into account when exploring this situation. Otherwise, we would fail to effectively analyze the causes of the problems we are facing today, therefore fail to generate any permanent solutions.

In order for the primary market to achieve its synergy, the secondary market has to work successfully. The environment where the primary market traders and the secondary market traders meet should be well organized so as to facilitate the buying-selling transactions. Obviously, the properties of tradable securities are equally important.

As things were going great in theory, toward the late 1990s, there have been instances where the financial instrument prices in the secondary market exceeded the actual price of the instrument. To clarify, stock exchanges had started to sell neither the present nor the future but the expectations, or rather dreams, based on different scenarios. As companies kept talking to the media about their financial statuses in accordance with the market transparency, some groups began manipulating the stock prices through unrealistic comments. Reports and comparisons showing that even the rapidly increasing prices were still cheap caused frenzy in stock markets. The infrastructure for virtual earnings has been established by running technical analyses of unprecedented levels. To confirm the soaring prices, time examples from national and international markets have been presented. In 2008, when the market cap of publicly listed companies in developing countries approached closer to the market cap of similar companies in the developed countries, the time had come for the bubble to burst.

Perhaps the biggest advantage of removing boundaries through financial liberalization would be to be able to create markets that move in harmony with perfectly synchronized regulations. I must say that serious efforts have been made to turn this aspiration into reality. However, it would also not be wrong to say that the desired result was unfortunately achieved. Today, investors trade in markets that are different from each other in terms of session and transaction rules, trading hours, guarantee terms, investor rights and privileges, and so on.

> Eliminating such differences will require a longer amount of time than estimated, because the markets in emerging economies generate large amounts of profits. However, no stable solutions can't be found to address both tax and profit transfer problems involving these earnings. Legislation in emerging economies is typically vague and is always open to interpretation. Regulations governing the Monetary and Capital Markets in these countries are issued not in accordance with global and future standards, but they are rather based on government policies, the country's economic fragilities, or worse, on the basis of the then-current agenda. The pressure exerted by the media and the political leaders, as well as the long-established reservations of the society play an important role in the shaping of these laws and regulations, which gives foreign investors, or domestic investors who pretend to be a foreign investor to engage in trading in their own domestic market, freedom to trade as they please.

To illustrate, when governments want to achieve growth through public spending, they tend to discriminate the government domestic debt securities positively in a manner to prevent private sector bonds-bills markets and stock exchanges. Tax exemption being in the first place, they eliminate all kinds of impacts that might create "friction" in the domestic debt market, not to mention that they hand tax-free and risk-free earning opportunities to both domestic and foreign investors on a silver platter.

EFFECTIVE MANAGEMENT OF GOVERNMENT DEBT FOR THE SURVIVAL OF THE POLITICAL REGIME

As the government debt-to-GDP ratio goes higher, the government becomes incapable of net borrowing due to the interest rate multiplier fuelled by inflation, which means the government has to pay off its old debts using the money it borrowed without having a chance to use this money for public expenditures or investments. So, the debt spiral grows bigger and bigger while interest rates keep climbing up further; however, higher interest rates become less attractive for the investors due to higher risk. When this happens, governments tend to show two types of behaviors:

First, if it's newly elected government, it usually offers the solutions of "moratorium" or "debt consolidation." Russia too has used the same method in the early years of Putin's presidency. Although it might not always bring positive yields, this method, however, might lead to some major side effects. If the country is barren in terms of strategic resources like natural gas and petroleum, this might result in panic among the creditors. A drastic downgrade of the country's credit rating would lead to the very high probability that the interest rates on the future debt will not fall to competitive levels for a very long period of time. However, as foreign funds are crucially important to countries that lack savings, they don't have the luxury of financially isolating themselves from the rest of the world. Even the least democratic governments should not choose the option of impoverishing their people just to pay off the national debt. A most obvious example of this is the era of Nicolae Ceauşescu in Romania. While the debt repayment operation which began in 1982 and continued until 1989 caused famine and poverty in the country, it paved the way for a regime change. This example alone shows that even the most repressive dictatorships can't survive without debt.

The second type of behavior involves improving creditworthiness by preparing a program with the help of organizations like the IMF, so as to extend debt payment terms and reduce the interest rates. Obviously, agreements with the IMF bring about specific conditions. As developing countries are required to pay high levels of interest, the IMF would want the government budget to run a certain surplus in its expense-revenue equilibrium at a certain proportion of the GDP, "except for interest payments," with the purpose of preventing the government from spending excessive money with populist intentions while forcing it to be more selective in investment and spending decisions. On the other hand, the IMF would also want to see some serious privatization efforts so as to put an end to the era of fund transfer to GBEs. Oftentimes, governments resist such changes; seeing privatization only as a mechanism to generate one-time revenue, they sell the shares of GBEs through public offering, which enables them to raise large amounts of funds while not being obliged to renounce power. By choosing the remedy of public offering, however, they recall the "crowding-out effect" they had created in the past through domestic borrowing. This way, the savings of the people go directly to the government, not the private sector, for public spending purposes, which is another example of the government abusing financial liberalization.

When governments refuse to renounce the management of GBEs by offering their shares to the public instead of privatizing them, IMF and other institutions resort to "deregulation," which means they force the governments to make GBE-related rights and privileges available for the use of free market. Although this leads to unfair competition due to the large size and major market power of the GBEs, after a while, privatization becomes inevitable. Mostly, this has been the case for telecommunication and energy sectors. Usually, the government issues privatization specifications to try to even out the National Private Capital Stock's inadequacies against the foreign competitors in terms of resources and know-how. By doing so, the government actually causes the national capital stock to struggle under a heavy burden of debt. The purpose is to restructure the country that tries to stay afloat amid a rising tide of debt. Consequently, the country's international reputation will increase; new borrowing opportunities will emerge after the improvement of its creditworthiness. But, the process of reformation which is underway and pushes all the limits of financial liberalization will eventually cause further current account deficit and a bigger pile of debt. The only relieving factor of this process is the fact that the net public debt-to-GDP ratio is remaining quite low compared to previous periods, which can help the country regain its credit eligibility status. Given the fact that, as a side effect of this remedy, the obligation for internal debt interest rates to remain at a level that satisfies the investors eliminates the opportunity to invest with the national currency, the business world becomes obligated to borrow mostly foreign currency-denominated debt; because, in foreign currency debt, the costs are low, and FX rates mostly remain low as well due to both high interest rates and the increasing creditworthiness of the country, which, in consequence, leads to further vulnerability to external impacts.

As can be seen, the first method that is used to get rid of the debt spiral causes major problems over the short term, leading the country to become even more introverted. However, although a Moratorium or Debt Consolidation creates problems in the short run, countries like Russia and Brazil that have abundant natural resources (oil and natural gas in particular) have succeeded to overcome such problems in the long term. Countries that do not have any natural resources, on the other hand, do not have the luxury to test this theory.

The political power Turkey possesses today due to its status as an energy corridor is in fact questionable. Turkey needs Political and Economic Stability for Oil and Natural Gas Pipeline security, but country cannot behave freely in those policies. For instance, Hungarian prime minister was stuck in a difficult situation during the "natural gas pipeline" negotiations between Hungary and Russia. Driven to the verge of resignation, the Hungarian PM had learned that in any future action he might take he will need to pay special attention to US "Red Lines."

Reading too much into the notion of "geostrategic advantage" and engaging in actions that can harm economic interests is apparently not the right thing to do. So, the only thing that is left to be done is to extend the debt repayment term and reduce the interest burden by improving the long-run creditworthiness in the eyes of the IMF and other international institutions. However, as can be seen, this only thing that is left to be done leads to a vicious circle in which

> national currency appreciates-current account deficit increases-interest rates go down-devaluation-interest rates go up-inflation increases-national currency appreciates again-current account deficit goes up again-interest rates go down again-devaluation again-inflation rises again-interest rates go up again.

In conclusion, the process of reducing internal and external debt to an acceptable level vis-à-vis GDP with the help of international institutions is quite a fragile process due to political developments. A decline in debt-to-GDP ratio doesn't change the fact that it continues to grow as an absolute number. Accordingly, the economy will always face certain risk factors unless the debt burden is not reduced nominally. Maybe the first action to achieve reduction is to balance the public budget, including interest payments.

So as to achieve this goal, unprecedented and drastic actions are needed, such as actions aimed to rapidly increase national savings. However, as we all know, making more savings at the same income level negatively affects the GDP growth rate. So, what needs to be done?

REVISITED: PRIVATE SAVINGS ARE THE SOURCE OF ECONOMIC GROWTH

Closing the savings gap shall not be a short-term goal. On the one hand, the government budget and need for borrowing should be reduced, while on the other, funds should be granted free passage in order to facilitate private investments which will create an economic growth momentum. A determined implementation of such a project might be able to help achieve significant progress in investment-savings balance over the next twenty-five years.

The challenging thing about the project is that whether or not each new government will want to work toward the same goal in a stable manner. After all, macroeconomic policies are determined by political leaders who have the option to choose a project over another. After the 1990s, while governments of developing countries, such as Turkey, have been trying to finance their expenses first using internal and then external debt securities, finally through capital markets, they did not make too much effort to increase private savings, because experts were saying that private savings would automatically increase as GDP grows. Even today, they are still saying the same thing. According to the Price Theory, higher income levels lead to higher saving rates. So, the abovementioned argument of those experts is based on a valid reference. But, there isn't any economics book that says what is exactly the income level, which can be considered "high," and when this level can be achieved.

The generalization of the "higher income levels lead to higher saving rates" theory, which was essentially based on the prosperity of rich countries, constantly redirects researchers to dead-end streets; because this topic covered by the Price Theory is actually not a generalization, but a phenomenon that needs to be analyzed on an individual basis. Considering the fact that US citizens have been consistently spending more than they earn for the last ten years, it becomes even clearer that it is impossible to generalize about this phenomenon. Just like the concepts of economic growth and economic development are often confused with each other, income and wealth too have the same confusing similarity between them.

Assuming that the notion of "disposable income" is connected to the income earned from production factors, we could hardly say that a significant savings progress was made over the last ten years. If increasing people's prosperity and welfare are among the duties of a government, increasing the disposable personal income should be the number one priority. However, governments tend to give priority to ensure the nominal expansion of incomes, for a very simple reason: government spending must be reduced in order to increase disposable income, which makes it possible to create budget surplus without even hiking tax rates. As less tax cuts would mean more savings or more investments at the same income level, the government would be able to create a foreseeable economic environment for the private sector.

The governments, however, cannot rule in a predictable climate. Political choices lose their significance in an economy that grows only through private sector investments. Private investments do not make negative selection as the public sector does, which means that the decisions made by and within the private sector are purely economic.

These investments will eventually turn into social benefits, which will apparently turn into monetary benefit, in other words, the profit. Governments, on the other hand, prefer creating such a development, rather than preparing the right environment for it. Besides, the tendencies that support government actions are already present within the society. Governments never want to give up the power of generating employment. They have priority actions in private sector employment.

Contrary to what is believed, the impact of public expenditures does increase the cost of living. Most of the attempts made by the government with social/economic benefit purposes unfortunately lead to non-productivity, economic damage, and budget deficits. When the government spends money in a manner that does not generate economic benefit, it must do something to cover the resulting deficits. So, the government uses two methods to finance the deficits through household and corporate revenue.

The first method is indirect taxation. Not only in developing countries but in almost every country in the world, the share of indirect taxes in total tax revenue has reached between 60 percent and 80 percent. The fact that revenues grow nominally has caused the share of essential expenses in total income to gradually increase, which led governments to levy higher indirect taxes. The increase in inflation helps the government to achieve its indirect tax target more easily.

The government's ever-increasing need for funds leads to some unfair practices I have mentioned in the earlier pages of this chapter. For instance, the government offers tax advantages to bonds and bills investors so as to ensure more effective management of the internal debt pile. But it doesn't provide the same advantage to the real sector. Due to the fact that the number of Income and Corporate taxpayers is quite low in total population, high taxes are imposed on all the domestically produced and imported goods and services. The purpose here is to levy taxes on informal earning activities that can't be monitored.

As a matter of fact, government engagement in markets to generate funds does increase the informal economy further. What's worse, this situation leads to a lack of interest in the real sector but a higher interest in capital market earnings. The difference between the attraction of real sector investment and that of bonds and bills investment quickly increases in favor of the latter. In situations where the supply cannot meet the demand, which is accelerated by interest-fuelled bank money, it is observed that the general price level, that is, inflation, climbs higher.

That is the reason why Central Banks have always warned about government spending while anti-inflationist policies were in effect. It's impossible to implement a successful anti-inflationist policy without bringing government spending under control. When the most important pillar of politics is missing, reducing inflation permanently through monetary policies alone is simply not possible.

Today, some experts that criticize the capitalist system due to the ongoing global crisis are arguing that the economic growth must be achieved by increasing government spending. The economic debates are one of the impediments to the disciplining of government spending growth. Whenever governments feel pressure about public spending, they tend to present the necessity of economic growth and employment as an argument for their actions. The real impediment to economic growth, however, is excessive government spending and the resulting debt.

The economic crisis we are going through today is a real ordeal for the capitalism. The capitalist system is being criticized in every aspect; there are great efforts to ensure that the state assumes a position where it serves as a regulatory, fund generating, and goods/services producing authority. Frankly, any fruit from these efforts would mean a waste of centuries of struggle for the evolution and maturation of liberalism.

For years, we have listened to theses where Keynesian economics and Welfare State concept have conflicted with each other. Today, those who demand state intervention by constantly emphasizing the importance of the Welfare State are following in the footsteps of Keynes, which made liberalism a philosophy that represents a freer way of life, more welfare, and production of more goods and services when compared to all social democratic ideas. It's not easy to get out of this dilemma.

Perhaps, capitalism needs to abandon the burden of fully representing liberalism and social democrats should accept the fact that they are not liberals, but actually the supporters of a statist economy. As mentioned in the early paragraphs of this chapter, given that the capitalism is not able to grow without the state's permission, ascribing too much meaning to its connection with liberalism should be avoided, because the current state of the liberal system does not provide equal opportunities to everyone.

On the other hand, we witness that democracy feeds on capitalism while its interaction with liberalism is gradually diminishing.

Chapter 3

In the Wake of the Outbreak, Income Distribution, and Poverty in Turkey

Ayşe Aylin Bayar and Öner Günçavdi

The COVID-19 outbreak caused unprecedented effects on the world economy and led the world to an economic crisis that has not been seen, to this extent, since the Great Depression (Baldwin and di Mauro, 2020; Roubini, 2020). According to the projection of the IMF, the world output is expected to fall almost by 4.9 percent in 2020. The IMF also estimated that advanced countries are likely to be hit more than the rest of the world (IMF, 2020). In particular, the economic output of the United States and European Union is expected to decline by 8 percent. The emerging market economies, on the other hand, are expected to perform relatively better, shrinking only by 3 percent. The only exception would be China with 1 percent positive economic growth. The economic growth rate in the same projection is estimated to be −5 percent for Turkey in 2020. However, the Turkish government has foreseen a relatively more optimistic growth rate of 0.3 percent for 2020 in its new economic program.[1] Even if the expected economic growth varies over countries, it will take some time to establish a new macroeconomic equilibrium for all countries.

One thing that is certain is that the impacts of the COVID-19 pandemic have been widespread and at unprecedented levels. Along with low growth rates and an increase in unemployment rates all over the world, the distributional and poverty effects of the pandemic must not be ignored. The World Bank, in this regard, draws the attention of the public to the fact that 40–60 million people are already in danger of falling into extreme poverty (World Bank, 2020), and they need international cooperation to finance the policies to combat these problems. According to the IMF, the great majority of these countries are in the Sub-Sahara and Southeast Asia regions. However, other countries are surely not an exception to this problem. For example, income distribution in Turkey is expected to increase drastically due to this pandemic, and the Gini coefficient, a well-known measure of inequality, is estimated to rise to 0.45 from 0.407, the level before the pandemic (Bayar et al. 2020a and 2020c). To mitigate the deteriorating effects of the pandemic on income distribution and poverty, governments are certainly required to implement sustainable redistributional income policies. It will definitely take some time after the pandemic to bring the Gini coefficient down to the level before the pandemic, and this will inevitably occupy the public agenda for a while in the post-pandemic period. These redistribution policies implemented by the government must then be long term and must be secured by financial resources available in the economy. In this regard, to calculate how long it will take for inequality and poverty to return to their pre-pandemic levels will be another issue in the chapter. Most importantly, the economic constraints and international environment that countries encounter in the post-pandemic world will determine the time required for this adjustment.

Governments all over the world will mainly face two important challenges in the post-pandemic world. *Firstly*, the world economy is most likely to enter into a period of moderate and low economic growth period after the pandemic, and the high economic growth rates that have been seen in many emerging market economics after 2001 will be difficult to find in the post-pandemic period. Emerging market economies such as Turkey will most likely experience relatively modest economic growth rates of around 3 percent or even lower for some time. *Secondly*, developing countries such as Turkey will face difficulties accessing the international financial market and borrowing at low interest rates as they have before. This will constitute the main restriction on public decision makers, keeping them from redirecting necessary financial resources to combat inequality and poverty.

In the midst of unprecedented contractions in economic activities and drastic jumps in unemployment rates in almost all countries in the world, policymakers have introduced massive fiscal and financial measures and drastically increased their debt stocks to raise finance for this spending. The burden of this massive debt stock will be more visible in the post-pandemic period than now and will be a burden hanging overall economic activities. However, given the limited financial resources, reviving economic growth will have priority for governments, and the impact of the pandemic on inequality and poverty will be widely ignored.

International organizations like the IMF and the World Bank estimate positive economic growth rates for the world economy in 2021. However, economic measures undertaken to ease the impacts of the pandemic will most likely result in many unsolved economic problems such as drastically increased budget deficits, high debt stocks, and, in the case of some countries, difficulties in accessing international financial markets. These new problems could constitute constraints on reviving economic growth next year, at least in some countries. Besides, economic risks arising from country-specific political problems also raise further concern about reviving economic growth sufficiently.

Economic growth is an important measure in poverty reduction policies and alleviates inequality without disturbing the shares of different income groups in the economy. Therefore, positive and high economic growth would be greatly helpful for governments to mitigate inequality and poverty without losing their public support.

The aim of this chapter is in general to estimate the likely effects of the COVID-19 pandemic on income distribution and poverty in Turkey. Most importantly, it is to examine the importance of direct cash transfers to households in controlling an increase in poverty. A short-time working payment system that has already been implemented in Turkey is used as a basis for this examination. This chapter will also investigate how long it will take to reach the level of poverty before the pandemic especially under the unfavorable economic conditions that will be prevailing in the post-COVID-19 world.

This issue is crucial mainly because many developing countries will face a noticeable increase in poverty and deteriorating income distribution due to the choice of inappropriate policy actions during the COVID-19 pandemic. The distributional issue will surely be more important in developing countries than in advanced countries, but it is certain for the time being that none of the countries that are already exposed to the spread of COVID-19 will be exempt from these effects.

We investigate the answer to the questions that we put forward in five sections. Following this introduction, section "Measuring the Impact of the COVID-19 Outbreak: Methodology" presents a general account of the pandemic and introduces containment measures and their economic results. The methodology of our empirical examination is introduced in section "Summary Statistics and the Impact of the Pandemic." The effects of the COVID-19 pandemic on inequality and poverty are discussed in section "A Rise in Poverty due to the COVID-19." Finally, concluding remarks and likely policy recommendations are presented in section "Conclusion."

TURKEY'S POLICY RESPONSE TO THE OUTBREAK

Turkey officially announced the first death due to the COVID-19 virus on March 11, 2020, and immediately undertook some preventive measures, all of which had negative impacts on economic activities. The aim of these measures was to contain the spread of the virus, but they also paved the way for a change in business practices and household preferences, which in turn brought about lasting effects on the economy. *Education* requiring physical contact with students was terminated, and it was taken into homes via the internet. Turkey gradually closed its borders to neighboring countries, suspending outbound and inbound flights. All *shopping malls* were closed as a precautionary measure to reduce physical contact among people. *Offices*, with mostly white-collar workers, were abandoned and moved into homes. Restaurants, eating out, shopping, and business meetings were all replaced with online deliveries, online shopping, and video conferences, respectively. These new business practices, some of which were by force, unexpectedly emerged in our life by changing the structures of economies in the world and caught many countries unprepared. However, the challenges of adjusting economies to the new conditions after the pandemic remain on many fronts.

As the spread of the pandemic continued at full speed in April and May, the Turkish government announced further measures such as lockdowns, bans on domestic travel, and restrictions on going out for people older than sixty-five. Even *curfews* were imposed on some occasions. Despite drastic effects on the economy, these measures continued until the beginning of June. The Turkish government, along with other governments in the world, could not afford the huge economic costs of the pandemic, and finally decided to open up the economy by removing some of these measures. However, the death toll began to increase once again starting from September, most probably heading Turkey toward the second wave of the outbreak.

Despite the disagreement on the official number of people infected by the virus, there is a general understanding in the public that the pandemic has recently revived and begun to endanger the daily life of households. The most recent official data available on the pandemic reveals the course in figure 3.1. It seems that a rise in the number of confirmed new cases stopped almost

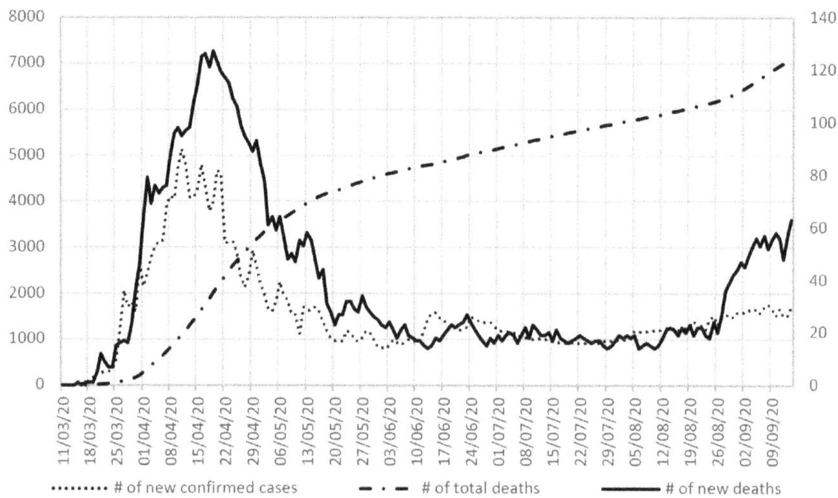

Figure 3.1 COVID-19 Cases and Deaths Toll in Turkey. *Source*: The Ministry of Health, https://covid19.saglik.gov.tr/.

one month after the outbreak, and even began to fall afterward. The pace of increase in the number of deaths seems to have slowed down significantly after the middle of May, and it almost stabilized before the removal of the lockdown on June 1, 2020. Although the number of tests has often been criticized as being insufficient, the number of people being tested continuously increased. Interestingly, the number of new deaths stabilized at around twenty during the entire summer, but *this suddenly began to increase on August 28, leading Turkey toward the second peak in terms of the number of deaths.*

The measures undertaken between March and June simply meant a pause in many economic activities, mostly in the service sector. For many people earning income from these activities, it was something like doomsday coming early. The measures inevitably halted some sectors and slowed down others, resulting in massive job and income losses. According to the official death toll announced by the *minister of health*, the effects of the pandemic reached its maximum in April. Its economic effects also became visible in the industrial production index in April. Figure 3.2 shows changes in the values of industrial production indices with drastic falls in the production levels of all industries in April. The total production index showed a decline of over 30 percent only in April. The fall in service sector production, although the data is unavailable, must have been even more than this in the same period.

After April 2020, the pandemic was controlled, and its spread, to a great extent, slowed down. The official death toll began to decline significantly (see figure 3.1). This was seen as an opportunity to relax some of the containment measures by many sector representatives which were badly affected by the

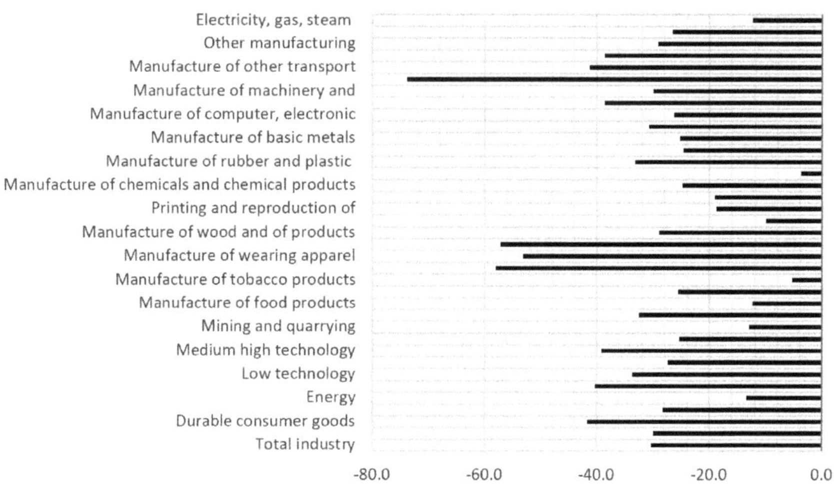

Figure 3.2 COVID-19 Cases and Deaths Toll in Turkey. *Source*: Turkstat, Industrial Production Index via https://data.tuik.gov.tr/.

pandemic and its economic outcomes. They then increased their pressure on the government to remove some of the COVID-19-related measures that previously either halted or slowed down economic activities in their industries.

As the economic cost mounted, the government could not resist these sectoral demands anymore. Besides, the government had an additional concern about losing foreign exchange revenues from tourism due to restrictions on international travel. More importantly, the harvest time in agriculture was approaching in summer, and this required the laborers to travel between cities. The government finally decided to gradually open up the economy at the beginning of June.

Gross domestic product performance in the second quarter—including April, May, and June—indeed gives us a clear impression regarding the economic impact of the lockdown period. It seems from figure 3.3 that the overall economy contracted by almost 10 percent in the second quarter. This unprecedented contraction was accompanied by a decline in service sector production of almost 25 percent. This was the highest decline in comparison to those of other sectors. A fall in industrial output was only 17 percent in the same period. Financial and insurance activities, real-estate, information and communication, and agricultural were four sectors showing positive economic growth performance in the same quarter due to increase in demand for the products produced by them. These results overall clearly illustrate how devastating the economic effects of the pandemic were on the supply side of the economy. To compensate for this fallout in the economy, the government immediately announced a TL 100 billion fiscal aid program. TL 75 billion of this amount was used to finance fiscal measures undertaken, and TL 25 billion was directed to the amount in the credit guarantee fund. Unfortunately,

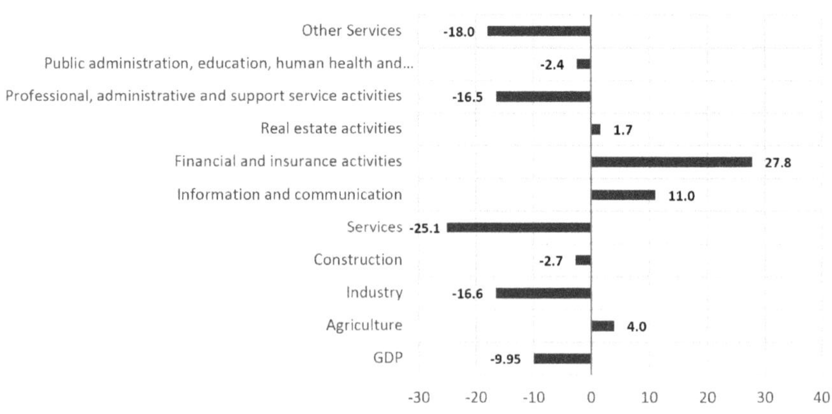

Figure 3.3 COVID-19 Cases and Deaths Toll in Turkey. *Source*: TurkStat, Quarterly Gross Domestic Product, Quarter II: April-June, 2020, via https://data.tuik.gov.tr/

the great majority of this program did not involve timely cash transfer to households but was rather given to firms and entrepreneurs to compensate for the falls in their cash flows. The financial program was not satisfactory in terms of either size or scope. In particular, the most vulnerable strata of Turkish society, such as poor and economically dependent women, were left untouched (Bayar et al. 2020b).

Producers were not the only economic units affected by containment measures and lockdown. Households, as the most important demand source in the economy, were also affected by the pandemic and encountered the danger of losing their jobs and incomes. As economic activities slowed down, the redundancy level of labor increased as expected for many businesses, and firms reduced their employment level and had to lay off workers. People's expectations of finding a new job in the present condition of the labor market eventually diminished.

The likelihood of finding jobs in the market fell drastically due to a fall in the employment rate. As seen in figure 3.4, the *employment rate* had actually been declining since August 2018, and this decline inevitably accelerated with the COVID-19 outbreak. The 45 percent employment rate in December 2019 dropped to 41 percent in April 2020. Without any hope of finding jobs in the present labor market, individuals stayed out and preferred to wait until the market conditions changed. As more and more people become unemployed and lose their hope of finding new jobs, their participation in the labor force continues to decline.

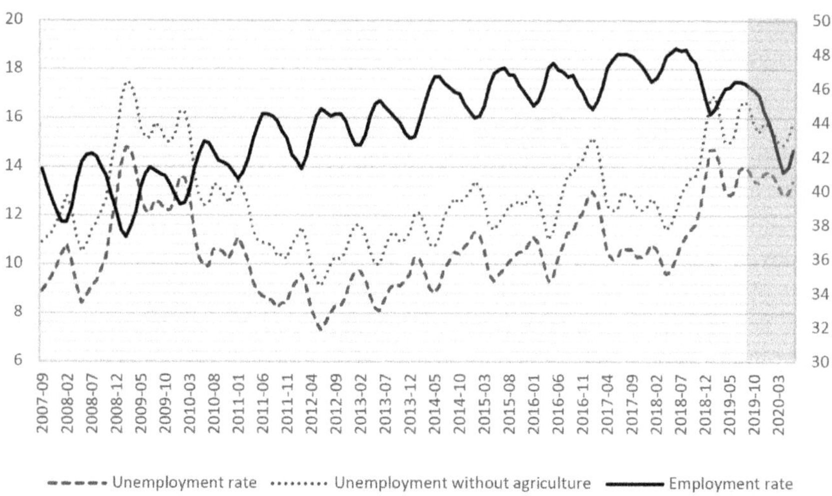

Figure 3.4 COVID-19 Cases and Deaths Toll in Turkey. *Source*: TurkStat, Labor Force Statistics, via https://data.tuik.gov.tr/.

TurkStat measures unemployment as the ratio of unemployed labor to the labor force. However, this definition has recently become the subject of political debate and has raised concern about the reliability of the labor market statistics announced by TurkStat. Despite the apparent fact that people without jobs increased, TurkStat's unemployment rate showed a slight decline in a number of successive months during the pandemic, and this has initiated a public debate. In figure 3.4, both unemployment rates with and without agriculture appear to have stayed stable in the period of the pandemic. This figure though is unable to capture the real state of the labor market. The employment rate, which indicates that people are increasingly staying out of the labor market, is surely a better indicator than the unemployment rate. It clearly shows the expected, declining trend in employment.

The Turkish government was wise enough to control the unemployment rate at least in official numbers and took some immediate actions to compensate for the economic impacts of the pandemic. Decree 7244,[2] for example, proposes to reduce the impact of the COVID-19 pandemic on economic and social life. The decree included financial measures to support minimum wage to decrease the cost of employment for employers. Dissolving labor contracts was also prohibited for three months, and this restriction could be extended if necessary. Employers were also given the right, in return, to release workers without payment. In that case, payments of 39 TL per day (1170 TL per month, which is equivalent to approximately $149 calculated with a 7.86 TL/$ exchange rate) were granted to those who were not eligible to receive unemployment benefits. Besides, the *short-term working allowance* was given to all workers who were employed in the firms' scaling down or stopping production. By April 22, 270,000 companies, comprising over 3 million employees, applied for the short-term employment allowance.[3] As of October 2020, the number of workers having short-term working allowances was 2.3 million.[4] Although this number was significantly higher at the beginning of the pandemic, the opening-up of the economy in June helped the number stay relatively low. This number alone is sufficient to prove how serious the employment effect of the pandemic would have been. However, not all employees can apply for this allowance. In order to be eligible to apply, first, an employee must have paid 450 premiums to the unemployment insurance fund. Second, he or she must have been employed for sixty days before his or her application. And most importantly, the eligibility for application does not cover non-registered employees, the self-employed, unpaid family workers, and immigrant workers. Turkey also gave 1000 TL (approximately $150) cash support to 2.1 million poor households.

In addition, the government, led by President *Recep Tayyip Erdoğan*, initiated a *Social Assistance and Solidarity Campaign* to raise money to help households in need. Nearly 180 million TL (approximately $23 million at the current exchange rate, 7.86) was donated to this campaign by individuals as well as private and public institutions. The government later put approximately 350 million TL (about $44.5 million) additional funds into this campaign.

Turkey so far has been unable to mobilize further financial resources in cash to combat the economic effects of the pandemic, and the government left the fate of the economy only to the market, particularly to the credit market. The pandemic caught Turkey in an ongoing economic crisis, and the government was under a strictly binding budget constraint. There was little room in the budget for the government to raise additional financial resources for the cash transfer to households in the pandemic relief program. The credit policy via the financial markets was an easy option left for the government. To keep the liquidity level of the financial market high, the money supply was increased by a tremendous amount, and the banking sector was able to extend credit to households and producers. The extent of fiscal and financial measures used in combating the COVID virus pandemic all over the world was examined by the IMF, and the result is summarized in figure 3.5.

The pandemic has inevitably increased the need for extra public spending on transfer payments, unemployment benefit payments, medical supplies, while also leading to the loss of tax revenue due to the fall in economic activities. Income has also paved the way for new financial tools and options to raise money to finance these expenditures. Because of the lack of adequate revenue on the public side, budget deficits have been extremely binding for some countries and led them to adopt unconventional measures for finance.

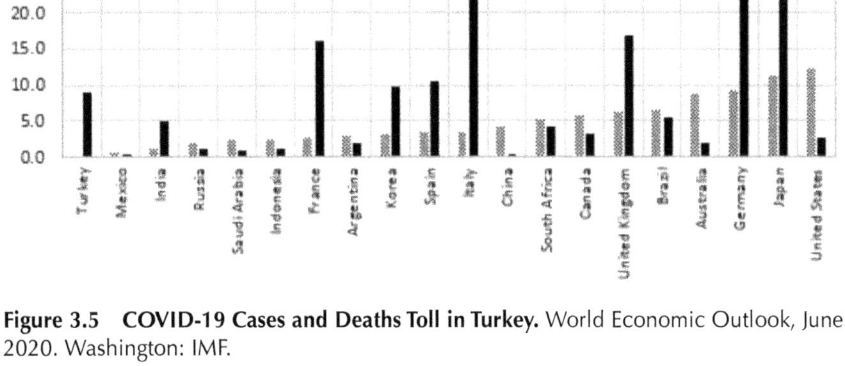

Figure 3.5 COVID-19 Cases and Deaths Toll in Turkey. World Economic Outlook, June 2020. Washington: IMF.

The IMF, in the latest World Economic Outlook, classifies countries based on their use of fiscal and financial measures in response to the COVID-19 pandemic. Countries use different combinations of both measures depending on their financial situation. Figure 3.5 shows the combination of economic measures for some selected countries. The most striking finding in figure 3.5 is that some countries such as Turkey overwhelmingly opted for financial measures rather than fiscal ones to raise money to finance extra spending (Günçavdı, 2020). This implicitly means that *the market, especially financial markets, gained importance in combating the undesirable economic effects of the COVID-19 pandemic.*

The somewhat insufficient economic measures to compensate for losses in the well-being of households could pave the way for a rise in poverty and deterioration in income distribution after the pandemic ends. Although the government was able to control a rise in unemployment by postponing layoffs in the labor force during the pandemic, it has failed to transfer an adequate amount of cash to low-income households to keep their income unchanged. Besides, the government was unable to provide cash support to individuals that were unregistered and were employed in occasional jobs. Most importantly, the cash support did not include any payment to small business owners and artisans whose businesses were badly affected and economic activities were drastically slowed down due to the pandemic. All these deficiencies of the cash transfer system in Turkey left a great number of households hopeless, abandoned, and afraid of falling into poverty. In what follows, a statistical methodology is proposed to measure the extent of this deterioration in income distribution both with and without the present scope of the cash transfer program.

MEASURING THE IMPACT OF THE COVID-19 OUTBREAK: METHODOLOGY

Unlike others in the literature (Özatay and Sak, 2020; Taymaz, 2020), the approach that we employ in this chapter is a microeconomic approach based on *heuristically* assigned impact coefficients to the sectors available in the Turkish statistics. The microdata from the *Survey of Income and Living Conditions* in 2018 is the latest available data source for public use, and we employ this data set to regenerate an alternative income and living condition which represents hypothetical situations after the outbreak.[5] Then, we estimate how much the pandemic, whose effects are measured by impact coefficients assigned to different sectors, might possibly change income and living conditions. Afterward, we calculate the various measures of income distribution and poverty for both cases and observe changes in these indicators.

The first essential step in our research is to determine the impact coefficients. We adopt a heuristic approach and assign coefficients to each sector from zero to five; zero representing no impact, and five indicating the maximum effect. It is assumed that each industry (or sector) is influenced to a different extent by the pandemic, and different impact factors, accordingly, are assigned to each sector by calculating the extent of these impacts. Then, a coefficient between zero and five is given to a sector by observing changes in both sectoral employment and sales that might likely be affected by initial containment measures in the short run.

After that, changes in employment and income level of individuals are calculated as the difference between the original ad hoc values of employment and income given in the Survey of Income and Living Conditions and those values obtained in the scenario-based generated hypothetical cases. The impact factors that are assigned to different sectors are pre-determined by looking at the responses of each sector after the outbreak of the pandemic. These observation-based impact factors are reported in table 3.1. These groups of sectors are already given by *TurkStat* and are available in the Survey of Income and Living Conditions. Individuals in households are

Table 3.1 Sectors and Their Hypothetical Impact Factors

	Sectors	*Assigned Impact Factors*
1	Agriculture, forestry, and fishing	Normal (3)
2	Mining and quarrying	Normal (3)
3	Manufacturing	Bad (2)
4	Electricity, water, gas, steam, and air conditioning supply	Normal (3)
5	Construction	Very bad (1)
6	Wholesale and retail trade	Good (4)
7	Transport and storage	Normal (3)
8	Accommodation and food service activities	Very bad (1)
9	Information and communication	Very good (5)
10	Financial and insurance activities	Bad (2)
11	Real-estate activities	Very bad (1)
12	Professional, scientific, and technical activities	Bad (2)
13	Administrative and support service activities	Bad (2)
14	Public administration and defense; compulsory social security	Normal (3)
15	Education	Normal (3)
16	Human health and social work activities	Very good (5)
17	Arts, entertainment, and recreation	Very Bad (1)
18	Other service activities	Bad (2)

Source: Authors' assumptions.

employed and generated an income flow from economic activities in these sectors.

After the official announcement of the pandemic and implementing containment measures, their effects on the economy immediately appeared in both the service and service-related sectors. For example, one part of retailing overwhelmingly increased their economic activities due to the sudden rise in online shopping. The health sector is another sector that outperformed during the pandemic, and the highest score is assigned to it.

The second step of our empirical study is to decide how income flows of households and individuals in different sectors are affected by the pandemic. For this purpose, we propose another scenario of impacts on income flows. We first distinguish different income types of households such as wage income, entrepreneurial income, financial income, real-estate income, retirement income, and transfer income. Immediate impacts of the COVID-19 pandemic appear on labor and, to a lesser extent, on entrepreneurial income, and the effects of economic measures can, gradually and with lag, be seen on income levels of other groups. It is assumed that all transfer incomes remain unchanged during and after the pandemic. Also, since real-estate income is constituted by rental income and they are bound to fixed-term contracts, then they are initially assumed to remain constant. Unlike others, only wage and entrepreneurial income are the two crucial income sources that are highly affected by economic conditions. Therefore, we concentrate our attention on these income sources, and come up with more detailed impact scenarios for these income groups. Entrepreneurial income, for instance, is related to sectoral economic conditions, and it is assumed to be affected by the same amount of the industry-wide impacts given in table 3.2. Regarding labor income, individuals working in casual jobs are the first income group that is most likely to lose their jobs and become dependent on any cash transfers by the government. Following casual workers, regular workers are also exposed to the risk of losing their jobs and income depending on the impacts that arise due to the pandemic-related economic measures.

In addition to the impacts of the pandemic on economic activities in table 3.2, it is also assumed that the economic conditions created by the pandemic affect the jobs of wage earners employed in different sectors and the flows of their income. Entrepreneurial and self-employed incomes are assumed to be affected by the change in economic conditions in different sectors. Other income groups, such as real-estate income, transfer payments, and retirement payments, are all assumed to remain constant.

A *heuristic approach* is used to describe the effects of the pandemic on the flows of income and employment in different sectors. We first assume that causal workers have a higher probability of losing their jobs than regular wage earners once the economic effects of the pandemic appear (Scenario 1). We accordingly assign different probabilities to the employment status

Table 3.2 Discount Factors in Income and Employment due to the Pandemic

		Assigned Probability of Losing Jobs		*Income Discount Factors*	
	Sectors	*Wage Earners*	*Casual Workers*	*Entrepreneur*	*Self-employment*
1	Agriculture	0.1	0.3	1	1
2	Mining	0.4	0.4	1	1
3	Manufacturing	0.3	0.8	0.6	0.4
4	Electric, water, and gas distribution	0.2	0	1	1
5	Construction	0.6	0.8	0.2	0
6	All trade	0.2	0	1.5	1.2
7	Transportation and storage	0.3	0.1	1.3	1.2
8	Hotel and restaurant	0.6	0.8	0.3	0.3
9	Information and communication	0	0	1.3	1.2
10	Finance	0.3	0.8	0.6	0.4
11	Real-estate	0.7	0.8	0.2	0.2
12	Professional and technical activities	0.4	0.8	0.6	0.4
13	Administrative and support	0.3	0.8	0.6	0.4
14	Public service and defense	0	0	1	1
15	Education	0	0	1	1
16	Health and Social service	-0.3	-0.3	1.5	1.5
17	Culture and Art	0.7	0.8	0.2	0.2
18	Others	0.5	0.8	0.4	0.4

Source: Authors' calculation.

in each industry. It is now necessary to repeat that the assigned probabilities are *heuristic* numbers, and they are not a precise number that appears from a detailed econometric study.

We also assume that entrepreneur and self-employment income flows are affected by the economic conditions of the pandemic, and different discount factors to the adjustment of their income in the post-COVID-19 period are heuristically assigned to the income flows of these groups. They are all seen in table 3.2. The adjustment of the sectoral economic activities is given in table 3.1 and the discount of income and employment in different sectors due to this adjustment in sectoral economic activities all together give us Scenario 2. This scenario describes the worse economic condition after the pandemic emerges, where there are no compensation policy measures by the government.

The condition after the government implemented the selective short-term working allowance is described by Scenario 3. This policy measure is selectively applied to wage earners who comply with certain conditions determined by the government. Those who lost their jobs but don't comply with application conditions are kept exempt from this allowance. The comparisons among various distributional and descriptive indicators calculated for these three conditions allow us to predict the distributional results of the COVID-19 pandemic. Most importantly, this methodology also reveals information regarding the capacity of the measure of the short-term working allowance to mitigate income inequality and poverty after the pandemic.

SUMMARY STATISTICS AND THE IMPACT OF THE PANDEMIC

The Survey of Income and Living Conditions is regularly conducted every year by TurkStat based on the previous year's income levels of households. Although the summary results of the survey are announced after a year, the microlevel data including the detailed information about the income and living conditions of individuals become available for the use of researchers with almost a two-year gap. For the time being, the detailed data is available for 2018 which includes information about the income of households in 2017.

This survey is conducted with 23 million households in 2018 whereas the total population is 79 million 761 thousand. The mean household size in the same survey is 3.4. According to the results of this survey seen in figure 3.6, wage income seems to constitute the major income source with 72 percent

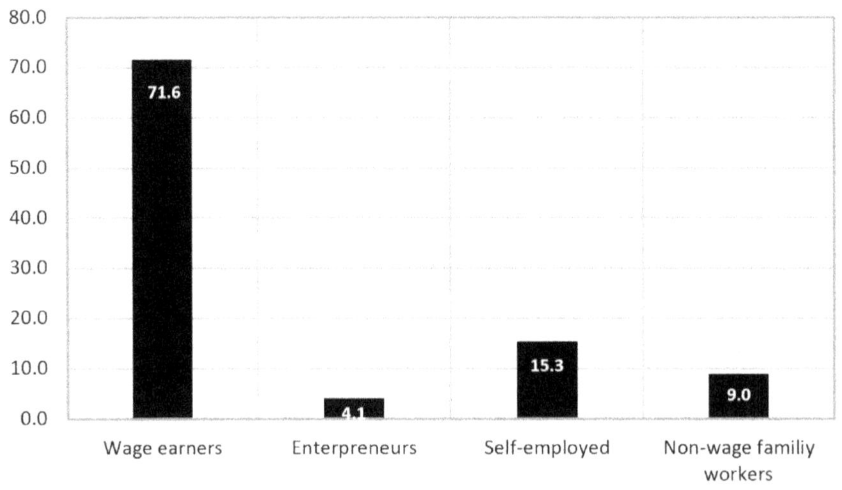

Figure 3.6 COVID-19 Cases and Deaths Toll in Turkey. *Source*: The survey of Income and Living Condition, TurkStat, 2018.

of total income. This is followed by income earned by self-employed economic activities at 15.3 percent. Entrepreneurial income is only 4.1 percent of total income. Another interesting feature of the Turkish economy is the presence of an income group that receives no income payment in return for their work in the business. They are basically family workers who work for free mainly in their family business. They are largely in the agriculture sector, and although they are not paid, the income created by their efforts implicitly constitutes 9 percent of total income.

The distribution of households over various economic activities available in the Turkish economy also reveals crucial information regarding who will be affected most by the pandemic. The members of households earn their income from employment in different sectors. As shown in figure 3.7, 55 percent of individuals earn income from economic activities in the service and service-related sectors, which to a great extent require face-to-face contact with people. It would not be an exaggeration to note that services are currently the major sources of employment and income in Turkey. The manufacturing sector is the second sector, with a19 percent share of employment that provides income to the households. The agriculture sector comes third with 16.3 percent.

To examine the extent of the effects on individuals of changes in household preferences and business practices after the COVID-19 pandemic emerged, the hypothetical impact factors in table 3.1 are imposed on economic activities. Then, households are grouped according to the extent of economic impacts on different sectors that are exposed to the pandemic. The results are exhibited in figure 3.8. 45.7 percent, almost half, of the entire households are

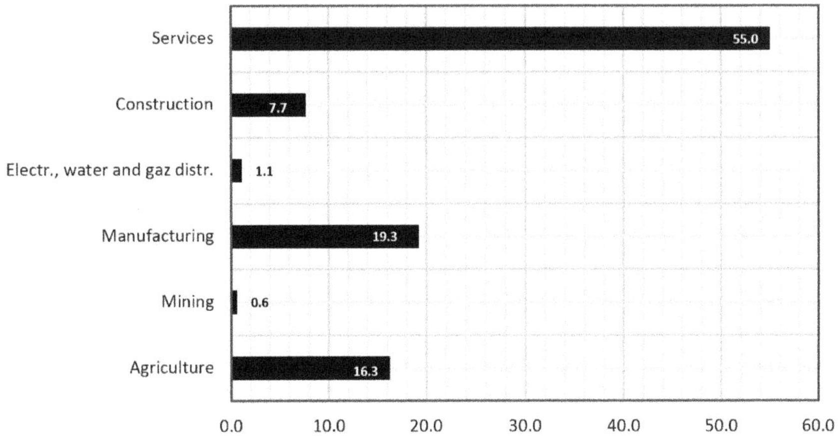

Figure 3.7 COVID-19 Cases and Deaths Toll in Turkey. *Source*: The survey of Income and Living Conditions, TurkStat, 2018.

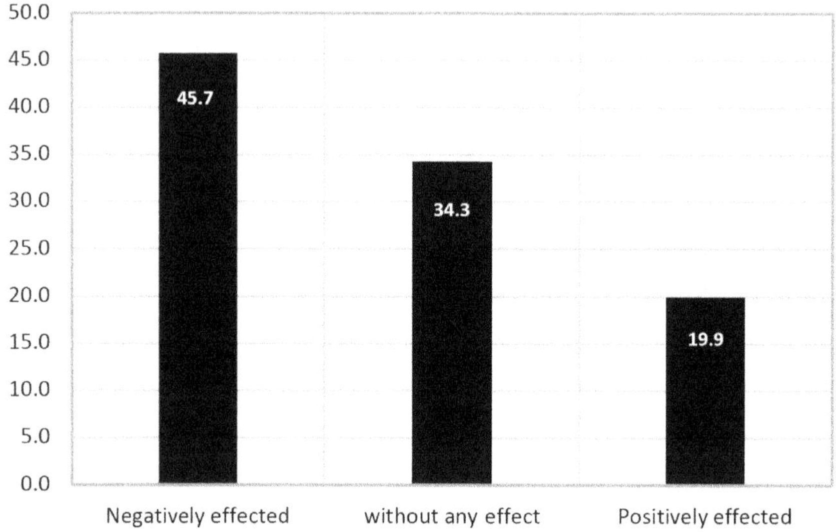

Figure 3.8 COVID-19 Cases and Deaths Toll in Turkey. *Source*: The survey of Income and Living Conditions, TurkStat, 2018.

found in the negatively affected sector group. Only 19.9 percent of households seem to be affected positively and benefit from the economic conditions that arise due to the pandemic. 34.4 percent of all households, on the other hand, remain in the sectors that are not affected by the pandemic at all.

To quantify the extent of the economic effects of the pandemic on households, average income levels of typical households can be calculated by imposing the hypothetical impact factors given in table 3.1. The results are reported in table 3.3 where the median income level, the most repeated income level in the sample, is shown. According to the Survey of Income and Living Conditions in 2018, the median income is calculated to be 17,914 TL. This income appears to decline to 14,9157 TL due to the pandemic. This apparently corresponds to a 16.5 percent reduction in income.

Table 3.3 Median Income by Income Group (TL)

	Total Income	*Income Group 1*	*Income Group 2*	*Income Group 3*	*Income Group 4*	*Income Group 5*
Before	17,913.8	7,873.9	12,883.1	17,901.8	25,156.5	43,516.3
After	14,957.1	6,336.6	11,582.3	16,461.9	22,842.1	38,833.7
% change	−16.5	−19.5	−10.1	−8.0	−9.2	−10.8

Source: *The Survey of Income and Living Conditions*, TurkStat, 2018 and authors' calculations.

The income levels of different income groups, however, fall disproportionately since each economic activity as a source of income is affected by the pandemic differently. Households are divided into five equal groups by their income, each of which corresponds to 20 percent of total income. The first group represents the poorest income group whereas the fifth one is the richest in the survey. In table 3.3, the income of the poor households seems to have declined by 19.5 percent whereas the income of the rich group falls by only 11 percent. This is simple and clear evidence to show the distributional impacts of the pandemic among households. It is also evident from table 3.3 that the pandemic deteriorated income distribution by reducing the income of the poor more than the rich.

It is clear from these calculations that Turkey is very likely to encounter a decline in overall household income presumably leading to a contraction in economic growth in 2020. *Besides, this decline takes place disproportionately among different income groups, and this gives us the initial clues of a deterioration in income distribution.*

The Turkish economy will likely be impacted by an escalation in income inequality and increased poverty after the COVID-19 pandemic ends. In what follows, the extent of these increases in income distribution and rise in poverty are to be estimated and the likely policy measures to bring them at least to the level before the pandemic are to be discussed.

Income Distribution and the Pandemic

How the COVID-19 pandemic influences income distribution at the micro-level is measured in this section. There are various statistical indicators to measure income distribution, each of which has its advantages and disadvantages (Cowell, 2011). Two of them are particularly worth mentioning. One of them is the Gini coefficient, whereas the second one is the coefficient of variation. Both measures are well known in the literature, but each put a different weight on different income groups in measurements. The former one is more sensitive to any variations in the income of high-income groups. The coefficient of variation, on the other hand, puts more weight on variations in the income of low-income groups and could be more appropriate to be used in the examination of the effects of the variations in the income of low-income earning groups.

Figure 3.9 shows the results of both measures. Each measure is calculated for three different cases based on the data from the Survey of Income and Living Conditions in 2018. The first case refers to the original case of income and living conditions *before* the pandemic. The second one describes the condition under the hypothetical income and living conditions *after* the COVID-19 pandemic and without any cash transfer to households. The third case is

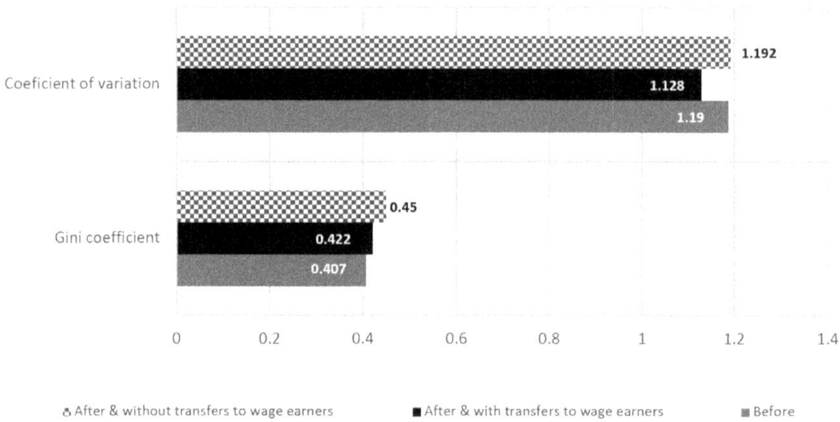

Figure 3.9 COVID-19 Cases and Deaths Toll in Turkey. *Source:* The survey of Income and Living Conditions, TurkStat, 2018 and authors' calculation.

the income and living conditions after the pandemic with cash transfers to wage-earner households.

According to both measures, income inequality increases after households are exposed to the economic effects of the pandemic and if they receive no cash transfer. This increase is greater using the Gini coefficient than using the coefficient of variation. The present income distribution of 0.407 immediately jumps to 0.45 after the pandemic. The change in the variation of coefficient remains fairly limited increasing from 1.19 to 1.20. However, a drastic difference between both measures appears when short-term working allowances are paid to wage-earner households that become unemployed as a result of the containment measures of the pandemic. Although this cash transfer has been considered insufficient and has become the subject of public debate, its effect on income distribution, with respect to both indicators of inequality, is evidently in the direction of mitigating inequality. The coefficient of variation declines from 1.2 to 1.13, whereas the Gini coefficient falls from 0.45 to 0.422. Besides, according to the coefficient of variation, the payment of short-term working allowances to relatively low-income households seems to alleviate the overall income distribution that prevailed in the economy before the pandemic. This is actually an expected result that occurs due to more weight being given to low-income households in the calculation of the coefficient of variation than in the Gini coefficient. *The one certain thing that this exercise clearly shows is that the short-term working allowance is an appropriate measure to control the adverse effects of the pandemic on income distribution.*

To examine the sources of changes in inequality due to the pandemic as well as short-term working allowances, the decomposition of total income into its income sources is of great help. Seven distinctive income groups are available in the Survey of Income and Living Conditions in Turkey. They are namely the wage-earner group, entrepreneurial income group, interest rate earner group, real-estate income group, retirement income group, and transfer income, and unemployment benefit groups. Among others, Jenkins' decomposition method is well known and the most appropriate one for our purpose here. Most importantly, Jenkins' decomposition method allows for a dynamic decomposition of a change in inequality either between two points over time or between two distinctive states (Jenkins, 1995).[6]

Accordingly, we first calculate changes in income inequality between the two states of income and living conditions before and after the pandemic. We denote these two states by 1 and 2, respectively. Then a change in inequality between two states can be formulated as follows:

$$\Delta I = I(Y)_2 - I(Y)_1 = \sum_k \Delta S_k \tag{3.1}$$

where Δ indicates changes in inequality in level. In our empirical study, the percentage of change in inequality can also be derived from equation (3.1) as follows:

$$\nabla I = \Delta I(Y)/I(Y) = \sum_k s_k \nabla S_k \tag{3.2}$$

where ∇, instead of Δ, shows the percentage of changes in inequality. Equation (3.2) is applied to the data from the surveys of income and living conditions.

Equations (3.1) and (3.2) are applied to the data from two different hypothetical cases to examine the importance of short-term working allowances given to individuals in firms whose business slowed down or was shut down. In the first hypothetical scenario, there are no extra transfer payments to households or any additional payments to other income groups. It only allows us to see the immediate effects of shutdown and containment measures undertaken just after the pandemic started. The effects of this scenario can be seen in figure 3.10 by dark bars. The immediate effects of the pandemic increase inequality, measured by the coefficient of variation, by 3.3 percent in the case where the government takes no action to compensate for the deterioration in income distribution. It appears in figure 3.10 that all income groups, except entrepreneurial income, contribute to changes in inequality positively.

The second scenario is set up by imposing the short-term working allowances scheme on some members within the wage-earner income group. The effects of this measure obviously mitigate the severity of increases in inequality in the first instance, as seen by the light-dark colored bars in figure 3.10. According to the results, the short-term working allowance scheme helps

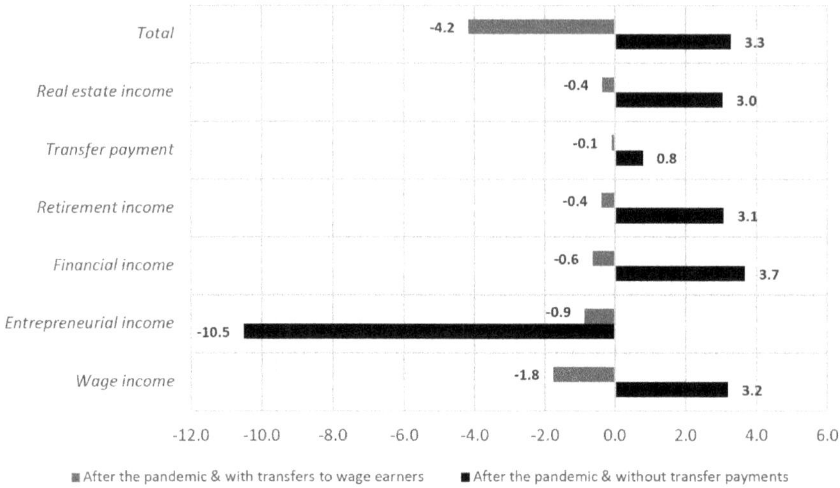

Figure 3.10 COVID-19 Cases and Deaths Toll in Turkey. *Source*: Authors' calculation.

the government to control the increase in inequality by alleviating it by 11.7 percent. The adverse impacts of all income groups, the only exception being the entrepreneurial income group, seem to be eased by this additional income support given to some members of the wage-earning group. This clearly implies that direct cash transfers to households whose income sources are badly affected by the shutdown and containment measures are an essential tool to control the distributional effects of the pandemic, and even to mitigate the deterioration in income distribution. *Although this measure imposes an extra burden on the public budget in the short term, the containment of the spread of the virus strictly requires scaling down the mobility of people and easing the worries of individuals about the fate of their income in the future in such a depressed economic condition.*

In addition to the distributional effects, the World Bank also estimates 40–50 million people, mostly in Sub-Saharan Africa and Southeast Asia, face the danger of falling into extreme poverty.[7] Even if the situation in Turkey is not as bad as in these countries, it is normal to expect a rise in the poverty rate. It is then important to observe the extent of this rise and to discuss the policy mix which alleviates a likely increase in the poverty rate due to the COVID-19 pandemic.

A RISE IN POVERTY DUE TO THE COVID-19

The poverty issue is particularly important because Turkey has been one of the worst countries in the OECD regarding the poverty rate for a long time. According to our calculation based on the Survey of Income and Living

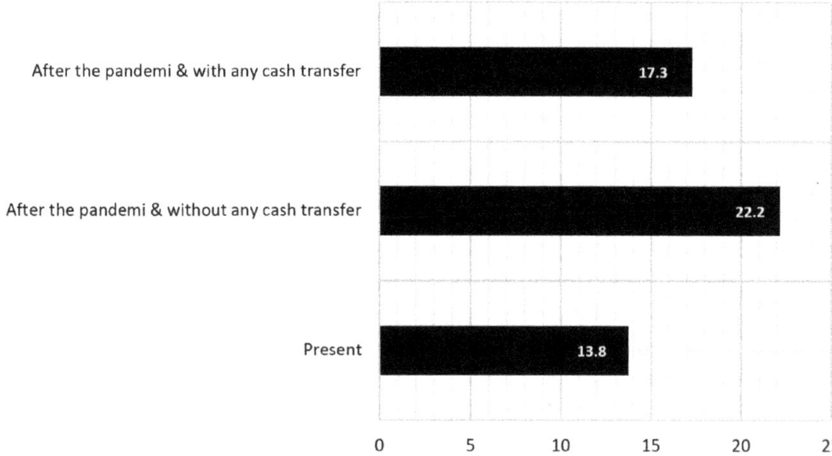

Figure 3.11 COVID-19 Cases and Deaths Toll in Turkey. *Source*: Authors' calculation.

Conditions in 2018, the poverty rate calculated as the share of the population with their income below 50 percent of the median income in 2018 is 13.77 percent.[8] This ratio is most likely to rise to 22.18 percent in case of no government intervention after COVID-19. The same ratio, however, is estimated to fall to 17.31 percent from 22.18 percent if the government intervenes in the economy by paying extra income such as short-term working allowances to individuals who are affected badly economically by the pandemic (see figure 3.11).

Another well-known measure of poverty is the poverty gap ratio which shows the stringency of poverty. This indicator of poverty measures the distance of the income level of individuals from the pre-determined income level. The closer the distance to the poverty line, the less costly reducing poverty is. A high value of the poverty gap ratio, on the other hand, means an increased stringency of poverty. According to the survey in 2018, the poverty gap ratio is 3.7 percent. This is a relatively low level and indicates that most of the poor individuals cluster around the poverty line, and mitigating poverty requires relatively low resources. However, the pandemic increases the poverty level by raising its stringency from 3.7 percent to 11.1 percent, then falling to 8.0 percent after paying a short-term working allowance. These results also imply that *a fall in poverty at least to the pre-pandemic level of poverty will be more costly in the post-pandemic period than before. This is mainly because the income level of more and more poor individuals drops further away from the poverty line after the pandemic hits them economically.*[9]

According to the IMF and the World Bank, the immediate effects of the pandemic can be seen in the changes in the poverty rates in the countries exposed to COVID-19. Whether this increase in poverty becomes permanent or temporary will be dependent, to a great extent, on the economic growth performance of these countries in the post-COVID era. However, what is more important than this is the expected increases in the extreme poverty rate in some developing countries. Following Roser and Ortis-Ospina (2013) and their revised extreme poverty measure for 2018, we assume $1.9 per day as the minimum income measure of extreme poverty for an individual. The annual extreme poverty income for an equivalent household is then calculated as 3,282.2 TL based on this assumption. Remembering that 8,957 TL in 2018 was the poverty income line, it can be seen that the extreme poverty income line is almost 5,675 TL lower than the poverty line income level. In other words, the annual extreme poverty income is about 36 percent of poverty line income. Without imposing the effects of the pandemic on sectoral economic activities and income flows, our calculation shows that there are almost 560,000 individuals who are already under the extreme poverty line. Since the total number of the poor in the 2018 survey is calculated as 10 million individuals, this corresponds to only 6 percent of the total poor population. In figure 3.12, the extreme poverty measure (the ratio of the number of individuals under the extreme poverty line to the total population, which is 79 million 760 thousand in 2018) is shown. Whereas only 1 percent of the population was under the extreme poverty line before the pandemic, this ratio increases to 10 percent after the containment measures of the spread of the virus emerge. However, the introduction of the short-term working allowance obviously helps decrease the ratio of people in extreme poverty in the entire population.[10]

It is clear from figures 3.11 and 3.12 that the pandemic certainly results in a rise in the poverty rate irrespective of the presence of any cash transfers to households. However, *the presence of this transfer and even cash allowances*

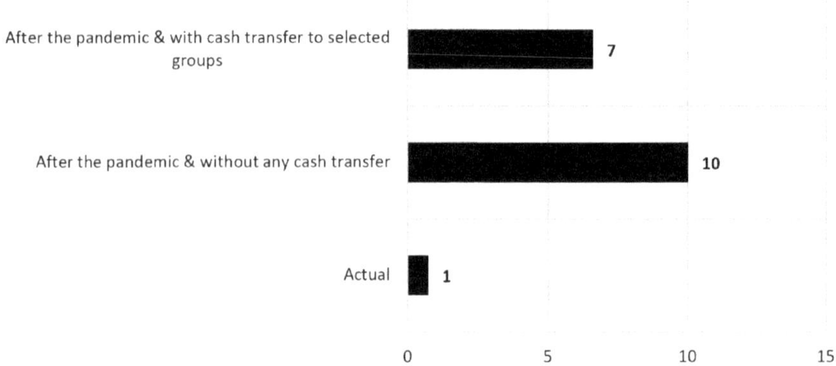

Figure 3.12 COVID-19 Cases and Deaths Toll in Turkey. *Source*: Authors' calculation.

to those whose incomes are negatively affected by the pandemic only mitigate the extent of a rise in the poverty rate. The important issue under this given condition is to find out how this increase in poverty rate could be compensated for, and, to some extent, be brought back to the level before the COVID-19 pandemic began. In the first instance, the literature suggests several methods to examine the answers to these questions. For example, in various empirical papers, Datt and Ravallion (1992) distinguish two important components that determine a change in the poverty rate; they are namely *economic growth* and *redistribution.* Each component exhibits a separate effect on poverty, and the direction of a change in the overall poverty rate depends on the net effects of these two components. If both components have impacts in the same direction on poverty, then the direction of the change in the poverty rate will also be in the same direction as these components. In some cases, each component has an effect in the opposite direction, and then the overall effect is in the direction of the net effect, which depends on the relative sizes of the impacts of the growth and redistribution components.

There has been a great deal of literature on the income distribution and poverty issues in developing countries after the 1990s, and various studies have put particular emphasis on the relationship between economic growth, income distribution, and changes in poverty. Some have especially drawn attention to the importance of having high but inclusive economic growth and a relatively fair distribution of income in combating poverty. International organizations such as the World Bank have also played a leading role in promoting this research. The reason for this pioneering role was the strong resistance encountered by the World Bank and IMF-supported policies due to the adverse effects of these economic reform programs. This has, in turn, necessitated measuring the distributional consequences of the reform programs, and appropriate social net programs which ease the distributional effects of the reform programs have been implemented.

Mitigating the poverty rate in the post-pandemic period in Turkey is a challenging economic as well as political issue, and designing appropriate policies to bring this ratio down has to be given priority. In this regard, attaining high economic growth rates and introducing redistribution policies both during and after the pandemic period will be the key to controlling the effects of poverty in the post-pandemic period. In what follows, the importance of economic growth and redistribution policies are empirically examined for the Turkish economy.

In various studies, Datt-Ravallion (1992) and Ravallion (2000) decomposed changes in poverty into economic growth and income distribution components. Besides, Ravallion (2004) has written a policy paper that established a quantitative relationship among changes in poverty, economic growth, and income distribution for policy concern. He defines a simple formula describing this quantitative relationship between poverty, economic growth, and income distribution as follows:

$$\Delta p = -9,33 \times \left(1 - Gini_0\right)^3 \times g \tag{3.3}$$

where Δp is the changes in poverty, $Gini_0$ is the initial level of the Gini coefficient; g is the economic growth. The coefficient appearing on the right-hand side of equation (3.3) is obtained as a simulated coefficient from a panel study on group developing countries by Ravallion (2004).[11] He also calculates the time which is required to reduce a certain proportion of changes in poverty (Δp) as follows:

$$t = \frac{ln\left(1 - \Delta\pi\right)}{ln(1 - \Delta p)} \tag{3.4}$$

where $\Delta\pi$ is the proportion of a reduction in the change in poverty that is hypothetically to be 50 percent, 25 percent, and 10 percent.

Table 3.4 reports the results of how long it takes to reduce the likely increase in poverty by 50 percent, 25 percent, and 10 percent. Besides, our empirical investigation also reveals that the poverty rate, measured by the headcount ratio, is likely to increase from 13.8 percent before the outbreak to 22.2 percent in 2020. This is an 8.4-point increase in the poverty ratio. Our examination in this section requires us to find out how much economic growth is necessary to eliminate these increases in poverty. Given Δp = 8.4

Table 3.4 How Much Economic Growth Is Necessary to Eliminate the Rise in Poverty?

	Hypothetical Growth Rates (%)	*Expected Changes in Poverty under a Certain Growth Scenario*	*The Number of Years Which Are Required to Eliminate by the πp Proportion of the Expected Change in Poverty*		
			πp = 50%	*πp = 25%*	*πp = 10%*
		Gini Coefficient = 0,407			
Scenario 1	5.0	9.8	7	3	1
Scenario 2	4.5	8.8	8	3	1
Scenario 3	4.0	7.8	9	4	1
Scenario 4	3.5	6.8	10	4	1
Scenario 5	3.0	5.9	11	5	2
Scenario 6	2.0	3.9	17	7	3
Scenario 7	1.0	2.0	35	15	5

Source: Authors' calculations.

and the Gini coefficient is presently 0.407, a required economic growth rate can be calculated by equation (3.3) as follows:

$$8.3 = -9.33 \times (1 - 0.407)^3 \times g \tag{3.3a}$$

From equation (3.3a), *the required economic growth* can be found to be 4.5–5.0 percent. Moreover, it takes almost eight years to reduce an 8.4-point increase in poverty only by 50 percent, and three years to reduce it by 25 percent, and finally one year by 10 percent. It is possible to shorten this time by increasing the economic growth rate. However, *in the case where the country has difficulties growing fast and the economic growth rates rise below 4.4 percent, the time to compensate for the increase in poverty takes longer.* Even so, there is a way of avoiding this problem of requiring a high economic growth rate, especially in the post-pandemic period where economic growth overall will likely be very difficult. If governments introduce a social transfer system in a wide scope, then the change in poverty rate can be kept to a very small size ($\Delta p = 3.5$), and the required rate of economic growth is expected to be smaller; most probably, any economic growth rate between 2 and 3 percent would be enough to compensate for this increase in poverty. Nevertheless, this relatively low economic growth rate will call for a longer period than in the first case to reduce the increase in poverty by at least 10 percent. Given the initial inequality level (i.e., 0.407), the expected changes in the poverty rate for different economic growth rates and their decaying time for different proportions are given in table 3.4. *High economic growth rates allow for compensating for relatively large increases in the poverty rate and require shorter periods than low growth rates to adjust for a given level of decay.*

Based on this finding, it is important for the Turkish policymakers to keep the poverty rate as low as possible while requiring relatively low economic growth in the post-pandemic period to bring the poverty rate to its initial level. *In this regard, social income transfers in different forms and in a wide scope become necessary to restrict the increase in the poverty rate caused by the COVID-19 pandemic.*

CONCLUSION

The COVID-19 virus effectively took hold of the world starting at the beginning of 2020 and caused unprecedented economic costs in all countries. Economies drastically contracted; unemployment rates rose to the levels that hadn't been seen before; public budget stance deteriorated; financial stability was maintained for the time being but at the expense of an increase in liquidity and debt stocks of the countries. The emergency additional spending on health care and social transfers to people who became in need after the pandemic and a drastic increase in public budget deficits are perfectly understandable for the time being. But the macroeconomic disequilibrium that will emerge due to emergency spending by the public as well as the private sector in the post-pandemic period is another issue to be considered. Worsening macroeconomic conditions today inevitably will lead to additional economic problems in the future. In particular, excess borrowing for almost a decade will leave high debt stocks for countries as well as multinational companies and constitute a danger threatening the stability of the international financial system. An important challenging issue of the post-pandemic world is to solve this macroeconomic disequilibrium and to reduce debt stocks. In this regard, austerity measures are the conventional tools that first come to the mind of government policymakers. However, macroeconomic disequilibrium this time is widespread all over the world, not just in a single country, and such austerity measures might create the danger of the world economy falling into a recession without reviving economic growth and might cause further deterioration in both income distribution and poverty.

The present research is an empirical attempt to estimate the likely impacts of the pandemic on income inequality and poverty in Turkey and suggest ways of coping with these effects. Two important conclusions emerge from our empirical research in this chapter. *First*, the present research for the Turkish case confirms the findings of the IMF and the World Bank, which indicate deterioration in income inequality and poverty in the developing world. *Second*, it is almost inevitable that inequality and the poverty rate will become worse, but introducing an adequate amount of social transfer in a wide scope, such as *short-time working allowances* and maintaining *economic growth* at as high a level as possible would, for the first instance, be a solution to cope with poverty and the distributional problem due to the pandemic. However, how the policy makers in Turkey must act to reach these solutions in the unfavorable economic conditions of the world economy in the post-pandemic era is another challenging task on the agenda of the present government.

NOTES

The authors thank *Haluk Levent* of İstanbul Bilgi University for insightful comments on the earlier version of the paper. We are also grateful to the editor of this book for allowing us to express our views on the distributional impacts of the pandemic in Turkey. However, any remaining mistakes are the authors'.

1. See https://en.hmb.gov.tr/. There are several studies for Turkey that empirically attempted to estimate the likely effects of the COVID-19 pandemic on economic

growth and employment in Turkey. Özatay and Sak (2020) estimate a 10 percent contraction in GDP under the assumption that the pandemic, the lockdown, and containment measures continue for the entire year. Taymaz (2020) employed an input-output approach under a very restrictive technology assumption and estimated that the unemployment rate would jump to a 28 percent rate during the pandemic. Bayar et al. (2020c), on the other hand, estimate a 3.5 percent decline in GDP under the assumption that the pandemic ended and the economy opened up in June 2020. These estimates, along with those of international organizations, are all worse than the estimates of the government for the year 2020.

2. Decree 7244 was the first comprehensive legislative action taken after the official announcement of the pandemic on April 17, 2020 (retrieved from https://www.resmigazete.gov.tr/eskiler/2020/04/20200417-2.htm).

Dünya Newspaper, May 16, 2020 (retrieved from https://www.dunya.com/kose-yazisi/COVID-19-salginina-karsi-alinan-tedbir-ve-onlemler-iii/470450).

3. Retrieved from https://www.aa.com.tr/tr/turkiye/bakan-selcuk-kisa-calisma-odenegine-su-ana-kadar-3-milyonu-askin-basvuru-oldu/1814696.

4. Basing on the Social Security Institution Database (retrieved from https://www.sozcu.com.tr/2020/ekonomi/kisa-calisma-odenegi-yil-sonuna-kadar-uzar-mi-6034643/).

5. It must be noted that TurkStat announces the data of the Survey of Income and Living Conditions with a one-year delay. Since any recent survey data is not available, the income and living conditions in 2018 is employed as the starting point in our empirical analysis and it is assumed it accurately reflects the income and living conditions in 2020.

6. The Shorrocks decomposition is another method, but it is static and only allows us to distinguish the different sources of inequality in a given year. It is unable to take into account the income sources that explain changes in inequality between periods (Shorrocks, 1982).

7. The World Bank defined extreme poverty as living on $1.90 or less a day in 2018. Since the equivalent household size is about 1.6, the extreme poverty income for an equivalent household is $3.04 per day, $1,094.4 per year. If we assume that the average exchange rate for the $ is roughly 3 TL in 2018, then the annual extreme poverty income for an equivalent household is 3,283.2 TL in 2018 (Roser and Ortis-Ospina, 2013).

[Retrieve from https://blogs.worldbank.org/opendata/impact-COVID-19-coronavirus-global-poverty-why-sub-saharan-africa-might-be-region-hardest].

8. The poverty line is established as 50 percent of the median income in 2018, and it is calculated as 8,956.9 TL (about $1,125 at the foreign currency rate 7.95 TL/$) (see Ravallion, 2008).

9. Based on the income and living conditions in 2018, we calculate over 11 million people under the poverty line before the pandemic. Due to the pandemic, this number is expected to rise to the level of around 18 million. This dramatic increase in the number of poor falls to 14 million after the short-term working allowances.

10. According to our calculation, there seem to be almost 600,000 individuals under the extreme poverty line before the pandemic. This number is expected to

rise to almost 8 million during the pandemic. However, it falls to 5 million after the introduction of the short-term working allowance. *This means a substantial amount of extra financial funds is required to evade this dramatic increase in extreme poverty in Turkey.*

11. In nonlinear least square estimates of θθ, the term on (1-Gini)θθ in (3), on a sample of estimates of the changes in the log of the $1/day poverty rates for a sample for sixty-two countries, θθ turns out to be 3.031. The coefficient of −9.33 is also estimated with the same sample with a standard error 0.75 and R2 = 0.71 (Ravallion, 2004, p. 13).

REFERENCES

Baldwin, R. and B. Weder di Mauro (Eds.) (2020). *Economics in the Time of COVID-19*. A VoxEU.org eBook, CEPR Press.

Bayar, A. A., Ö. Günçavdı and H. Levent (2020a). "Evaluating the Impacts of the COVID-19 Pandemic on Unemployment, Income Distribution & Poverty in Turkey." Unpublished manuscript. İstanbul: İTÜ.

Bayar, A.A., Ö. Günçavdı and H. Levent (2020b). "COVID-19 Salgınının Kadınlar Üzerine Etkileri." *The Impacts of COVID-19 Pandemic on Women*. İstanbul Politik Araştırmalar Enstitüsü. May 2020 – 010. [Retrieve from https://d4b693e1-c592-4336-bc6a-36c134d6fb5e.filesusr.com/ugd/c80586_86b8dec8fdba4de6afbe1bf1136fa068.pdf].

Bayar, A. A., Ö. Günçavdı and H. Levent (2020c). "COVID-19 salgınının Türkiye'de gelir dağılımına etkisi ve mevcut politika seçenekleri" (The impacts of COVID-19 pandemic on income distribution and possible policy implication in Turkey). İstanbul Politik Araştırmalar Enstitüsü. April 2020 – 07. [Retrieve from https://www.sivilsayfalar.org/wp-content/uploads/2020/04/c80586_60d5c23e00664d9dbb95b3c43f2a52d7.pdf].

Cowell, F. A. (2011). *Measuring Inequality*. Oxford: University Press.

Datt, G. and Martin Ravallion (1992). "Growth and Redistribution Components of Changes in Poverty Measures: A Decomposition with Applications to Brazil and India in the 1980s." *Journal of Development Economics*, 38, 275–295.

Günçavdı, Ö. (2020). "Salgınla mücadelede piyasanın artan önemi ve ekonominin büyümeye olan bağımlılığı" (An increase in the importance of market in combating the pandemic and the dependence of the economy on economic growth). In Ö.F. Çolak (Ed.), *Salgın Ekonomisi* (*The Economics of Pandemic*), Ch.13, pp. 251–288. Ankara: Efil Publishing Company.

IMF (2020). *World Economic Outlook: Update*, June. Washington, DC: IMF. [Retrieve from https://www.imf.org/en/Publications/WEO/Issues/2020/06/24/WEOUpdateJune2020].

Jenkins, S. P. (1995). "Accounting for Inequality Trends: Decomposition Analyses for the UK, 1971–86." *Economica*, 62, 29–63.

OECD (2019). Society at a Glance, OECD Social Indicators. [Retrieve from https://www.oecd-ilibrary.org/docserver/soc_glance-2019-en.pdf?expires

=1592689000&id=id&accname=guest&checksum=01A9808E1CF78A2AD55 3E0C8960A2231].

Ravallion, M. (2008). " Poverty Lines." In N. Durlauf and L.E. Blume (Eds.), *The New Palgrave Dictionary of Economics*, Vol. 6, pp. 5068–5073. Palgrave-MacMillan.

Ravallion, M. (2004). "Pro-Poor Growth: A Primer." *World Bank Policy Research Working Paper 3242*. Washington, DC: The World Bank.

Roser, M. and E. Ortiz-Ospina (2013). "Global Extreme Poverty." *Published online at OurWorldInData.org* [Retrieved from: https://ourworldindata.org/extreme -poverty].

Roubini, N. (2020). "The Coming Greater Depression of the 2020." April 28, 2020. *Policy-Syndicate*. [Retrieve from https://www.project-syndicate.org/commentary /greater-depression-COVID19-headwinds-by-nouriel-roubini-2020-04?barrier =accesspaylog].

Sak, G. ve F. Özatay (2020). "COVID-19 Nedeniyle Sokağa Çıkma Yasağı Uygulanırsa." (What If a curfew is imposed due to COVID-19?). Ankara: TEPAV. [Retrieve from https://www.tepav.org.tr/upload/files/1585713990-3.COVID_19 _Nedeniyle_Sokaga_Cikma_Yasagi_Uygulanirsa.pdf].

Shorrocks, A.F. (1982). "Inequality Decomposition by Factor Components." *Econometrica,* 50, 193–212.

Taymaz, E. (2020). "COVID-19 tedbirlerinin Türkiye ekonomisine etkisi ve çözüm önerileri." (The economic impacts of COVID-19 containment measures and suggested solutions) Istanbul: Science Academy. [Retrieve from https://sarkac.org /2020/04/COVID19-tedbirlerinin-turkiye-ekonomisine-etkisi-cozum-onerleri/].

TurkStat (2019). *The Survey of Income and Living Condition*; 2018. Data set.

World Bank (2020). *Global Economic Prospects*. [Retrieve from https://www.worldbank.org/en/publication/global-economic-prospects].

Chapter 4

Wealth Effects of New Tariff Measures during COVID-19

Pınar Kaynak

INTRODUCTION

The COVID-19 pandemic introduced the world exceptional health, social, and economic challenges. More than 2 million individuals have lost their lives due to the pandemic since the 2019 COVID-19 outbreak,[1] and the global economy is predicted to contract by 3.9 percent in 2020.[2] While these figures represent the tremendous difficulties created by this pandemic, an end to it is also not yet in sight. The number of new COVID-19 cases is still growing at an unprecedented pace in many countries. There is a lot of confusion about how and when the pandemic will run its course. Still, the unprecedented economic shock created by the global health emergency has already clearly exposed the preexisting vulnerability of the global economy.

Although the current crisis showed how vulnerable the economies are globally, not all countries were affected to the same extent. Some developed countries were hit much heavier than their less-developed counterparts. According to the UNCTAD, in 2020, developed economies are predicted to be more affected by −4.8 percent than developing countries (see figure 4.1), and expect a slower rebound in 2021. European countries are expected to experience substantial negative growth in 2020, with France at −8.1 percent, Germany at −4.9 percent, Italy at −8.6 percent, and the UK and Ireland at −9.9 percent. Moreover, the recession was projected in the United States in 2020, both developed and emerging: Argentina at −10.4 percent, Brazil at −5.7 percent, Mexico at −10 percent, and the United States at −5.4 percent. To sum up, almost all countries except for China and the Republic of Korea which expect a positive growth of +1.3 percent and +0.1 percent, respectively, in 2020, suffered from a recession.

This recession surely had repercussions regarding the world trade as well. The early impacts of the pandemic on trade were felt in the first quarter of

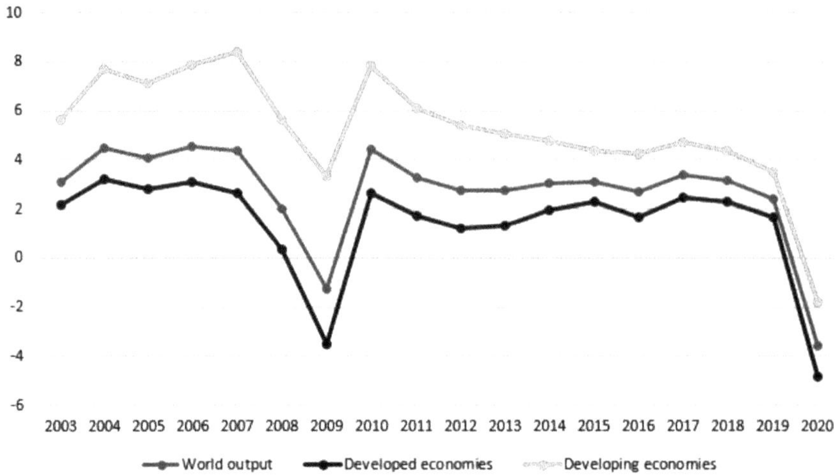

Figure 4.1 Global Economic Growth (Annual Percentage Change). *Source*: UNCTAD (2020).

2020, as growth in (merchandise) trade shrank by 3 percent year on year (YoY).[3] In the second quarter, trade in both goods and services decreased by 19 percent YoY which is much larger than in the first quarter. Global trade started to recover in the third quarter. Overall, world merchandise exports fell by 7.5 percent in 2020 (see figure 4.2).

Following the economic downturn, no region was spared from the decline in international trade. Figure 4.3 below shows that trade has fallen dramatically in most areas except in East Asia and the Pacific in the aftermath of the

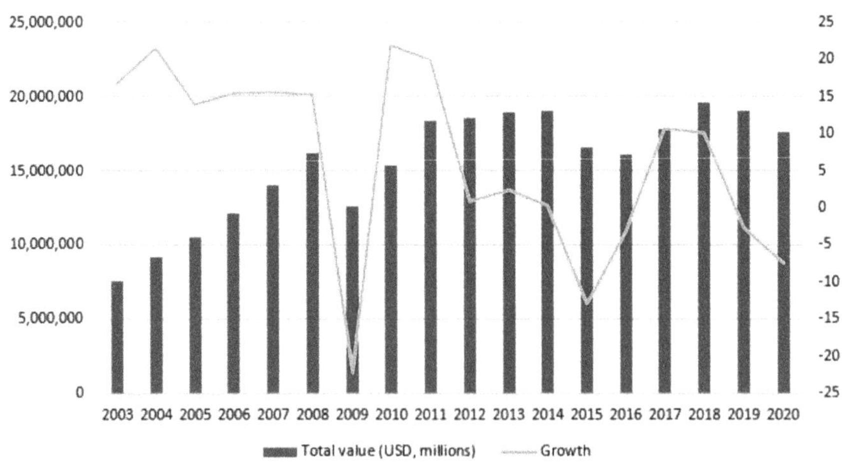

Figure 4.2 World Merchandise Exports, Annually. *Source*: UNCTAD, 2020.

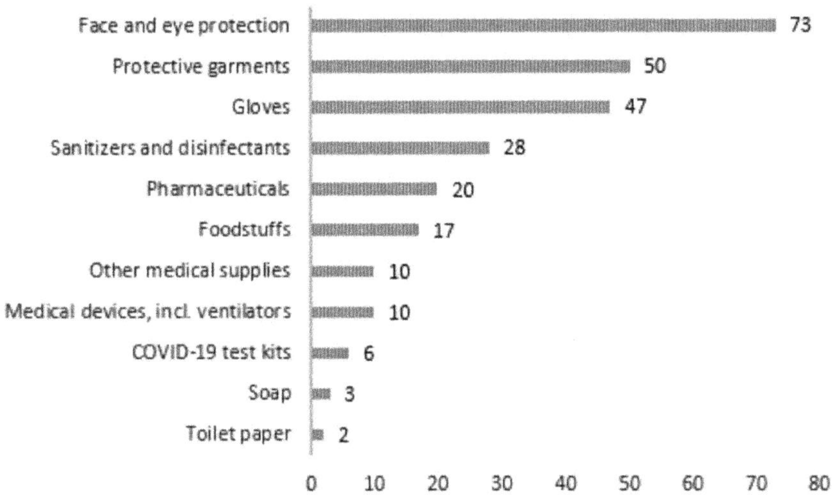

Figure 4.3 Top 10 Sectors Hit by the Export Ban. *Source*: WTO Secretariat.

first wave of COVID-19. West and South Asia were the regions that were hit the most: they faced a 35 percent decline in imports and a 41 percent decline in exports.

Likewise the effect of the pandemic on countries, its effect on sectors was quite heterogenous. Some industries have been substantially more affected by economic disruptions than others. The value of global trade in the automotive and energy industries in the second quarter of 2020 was about half of what it was in 2019. In chemicals, machinery, metals and minerals, and precision instruments, trade declined significantly. On the other hand, medical products related to COVID-19, such as personal protective equipment, ventilators, thermometers, sanitizers, and the like, experienced very high growth; for example, in May 2020, these products were 186 percent higher than in the same period in 2019. Imports of office equipment, textiles, and clothing increased as well. As these industries include home office equipment and protective equipment such as masks, such rises are related to the COVID-19 pandemic.

Due to the economic downturn and the disruptions in international trade, national authorities were forced to introduce emergency measures to avoid a shortage of necessary goods to cope with the disease's spread. Consequently, countries adopted new protective trade measures to protect their economies and satisfy the necessity goods' upward shock.

In April, thirty-nine WTO member states, including Albania, Australia, Bangladesh, Colombia, Costa Rica, Egypt, the EU, Georgia, the Republic of Korea, the Kyrgyz Republic, North Macedonia, Thailand, and Ukraine,

Table 4.1 Turkey's Trade in Affected Products from the Countries that Are Subject to New Regulations

Year	*Exports*	*Imports*	*Net Exports*
2015	7.4	6.9	0.5
2016	6.8	6.8	0.0
2017	8.0	6.9	1.1
2018	9.1	6.2	2.9
2019	9.2	5.1	4.1

Source: TEPAV *Note*, May 2020.

introduced new export prohibitions or restrictions due to the pandemic. Table 4.1 below shows the list of products that were most heavily affected by export bans. As we see from figure 4.1, such products are all necessary goods showing that export restrictions were targeting to prevent any lack of aforementioned substantial goods, like in the war times.

On the other hand, some countries reacted to the pandemic by easing measures on imports, especially on medical goods (Espitia et al. 2020). According to the Global Trade Alert, some of the twenty developing countries most impacted by COVID-19 introduced import reforms to decrease taxes on imports. For example, for medical and testing facilities, Pakistan implemented tax and import duty exemptions, while Brazil abolished tariffs on medical and hospital goods. Although many of these reforms were temporary, meaning that they were postponed rather than removed, this was a step in the right direction considering the existing circumstances.

In contrast to most countries, Turkey responded to the pandemic in a different way trade-policywise. Instead of concentrating on export restrictions and easing import measures, Turkey introduced new tariff measures, concerning mostly intermediate goods. This move's motive was different from the policies mentioned above as this one targeted mostly increasing tariff revenues for the government along with protecting several industries.

Whether these measures served the governments' purposes and the public interest or not is a challenging question. While the introduction of such protectionist measures is understandable, all countries depend on international trade as a matter of fact. And the lack of international cooperation in these areas threatens global value chains, risking the global economy's recovery as well as countries' recoveries individually.

This chapter discusses the potential wealth effects of trade policy changes due to the pandemic in Turkey. The subsequent section presents the new trade measures introduced during the pandemic. Section "Potential Wealth Effects of Measures due to COVID-19" reviews the possible welfare changes due to the new regulations. Finally, "Conclusion and Policy Recommendations" concludes this chapter.

TRADE POLICY RESPONSE TO THE PANDEMIC IN TURKEY

Turkey announced the first set of new trade measures on April 18, 2020, followed by April 21, May 5, May 11, May 19, and June 27 enactments. These tariffs included 1,304 products in total and 187 (import) partner countries. EU countries, the UK, and the twenty-three countries that are partners of Turkey according to the Free Trade Agreement (FTA) were exempt from these new trade measures as Turkey had binding constraints regarding custom duties with them.[4]

By May 2020, Turkey's imports for the 859 products that were subject to new regulations amounted to a total of 5.1 billion dollars. 47 percent of these 859 products were imported from the EU countries in 2019, 5 percent were imported from the countries with STA agreements, and 2 percent were imported from the EFTA countries. While Turkey's imports concerning the same product groups from the partner countries that are subject to the new regulations have been declining over the years, its exports have been increasing. In 2019, Turkey exported 9.2 billion dollars, giving a trade surplus of 4.1 billion dollars in total (see table 4.1) from the countries subject to these customs duties, regarding the product groups of interest. Also, the imports have not increased in the last five years; on the contrary, they follow a decreasing trend after 2017 (see table 4.1). As EU, EFTA, and STA countries were exempt from the new measures, the customs duty on imports (on 859 items) was worth 2.32 billion dollars.

Even though Turkey gave a trade surplus regarding the products mentioned above, the government went on introducing new tariff measures. On June 27, the government announced further increases in tariff rates on twenty-eight sectors and introduced new measures on fifty-one sectors that were not subject to such regulations previously. So, taking into account the last regulations, the government introduced new measures on 188 sectors in total, including numerous number of products.[5]

The tariff increase was 10 percent on average. Previously, no tariffs were applied to any country regarding the respective product categories. Hence, these newly announced taxes can also be considered as a 10 percent increase in the corresponding sectors. Table 4.2 below shows the most heavily hit sectors in terms of tariff increases with May and June enactments. The largest increase in tariffs appeared in paper and paper products sector followed by rubber and plastics, and nonmetallic mineral sectors.

Twenty-seven products were introduced new import taxes within paper and paper products sector, whereas sixty-three products were subject to new regulations in rubber and plastics, and 184 products in nonmetallic mineral sectors (see table 4.3).

Although the magnitude of tariffs and the number of products affected by the change might stand as a benchmark, the total volume/value of trade

Table 4.2 Tariff Measures Introduced in May and June Enactments (Top 10 Sectors)

	Tariff Rates (weighted average) (%)			
Sector Classification ISIC Rev.4	*May 2020 Enactment-1*	*May 2020 Enactment-2*	*June 2020 Enactment-1*	*June 2020 Enactment-2*
Manufacture of rubber and plastics products	7.2	11.2	10.7	10.7
Manufacture of paper and paper products	7.4	12.4	20	20
Manufacture of other nonmetallic mineral products	10.1	14.4	8.3	15
Manufacture of basic metals	7.5	12.0	10.8	13.8
Mining of metal ores	-	-	8.3	12.3
Manufacture of electrical equipment	6.8	9.3	6.5	9.0
Manufacture of textiles	6.4	10.3	5.0	5.0
Manufacture of computer electronic and optical products	9.8	13.5	5.5	5.5
Manufacture of wearing apparel	-	-	20	20

Source: Author's calculations based on May and June 2020 Enactments published by the Presidency of the Turkish Republic.

matters too. Among the products that are the most affected by additional customs duties, products classified under the machinery sector, such as compressors for cooling devices, excavators, metal processing centers, accumulators, injection machines, stand out in terms of trade volume.[6]

Overall, the majority of products that are affected the most—either considering the magnitude of tariffs or trade volume—are products used as raw materials or intermediate goods within the production process. Therefore, it will not be an incorrect statement to claim that these tariff measures are targeting mainly raising government revenue rather than boosting import competition nationally which will have further repercussions regarding the total welfare of the country.

POTENTIAL WEALTH EFFECTS OF MEASURES DUE TO COVID-19

Why do trade costs matter for a country's welfare? Countries are largely excluded from global markets by high trade costs: customers in these

Table 4.3 Sector Composition of New Import Measures

Sector Code (GTIP)	*Sectors*	*May 2020 Enactment (Number of products)*	*June 2020 Enactment (Number of products)*
25	Mineral Materials	14	-
28	Inorganic chemicals	5	-
29	*Organic chemicals*	3	1
34	Soaps	1	-
36	Explosives	3	-
39	*Plastics and articles thereof*	15	1
40	*Rubber and articles thereof*	50	13
41	Raw hides and skins and leather	68	-
45	Cork and articles of cork	12	-
46	Manufactures of straw	29	-
48	*Paper and related products*	25	2
52	Cotton	6	-
54	Sewing thread of man-made filaments	69	-
55	Man-made staple fibers	9	-
56	Wadding, felt and nonwovens, and articles thereof	39	-
59	Impregnated, coated, covered, or laminated textile fabrics	-	9
63	Other made up textile articles	-	4
65	Headgear and parts thereof	-	2
67	Prepared feathers and articles made of feathers	-	11
68	Articles of stone	9	-
69	*Ceramic products*	8	7
70	*Glass and glassware*	21	17
71	Jewelry and precious metals	-	30
72	*Iron and steel*	7	26
73	*Articles of iron or steel*	106	45
76	*Aluminum and articles thereof*	29	1
84	*Nuclear reactors and parts thereof*	249	226
85	*Electrical machinery and equipment and parts thereof*	40	26
87	*Vehicles other than railway or tramway rolling-stock*	19	11
90	*Optical apparatus; parts and accessories thereof*	23	13

Source: Author's calculations based on May and June 2020 Enactments published by the Presidency of the Turkish Republic.
Note: Sectors in *italic* are the ones that are affected both by May and June enactments.

countries are unable to benefit from competitively priced products from abroad, and their businesses are unable to access high-quality international inputs or export them to overseas markets. Even though the distributional effect of trade costs varies across countries, lower trade costs are generally correlated with net reductions in poverty.

In a static sense, economic welfare will grow from lower trade costs. As new transactions occur, the actual economic cost of doing business decreases and GDP rises accordingly. There are also complex potential gains. In particular, access to international inputs has been described as being related to creative activities: as businesses gain access to new materials, they combine them in various ways to create new products. The development or adaptation of indigenous technology is at the heart of economic development over the medium to long term, and harnessing the process is likely to be an important part of pushing global value chains upward.

There is a vast literature on trade effects of wealth. Pioneered by Eaton and Kortum (2002), the versions of Ricardian trade model has become the dominant tool to explain trade mechanism and study the impact of trade costs (e.g., tariffs) for trade, prices, and consumer welfare (see Alvarez and Lucas Jr. 2007; Dekle et al. 2007; Costinot et al. 2011; Fieler 2011; Shikher 2012; Caliendo and Parro 2014; Egger and Nigai 2015; Levchenko and Zhang 2016).

In this section, I discuss the wealth effects of post-COVID trade policy change in Turkey. I distinguish the period in which the welfare effects are expected to be felt into two: (i) short run and (ii) long run. The short run is when the countries cannot adjust to a policy change, whereas the long run is defined as a sufficient time for countries to do so. Welfare change is defined as the change in real income (the difference between nominal wages and prices). The welfare effect for an average country is expected to be smaller in the long run (in absolute terms) than in the short run as countries have sufficient time to alter their consumption and production behaviors and develop new policies if necessary.

The welfare changes are estimated based on the methodology in Kaynak (2020)[7] where the trade model is an extension of the Eaton and Kortum (2002) model into a multicountry multisector setup. This framework supports structural estimation where all parameters of the model are estimated within the same data that the model is estimated on and calibrated to. Moreover, to calculate the welfare effect of trade policy changes, the approach proposed by Dekle et al. (2007) is adopted, where instead of solving for equilibrium under alternative trade policies, the notion of relative changes is exploited. Within this framework, one can identify the effects on equilibrium outcomes without solving each equation one by one and without estimating parameters such as iceberg trade costs. Hence, one can compute the welfare changes given the policy shift. Though this model comes in handy with a few parameter and data requirements, it should also be emphasized that the model provides an insight regarding the magnitude of the welfare changes rather than predicting the precise values.

As indicated in the previous section, Turkey increased tariff rates by 10 percent on an average. This will affect prices via two channels: first, the prices go up for consumers who use the products subject to new tariffs as final goods; second, producers who use the concerned products as inputs will face higher production costs, which will further drive up the consumer prices. Consequently, a welfare loss is expected due to the upsurge in prices. In line with the literature mentioned above on trade, on average, a 7 percent welfare loss[8] is estimated in the short run and a 3.8 percent welfare loss in the long run due to a 10 percent tariff increase. In the long run, the country can adjust its consumption and production behaviors repressing the welfare loss, but it cannot fully compensate for price increases.

CONCLUSION AND POLICY RECOMMENDATIONS

Following the economic crisis which appeared after the pandemic, many countries introduced trade restrictions. On the one hand, to offset price increases and potential shortages in domestic markets, some governments (especially developed economies) implemented export restrictions. These interventions had aggregate effects, exacerbating the initial shock and contributing to price rises (Giordani et al. 2016). Moreover, the high concentration of imports of some goods in developed economies made developing countries highly vulnerable to exporters' policy changes. Because of export restrictions, access to medical supplies and other essential goods was disrupted for developing countries that needed them urgently. For example, Armenia had a shortage of protective clothing, while Malaysia experienced shortages in hand sanitizers (Espitia et al. 2020).

On the other hand, some countries imposed tariffs on primary COVID-19 goods. In twenty developing countries with the largest number of incidents, the imposed tariffs on primary COVID-19 goods were, on average, over 6 percent. Personal security equipment items such as aprons, surgical masks, and protective clothing were subject to tariffs of more than 10 percent. Severely affected countries, such as Iran, implemented even higher import restrictions on essential COVID-19 items, in particular for personal protection devices. These developments increased the domestic price of basic goods and further decreased welfare for the consumers.

Focusing on the production side, companies of all sizes were impacted by the COVID-19 steps, but the most vulnerable were smaller companies with fewer reserves. Gourinchas et al. (2020) has calculated an SME bankruptcy rate for seventeen countries as an average of 12.1 percent, compared to a 4.5 percent base without a factor COVID-19, without any policy action (in the absence of political intervention). Business exits in the medium to long term are expected to increase further.

Turkey adopted a different trade policy than introducing export bans or increasing tariffs on necessities. The government chose to introduce import taxes on products mainly used as raw materials or intermediate goods. The analysis here suggests that there are welfare losses due to new tariff measures as they lead to price increases.

During the pandemic, the importance of openness over nontariff initiatives increased. The many problems exposed by the global health crisis need countries to step up cooperation efforts. As far as trade policies aimed at economic recovery are concerned, collaboration with trading partners through bilateral or regional mechanisms can be more effective in achieving a policy measure's multiplier impact than in circumstances where it is introduced unilaterally. Such cooperation could also pave the way for enhancing multilateral cooperation. Cooperation to minimize regulatory divergence will reduce the cost of trade by 25 percent (Knebel and Peters, 2019), which would reduce consumer prices in turn.

As countries lift emergency trade measures and adopt recovery plans (international currency fund, 2020a), they have to analyze the multifaceted effect of trade policy and use it to improve and resilience recovery. In general, trade policies that promote a rapid and resilient private sector return would help to reduce the government's "building back" burden more effectively.

In response to the COVID-19 pandemic, observed trade policy activism trends pose several questions about the determinants and underlying political economy of trade policy (Evenett et al. 2020). One fruitful research line is understanding the motivations underlying decisions in the design and implementation of trade policy responses to the pandemic, reflected in the considerable cross-country heterogeneity. Another issue is the quantification, both for the world and Turkey in particular, of the consequences of various trade policy strategies. A third policy analysis is concerned that the data can help around the broader topic of the importance of trade agreements. To what degree have countries complied with the necessary provisions of trade agreements that provide for transparency and temporary and essential trade restrictions in response to emergencies? These are just some of the research questions that the stylized details disclosed by this dataset indicate. There are, no doubt, several others.

NOTES

1. https://www.worldometers.info/coronavirus/.
2. https://www.imf.org/en/Publications/WEO/Issues/2021/01/26/2021-world-economic-outlook-update.
3. WTO (2020) Press Release.
4. TEPAV Note, May 2020.
5. See May 20 and June 27, 2020, Enactments published by the Presidency of the Turkish Republic.

6. Taşöz-Düşündere A., Avşar-Koyuncu İ. 2020. "Yeni İlave Gümrük Vergileri Türkiye için Ne İfade Ediyor?," *TEPAV Notes*.
7. See Kaynak (2020) for detailed calculations.
8. Welfare is measured as real income.

REFERENCES

Alvarez, Fernando, and Robert E. Lucas Jr. 2007. "General Equilibrium Analysis of the Eaton–Kortum Model of International Trade." *Journal of Monetary Economics* 54.6: 1726–1768.

Baldwin, R. 2020. "The Greater Trade Collapse of 2020: Learnings from the 2008-09 Great Trade Collapse." *Vox EU blog*.

Bown, C. 2020b. "EU Limits on Medical Gear Exports Put Poor Countries and Europeans at Risk." *PIIE blog*.

Caliendo, Lorenzo, and Fernando Parro. 2015. "Estimates of the Trade and Welfare Effects of NAFTA." *The Review of Economic Studies* 82.1: 1–44.

Costinot, Arnaud, Dave Donaldson, and Ivana Komunjer. 2011. "What Goods Do Countries Trade? A Quantitative Exploration of Ricardo's Ideas." *Review of Economic Studies* 79.2: 581–608.

Eaton, Jonathan, and Samuel Kortum. 2002. "Technology, Geography, and Trade." *Econometrica* 70.5: 1741–1779.

Eaton, Jonathan, Robert Dekle, and Samuel Kortum. 2007. "Unbalanced Trade." *American Economic Review* 97.2: 351–355.

Egger, Peter and Sergey Nigai. 2015. "Structural Gravity with Dummies Only: Constrained ANOVA-type Estimation of Gravity Models." *Journal of International Economics* 97.1: 86–99.

Espitia, A., N. Rocha, M. Ruta. 2020. "Trade and the COVID-19 Crisis in Developing Countries." *VoxEU. org*, 9

Espitia, A., N. Rocha, and M. Ruta. 2020. "Database on COVID-19 Trade Flows and Policies." World Bank.

Evenett S., M. Fiorini, J. Fritz, B. Hoekman, P. Lukaszuk, N. Rocha, M. Ruta, S. Santi, A. Shingal. 2020. "Trade Policy Responses to the COVID-19 Pandemic: Evidence from a New Dataset." *Vox EU blog*.

Fieler, Ana Cecilia. 2011. "Nonhomotheticity and Bilateral Trade: Evidence and a Quantitative Explanation." *Econometrica* 79.4: 1069–1101.

Giordani, P. E., N. Rocha, and M. Ruta. 2016. "Food Prices and the Multiplier Effect of Trade Policy." *Journal of International Economics* 101: 102–122.

Knebel, Christian, and Ralf Peters. 2018. "Non-tariff Measures and the Impact of Regulatory Convergence in ASEAN." In *Non-tariff Measures in ASEAN*, edited by Lili Yan Ing, Olivier Cadot, and Ralf Peters. Jakarta: Economic Research Institute for ASEAN and East Asia.

Levchenko, Andrei A. and Jing Zhang. 2016. "The Evolution of Comparative Advantage: Measurement and Welfare Implications." *Journal of Monetary Economics* 78: 96–111.

OECD. 2020. "COVID-19 and International Trade: Issues and Action."
Taşöz-Düşündere, A. and I. Avşar-Koyuncu. "Yeni İlave Gümrük Vergileri Türkiye için Ne İfade Ediyor?" TEPAV Notes, May 2020.
UNCTAD. 2020. "Global Trade Update." October.
UNCTAD. 2020. "Impact of the COVID-19 Pandemic on Trade and Development."
WTO. 2020. "Trade in Medical Goods in the Context of Tackling COVID-19." 20 April.
WTO. 2020. Press Release.

Chapter 5

Global Questions, European Challenges, Turkish Tasks

Bahadır Kaleağasi

INTRODUCTION

The global economy after World War II had been broadly defined by the Bretton-Woods agreement and the Soviet Union's areas of influence, but never materialized into a long-term system. After the Cold War, with the WTO being established, the United States and EU making progress in transatlantic cooperation, the internet growing rapidly, Russia recovering, India digitalizing, and China rising, globalization gained its momentum. When the 2008 financial crisis hit the world after a relatively long period of economic growth, the global economy was not being supported by a well-coordinated system. Reactivated with the hope of resolving this crisis, the G20 paved the way for a new international order in many areas, from financial markets to climate change. However, such attempts at global governance were unable to achieve the level of power that was needed for international policymaking. Globalization, on the other hand, was expanding in all directions.

Everything was moving with more freedom around the planet: Societies were embracing the irresistible opportunities of globalization. Bananas from Nicaragua traded through a Venezuelan distributor, bought by a Canadian company funded with American and German investment, sold to a Spanish importer with transportation on Greek ships, offered to consumers in the French market; US-brand sneakers produced in Vietnam; smartphones designed in California, manufactured in China; British internet games based on computer software originating in India, bringing children all over the world from Santiago to Cairo together into the same virtual reality; social media which has become the main communication platform for any dimension including political, corporate, and personal life; digitalization in all areas from tourism, retail, public affairs, and education to the most complex financial markets; transfer of big data and algorithms; rapidly growing energy consumption, unsustainable levels of waste, green technology innovation, the search for a socially and ecologically responsible consumer society, and so on.

Everything was moving with more freedom around the planet: money, goods, services, people, information, data, ideas, culture, and so on.

Everything was moving with more freedom around the planet—global viruses too: biological, financial, digital, and ideological viruses; the carbon dioxide virus; the terrorism virus; the organized crime virus; the corruption virus; the unemployment virus; the disinformation virus; and so on.

Human civilization entered the COVID-19 pandemic within the midst of this complex dynamic. Those same issues are now determining the new reality of the near future. Global trends in precrisis times shed light on the world beyond the pandemic. When dust and smoke have begun to dissipate, when our lifestyles have started to be cleansed from this disease, the existential issues which face our societies have started to deepen as well: security, freedom, technology, personal space, the nation-state, international cooperation, protectionism, urban mobility, oil prices, green energy investments, energy markets, climate change, income inequality, and so on.

And of course, the list of urgent problems which have emerged from this crisis continue to be at the forefront of our agenda: keeping the pandemic under control to prevent new waves of the outbreak; cross-border control; cross-border cooperation; the balance between safeguarding people's health, returning to business activities, and domestic and international travel; the financial situation of small companies and multinational corporations alike; invoices, loans, debts, insurances, investments, employment; and so on. The pandemic is projected to remove four years of growth from the global economy and push an additional 130 million people to poverty, according to a UN study. This will trigger another cross-border contagiousness: the poverty virus, income disparity pandemic, social and economic quarantines, and so on.

Public health first, or the economy first? It seems that unhealthy societies bring the economy down, but if the economy collapses, how will the health system work? Which political consensus, which model of transparency and accountability will find the right balance? Which systems of governance at the institutional, local, national, and international levels will be successful?

IN SEARCH OF A POST-COVID GLOBAL ORDER

In which direction will the needle move between the dilemma of security and freedom? Will governments that have systematized facial recognition, phone tracking, social behavior measurement, and drone technologies become widespread? Or, on the contrary, perhaps through the waves of increased social responsibility and individual initiative that arise in pandemic times, will a more democratic, transparent, social, scientific, and global understanding of politics prevail?

Will we pass through an initial phase where every country is introverted, protecting its own health order, its citizens, its companies that manage to survive the Darwinian process, and its physical geography?

Will we then dialectically move on to an era where the inevitable need for international cooperation becomes obvious? Will this be a world where the global governance of public health, the Eurozone's management system, the United States' multilateral approach toward global finance and trade policies, the impact of transatlantic and trans-pacific economic areas, the effect of 3D printers on trade, drone traffic airspace regulations, the impact of satellites orbiting the Earth in supporting economic and social development, artificial intelligence regulations, 5G infrastructure, and quantum computing competition become stronger?

What about the global supply chains? Not only for trade but also for logistics, finance, technology, agriculture, tourism, medical services, data management, and so on. Less dependency on few sources like China and more localization and diversification on the horizon? Will proximity become a fundamental criterion in the reorganization of the global supply chains? Is proximity being defined not only in geographic terms but in regulatory, institutional, and political terms as well?

At the same time, will this be a world in which OECD countries with common goals such as democracy, rule of law, fundamental freedoms, market economy, independent regulatory institutions, and social progress adopt such "broad West" values with a more progressive approach in the post-Corona era? Will this be a period in which China, despite its authoritarian characteristics, after taking into account its internal social and economic fragilities, becomes a more constructive player in this new paradigm of international cooperation? Will it be an order in which the G20, which represents 65 percent of the world's population and 85 percent of its economy, will attempt to design and implement policies at the global level?

After the fourth industrial revolution, will there now be a more focused search for "Society 5.0" which establishes the right equation for social, ecological, scientific, technological, and democratic development? Will the UN' Sustainable Development Goals (SDGs), grouped into seventeen global objectives, become the main framework for the achievement of all these developments in the West and maybe in the world? Will the progress that we make in these areas today, even if only in part, shape the history of the near future?

Yes.

EUROPE'S TURKISH EQUATION

The global challenges justify better relations between the EU and Turkey. They both need them. However, significant questions on Europe's future are still open. Shall the European states finally commit to sufficient coherence and solidarity as a prerequisite to redefine a global role for the EU? Will they agree to confer on the EU more effective competencies in the field of economic policies? Will the Eurozone's governance become more supranational? For a country like Turkey, will these be times in which an EU that is evolving toward flexible membership models provides it with the opportunity to revive its accession process? In which positioning itself as a Eurasian gateway of democracy and economic dynamism becomes the only realistic strategy to maintain its global competitiveness?

The Turkey debate's focal point is "Europe's geostrategic sovereignty" (Tocci 2021). Turkey should evolve to be a net contributor to Europe's security and global competitiveness. No matter how significant today's drawbacks are, such as freedom of expression and tensions like the life-consuming Cyprus imbroglio, the guiding question for the EU ought to be: "How can Turkey, in the near future, become a country that is progressively in convergence with the values and interests of European citizens?" This includes citizens of the Turkish Republic as well.

In this context, EU's policy on Turkey needs an approach which may avoid the recent past's mistakes, reinvigorate successful experiences, and better serve common European values and citizens' interests. At least five points were considered for brainstorming:

- A sound economic partnership
- Replacing political tensions with structural cooperation
- Promoting European values
- Thinking in terms of European integration's evolution and global challenges
- Open and effective communication with the public; avoiding disinformation and opacity

PROBLEMS? TENSIONS? CONFLICTS?

Since the 1990s, every time the EU engaged Turkey in the European integration, the results have been good for European values and policies; for EU and Turkish citizens. However, political tensions are real, challenging, and harmful. However, nonconstructive policies of engagement are also part of the problem. They have been stimulated by years of ever weaker partnership, deadlocks, prejudices, and policy errors from both sides. Thus, we cannot find in more negative policies—blocking, suspending, or sanctioning different aspects of the EU-Turkey relationship—a relevant solution to today's problems.

In fact, the cost of excluding Turkey from European integration is very high for both EU and Turkish citizens. If Turkey had been well-engaged in the EU accession process since the open-ended negotiations began in 2005—on issues from foreign policy, rule of law, and refugees, to economic growth and energy policy—today's picture would be very different. The EU would be a better global power, and Turkey would be a stronger European democracy showing greater convergence with European values and interests. The results of the EU's failed Turkey policy are clear.

WAY FORWARD

To negotiate a new status for Turkey, membership to the EU would not be timely before both the EU and Turkey are ready. Turkey's politics and economics are in transition, the EU has not yet evolved toward a better institutionalized model of differentiated integration; and from Brexit, to the "Biden effect," to transatlantic relations, and now post-pandemic global economic challenges, many factors justify not going in that direction at this time. Moreover, without the clear "conditionality" of the accession partnership process, the EU's transformative power would be diminished. However, there is a need for political courage and leadership to explain to the public that positive steps are not a gift to anyone—they are tools of action to protect European values, standards, and interests.

The EU has at its disposal an effective soft-power algorithm which has consistently proved its effectiveness in the past: accession chapters, especially those covering the supporting pillars of democracy—fundamental rights, justice, and freedoms (23 and 24). Already over a decade ago, the former EU Commissioner Olli Rehn warned:

> We need to apply rigorous conditionality. Experience shows that the better the new member states are prepared, the smoother the EU functions after enlargement. Difficult issues, such as judicial reform and the fight against corruption, must be addressed at an early stage of the negotiations. (European Parliament, December 13, 2006)

Meanwhile, this is not the right time to propose and negotiate a special status specifically for Turkey. Membership in the EU is not today's question. Turkey's politics and economics are in transition, and so is the European integration process. Moreover, without the clear democratic and economic governance conditionality of the accession partnership process, the EU's transformative power would be diminished with adverse consequences for Turkey's economic and social stability, whose side effects may then rapidly cross the waters toward the EU. The bottom line is drawn by a need for political courage and leadership to explain to the European public that positive steps in the relationship with Turkey are not a gift to anyone: they are tools of action to protect European values, standards, and interests. The timing is now right; European populism is in a period of temporary hibernation.

CONCLUSION

The successful achievement of the EU-Turkey customs union's modernization process is also an important asset in the EU's toolbox. By being part of the EU's customs union on industrial goods, Turkey has already moved to be in compliance with more than half of the single market's regulations. The next step involves the extension of this model to include services, agriculture, public procurement, and conflict resolution mechanisms. This needs to be a twenty-first-century version partnership, a customs union 5.0 which also covers the European digital single market, the European Green Deal, and more broadly Turkey's commitment to converge with the EU's SDGs policies. This would enhance Europe's global economic competitiveness and Turkey's trajectory in the European economic and regulatory sphere.

A policy of positive re-engagement with Turkey would also propel the prospect of convergences on various foreign policy fields such as Cyprus, the Northern Mediterranean, the fight against terrorism, refugee crisis management, and so on.

Yes, the EU and Turkey may well reload a new relationship algorithm accordingly with the twenty-first-century's post-pandemic challenges, and values.

REFERENCES

Adar Sinem, Bilotta Nicola, Denizeau Aurélien, Ekim Sinan, Schmid Dorothée, Seufert Günter, Toygür Ilke, and Wasilewski Karol, "Customs Union: Old Instrument, New Function in EU-Turkey Relations," Stiftung Wissenshaft und Politik, SWP Berlin, 2020.

Anghel Suzana, Strategic Sovereignty for Europe, European Parliamentary Research Service, September 2020.

Kaleagasi Bahadir, "Four Scenarios for Europe's Future," policy brief, German Marshall Fund of the United States (GMF), February 2013.

Kaleagasi Bahadir, "Global Viruses and Goals," Institut des Relations Internationales et Stratégiques (IRIS), Paris, 2020.
Kaleagasi Bahadir, "Europe's Geostrategic Sovereignity and Turkey," Atlantic Council, 2021, Issue Brief, March 2021.
Krastev Ivan, "Thirty Years after the 'Fall of the Wall': Aspirations, Illusions, Harsh Realities and the Future of the EU's Strategic Standing," Institut du Bosphore - Paris, September 2019.
Leonard Mark and Shapiro Jeremy, eds., Strategic Sovereignty: How Europe Can Regain the Capacity to Act, European Council on Foreign Relations, 2019.
Telò Mario, "The EU's Role in the World Should Be," Institut d'Etudes Européennes, Université Libre de Bruxelles, March 2021.

Chapter 6

Turkey-US Relations Post-COVID-19

Ahmet Salih İkiz

INTRODUCTION

There is little doubt that the global plague has implications on US-Turkish relations. This is not only pandemic, effecting countries' economic indicators, but it has also many impacts on world order. Following a Spanish flu a decade ago there was a drastic change in the globe, in countries, hegemonic powers, and so on. Even if during the pandemic, there is a lot of speculative forecasting for coming decades. In this chapter, my intention is to share my humble knowledge of post-pandemic US-Turkey relations.

US-Turkish relations can be categorized into two main pillars: the post–World War period shaped with polarized world order between USSR and United States, and post–Cold War period with dominant US hegemonic power in globe. Even though Turkey quite restricted in its foreign policy issues due to its involvement in Western block, following the disintegration of USSR, there was much more proactive foreign policy formation, especially toward Turkic Republics. Last decade, Turkish foreign policy had much more structural change in different parts of the globe with new partnerships with emerging hegemonic powers such as China.

The Cold War international era shaped by NATO and Iron Curtain countries was led by USSR. Therefore, Turkish NATO and UN involvement heavily designed the foreign policy formation. US-Turkey relations thus without some special cases such as the Cypriot issue in 1974 was in tolerable mood due to the Turkish precious contribution to NATO as a border country with USSR. Turkey's strategic location on Europe's southeastern flank and as part of the "Northern Tier" (with Greece, Iran, and Pakistan) reinforced America's policy of containment throughout the Cold War, and Turkey's inclusion in the "West" protected the country from Soviet aggression.

Following the disintegration of the USSR, new era for US-Turkey relations occur. Involvement in internal affairs with Turkic spoken countries and diaspora Turks became inevitable due to the lack of state authority in those regions. Even if US-Turkey relations lost its momentum for a decade, the NATO member Turkey became a significant ally after the transformation of the Russian Federation with special emphasis on Central Asia and new Pacific economic players.

THE HISTORICAL CONTEXT OF US-TURKEY RELATIONS

Turkish-US relations have always been so interactive and reflective in the historical context in different time spans due to the strategic geopolitical location of Turkey, neighboring main energy hubs and supply regions. During the Cold War, the USSR threat imposed two countries together as a strategic ally for their own interest in security issues. The relations do not harm regional development policies and internal political affairs on both sides. The traditional foundation of the US-Turkey alliance has always been bound on military cooperation, which is highly integrated into the context of a common NATO framework and because of sustained bilateral cooperation.

Even if Turkey has economic instability and lesser geopolitical capabilities, in the 1970s compared with today's, Ankara under a left-wing Prime Minister Bülent Ecevit government chose to intervene militarily in Cyprus in 1974 with over Washington's critics and subsequently imposed by Congress' banning military aid. This is one of the breaking points in Turkish-US relations during the Cold War where Turkey experienced a harsh US embargo (Walker 2010).

Even if US foreign policymakers have consistently reiterated that they do not involve in domestic political matters or support any political motivations, they have embroiled themselves in domestic Turkish politics from time to time. In his memories, former president of Turkey Suleyman Demirel gave detailed briefs of meeting with US president George Bush in Turkey, just a couple of months before the general elections in Turkey where he became prime minister after the downfall in a military coup in 1980. Another important example was the Bush administration's decision in December 2002 to invite then AKP leader Recep Tayyip Erdoğan for an official visit to Washington where he has not any official post due to his political bans. The election of President Obama ushered hopes among many in both Turkey and the United States that there would be a new era of relations following the Bush years with problems in different perceptions for Turkish border countries. In his speech in Turkey on his first overseas visit, Obama pointed out the importance of partnership. In those times, Turkey's relationship with Iran, Syria, and Hamas is very crucial for sustainable peace and prosperity in the Middle East. Ahmet Davutoglu, the foreign policy adviser to the Turkish prime minister, predicted that Turkish-American relations were about to enter a golden era, after several visits of US Middle East Envoy and Secretary of State Hilary Clinton visits to Turkey. This prediction was based on converging developments in Turkey and America's approach to the Middle East in particular and foreign policy in general. President Obama's visit to Turkey on April 6 signals that this new golden era has indeed begun (Aras 2009). US-Turkey relations are much more complex issues compared to the 1980s, because of the historic changes taking place in the Middle East and around the globe. Turkey has increased economic, political, and diplomatic influence and act as middle power country in regional affairs with his strength in both hard power and soft power vehicles and aiming to become a global player in next decade. The US approach to the Middle East has fundamentally changed from an interventionist agenda to bring democracy to the region under the Bush administration to a more minimalist outlook under President Obama (Üstün and Kanat 2013). During both administrations, US-Turkey relations had some vulnerability and fragility due to the major tests.

In the Obama administration after 2008, especially after 2012, the US-Turkey bilateral relationship was strong and independent of Turkey's relations with Israel or of the EU membership track. That bilateral cooperation helped to solve some conflicts in Middle Eastern affairs. At those times, Turkey has become an integral actor in Iraq, in the Israeli-Palestinian conflict, and in Egypt. What this means is that Turkey and the United States have a much broader set of common interests outside the traditional security-oriented frameworks. Kanat (2013) explains that security-oriented partnership in those words.

> As their relations become varied and more complex, there is always more potential for misreading one another's policies or intentions. However, both sides have learned to live with and overcome such differences during the AK Party decade. This is unlikely to change but Turkey, with its aspiration to become a regional and global power, is likely to keep regional issues on the US agenda. If both sides can reassure one another that they are mindful of each other's interests and concerns, the US-Turkey relationship has the potential to contribute to regional peace and stability. (Üstün and Kanat 2013)

Following the Obama administration, Trump on the contrary was much more self-oriented and direct manners in forming foreign policy. Rather than institutional relations in formal communications in most cases, he used direct informal communication with political leaders around the world including

Turkey. Even though that way of communication is fast-track solution it may jeopardize long-term sustainable foreign policy formation. He bypassed foreign policy advisers in some issues where there were several issues. In case of Turkey, although some issues such as Branson's case where he declared a very impolite message to the Turkish Presidency, his term were rather easy to deal process for Turkish partners.

Even if US-Turkish relations were strained by political disputes, the US secretary of state Mike Pompeo kindly appreciated NATO ally Turkey for their support to US companies during the COVID-19 period, where there is the highest dead toll in reported cases. Meantime even if doubts were to linger about the S-400 case, Biden administration would deescalate Iran-US tensions with Turkey as a solid actor in region. The prominent actor Turkey is the only secular Muslim country with a vibrant free-market economy and decades-long ties with Western institutions (Turkish Heritage Organization 2021).

THEORETICAL FOUNDATIONS OF US-TURKISH RELATIONS

The United States was rather inward-oriented country in foreign relations until the beginning of the twentieth century. The collapse of European hegemons and the establishment of post–world war institutions such as NATO and IMF made drastic changes in that policy where the country became a prominent global power in following decades. Some argue that the Spanish flue has inevitable effects on the globe in following years such as economic crisis and World War II.

Penetration in global sea routes and containment policy of eminent rival USSR were main pillars of that policy. US Grand Strategy after Rimland approach was based on the improvement of naval force and penetration in coastal parts in partner countries.[1] Turkish geographic location and NATO membership thus evolved in this. There is no doubt that the main element they wish to preserve is the Rimland. This is the structure preventing Russia (and China later) from expanding into the oceans, by trapping it into the Heartland of the Eurasian geography. Controlling world maritime trade roots is the key factor for US foreign policy after World War II. China, which has been catching up to the United States since the 1970s, is now one of the main targets of the Rimland strategy. In the end, the expansion of the Eurasian camp, which has grown stronger with the cooperation of Russia and China, taking some EU countries and Turkey into its sphere of influence, is a nightmare for the United States (Gürdeniz 2020).

During the two polar world systems until the disintegration of USSR, Turkey was one of the prominent members of the NATO alliance due to the geostrategic location. The second pillar of US foreign policy was the containment policy of Iron Curtain countries with religious affairs. Turkey is the only country where democracy and Islam stand together. That is why the US green belt policy in the Cold War and the following Greater Middle East Project consider Turkey as a reliable partner. Compared to most unstable countries in the Middle East, Turkey is in a much better position after the Arab Spring. This led the Neo-Cons of the United States to encourage a moral "mild" Islam that could enable the coexistence of democracy and Islam. Therefore, the G8 Group became the instrument to encourage dialogue for peace and democracy among religions. Even though almost all Islamic countries choose to talk about reform of their societies, very little actual progress was achieved (Taşhan 2016).

Even if USSR's hegemonic power diminishes from the globe at the beginning of the 1990s, it seems American hegemony did not persist globally in the following decades. That will be the end of history as Francis Fukuyama called that capitalist economic system with US dominance in the world became inevitable. Dugin's Eurasia strategy with OBOR of China amalgamated a new power block, which had some coincidences on US foreign policy sets. The premises of US foreign policy somehow struck on Cold War period theoretical foundation, which is mainly, depend upon hard power and world gendarmerie. That created sort of power erosion in the globe. In addition, the usage of hard power for decades created US antagonism even in Western spheres of the world. So far, the emergence of new powers from the Pacific region had different perceptions in world order and categorized much more soft power.

The moderate Islam project of the United States for a long time heavily supported Turkish membership in EU. The main US agenda in the theoretical foundations for Turkish-EU relations is creating an EU anchor for a sustainable democratic path for moderate Islamic country where it can also reach Muslim world with own cultural ties. Meantime some researchers claim that the growing regional penetration of Turkey until 2050 makes the country global power than a regional power. Turkey will be eminent economies on the globe after 2020 and would have highly committed naval, air force troops with advanced technologies. In that stage, there would be inevitable conflicts even wars between the United States and Turkey (Friedman 2010).

Controlling energy sources means the backbone of US foreign policy in Middle East countries. So Turkish partnership is important to deal with those regions. The dominant part of global energy resources in oil and gas are produced in countries where Turkey has borders. Meantime European countries soar vast amount of energy and depend upon those countries. Thus, Turkey plays a crucial role in that geostrategic energy hub. The increasing role of China with the Belt and Road Initiative in region after 2013 vis-à-vis had impacts on Turkey as well due to the different diplomatic missions of the Chinese intelligentsia.

There is no doubt that the gradual decline of the Western liberal international order has turned Turkey's attention away from normative principles toward hard power instruments. However, Turkey will be a more successful actor in its region if it combines the military achievements with diplomatic openings.

> Being aware of its strengths and weaknesses as a middle power, while Turkish policymakers should continue with their support for and investment in the country's thriving defense industry and be ready for military engagement when necessary, they also need to re-energize Turkey's soft power politics, and to revitalize the diplomatic path in order to improve the country's position in various regional and international institutions and alliances. (Pusane 2021).

POST-COVID-19 UNITED STATES AND RELATIONS WITH TURKEY

During the pandemic, the relations with those countries—like other parts of the world—became overshadowed and ignored by the massive impacts of the global crisis in Turkey like most of the globe. Since the relations became insignificant due to the mass effects, important issues such as Syrian issue and Northern Iraq became less evident for a while.

Trump administration's America First motto means steps towards less economic ties with increasing internal production created weaker United States in the international arena with the impacts of pandemic. Thus, rather than collaborating with other countries, the US declaration of self-treatment of pandemic also reveals the decline of United States which is the main supporter of liberal word order. During the pandemic, Trump administration, both ignored the crisis and have poor health services performance in hospitals. According to Duran, the United States failed to perform as a world leader during the pandemic (Duran 2020). "America First Motto" of Trump harmed the global corporation role in the international arena for the United States. Compared to China, the US regime, economic and market structure cannot cope with full lockdown of economy but that does not mean weak American power in the globe.

One of the main outputs of the severe economic crisis due to the pandemic was a sharp increase in the money supply of FED. It is highly expected that a quantitative fiscal boom means low interest rates and an increase in idle capital. Increasing financial liquidity will boost the capital accumulation of companies to lure new investment areas with high profit rates. Global US companies try to defend their global interests with technological innovation, renewable energy, robotics, artificial intelligence, digital chips, and flexible business methods. If the United States chooses protective, nationalist policies with the Western world, that means the miscalculation of dynamics of competition in global resistance (Aybar 2020).

When speaking about the US-Turkey economic relationship, the elephant in the room is the looming S-400 and related US sanctions. Predictions for Biden's policy about those sanctions vary widely. Fortunately, President Biden's foreign policy agenda has many overlaps with Ankara's interests. Strengthening NATO would be helped by a possible reset with Turkey. Reengaging with Iran would create new avenues of collaboration with Ankara. Stabilizing Libya to prevent further encroachment by Russian military assets is a common objective. There are many obstacles to a grand bargain between Ankara and Washington. Both sides would have to bend. Any road map would at the very least feature: a reappraisal of US support for the Syrian PYD; agreement on the conditions for operating the S-400-missile system; a concomitant lifting of the US sanctions; and Turkey's removal and a possible return to the US F-35 aircraft program. There would also need to be a role for Turkey in future negotiations with Iran, active American support for improved EU-Turkey relations, and an unambiguous commitment by the Turkish leadership to cease fueling anti-Americanism and skepticism of the west at home. This list may appear overly ambitious. However, it pales in comparison to the scale of the responsibility facing the US and Turkish presidents. At stake is Turkey's place in the wider world—and the future of the regional order (Ülgen 2021).

As in the past, today the United States and Turkey share the same strategic objectives in most aspects in the long-term issues. So that, there is no need to sacrifice those important long-term goals in reaching a consensus since establishing a agreement on most of these goals took so costly in past and rearranging same way of negotiation would take so long. There is no open option rather than to find common ground since those countries are indispensable to each other. Thus from every perspective (geostrategic, political, economic), those strategic partners depend on each other to realize their short-term and long-term objectives. While both governments might realize some of their short-term objectives without positive bilateral engagement, it will only be at a higher cost (Tan 2020).

Former US ambassador in Turkey Francis Ricardione has an admirable explanation about the strategic partnership of those countries.

> I believe that economic engagement between the two countries will continue to run its natural course based more on economic factors and regional developments than on any particular policy choices of either a Trump or Biden administration. I suspect that a historical analysis would indicate that both

> (traditional) Republican and Democratic administrations have approximately equally promoted foreign trade, investment, and security cooperation as a global principle, and especially with Turkey as a formal treaty ally and one of the top twenty world economies. Even the free-est of American "free traders" administrations have negotiated very elaborate measures to protect US industries, so US "free trade" agreements remain rare, and few would expect them to proliferate in future under either Republican or Democratic administrations. Likewise, administrations of each party have presided over regrettable (and usually regretted) periods of extreme tension with Turkey. Since at least the time of Presidents Johnson and Ford, neither party can claim a monopoly on the episodic US resort to imposing or threatening to impose various forms of sanctions, whether for specific expressed economic or regional security policy purposes. (Ricardione 2020)

Even if he has close relationships with Greece, new US president Biden has always been pragmatic, and he is appreciative of Turkey's geostrategic value. He will seek to alter Turkey's course, both domestically and externally as indicated in the following opinions of Alan Makovsky:

> But Biden and his Administration will face what has become a perennial problem: How to change Turkey's behavior without devastating its economy or causing—in the words of Turkey analyst Nicholas Danforth—"a permanent rupture" in US-Turkish ties. Biden will want to preserve a sound diplomatic and security relationship with Turkey, to the extent possible—but it may not be possible. Led by human rights and the S-400 purchase, many difficult issues are looming. The Biden Administration will almost certainly let Turkey know early on, what is expected of it, along the lines suggested in the first part of this paper. Perhaps it will even consider a senior-level dialogue, as Blinken and Sullivan have suggested at times. The wild card will be how Erdoğan—now seemingly bent on an assertive, nationalist, and independent foreign policy and a role as a leading regional power, and seeing these ambitions lashed to his domestic political prospects—will respond. It is not what Biden will seek, but further deterioration in US-Turkish ties in the early months of the Biden Administration seems almost inevitable, barring a sudden change in Turkey's domestic and regional posture. (Makovsky 2020)

Turkey has overwhelmingly close contact with the other parts of the world. The country itself has the highest aid contributor to African continent compared to other countries on the globe. Latest improvement in the air defense industry enabled military operations around the globe such as latest developments in Azeri Armenian conflict. Therefore, he created his own brand of diplomacy during the coronavirus pandemic, delivered medical supplies and plans for long-term cooperation on medical equipment. Turkish Presidency aims to handle this cooperative diplomacy with an assertive foreign policy illustrated by "Blue Homeland" defense concept for energy resources for legal order in the Eastern Mediterranean. This proactive foreign policy, which will lead the country to agenda 2023, when Turkey will hold both a presidential election and the celebrations of the country's centennial, would have some side effects with its partners such as the United States. The countries' and regions' medical deliveries are carefully chosen with geostrategic policies. In order to achieve this aim, to maintain stable ties (as with Italy, Spain, and the UK) or further geopolitical interests (as with the Western Balkans and various African partners) or attempt to win favors (as with the United States), Turkey sends masks, medical supplements, and any other devices to combat the pandemic. It is a way of public diplomacy in abroad showing soft power welcoming ceremonies for long-haul military cargo planes, carrying those cargos that were carefully choreographed by Turkish diplomats.

Meanwhile, Turkey aims to be alternative region for European companies' production plants, which are diagnosed by Chinese products due to the latest development in COVID-19 for supplying medical equipment, and defense industry items. The diplomatic objective is clear: use the pandemic to support countries in need and improve Turkey's image on the international stage (Pierini 2020).

In order to analyze the prospects of US-Turkish relations, one must resume the shortsighted view in all aspects and understand the US policymaking process overlaps generations and presidents. The long-term policy framework hardly changes in decades. Prominent academic figure and famous adviser to US president until today, Henry Kissinger, for example still has power in US foreign policy establishment.

For example, a recent speech of the Armenian genocide of President Biden would rather be paid a bit of lip service (which may be a rather strong way compared to former presidents) to the Armenian diaspora. It is quite obvious that the United States had left Pashinyan in Nagorno Karabakh case for long-term interests. We cannot ignore the fact that recent developments in Nagorno Karabakh where the occupation of Armenia was defeated by Azerbaijan army with support from Turkey. During the attack, the United States followed wait and see policy with appeasement to both sides. Thus, there was not a strong condemnation to Azeri forces during the operations.

As indicated in their research a decade ago, Taşpınar argues that the west as EU and the United States must win Turkey in order to solve Kurdish issue, prosperous Cyprus case, and stable Middle Eastern territories. In this case, Islamic democratic values and political movements seemed much more reliable rather than secular political parties and movements in US foreign policy for years (Gordon ve Taşpınar 2008).

CONCLUSION

COVID-19 epidemic is a global phenomenon and most probably would have long-lasting implications in the international political economy. Therefore, post-COVID world would have new dimensions in US-Turkey relations. However, the priorities of both parties somehow would be different from each other. The United States has long withstanding security issues about its hegemonic agenda in both Middle East and Asia. That means somehow leveraging Turkish hard power under the NATO umbrella. On the other side, Turkey would like to stabilize its territories and penetration areas in border countries with maintaining considerable economic growth rates. Turkey even revealed its intention for Shanghai Security Organization with Asian Development though the idea behind that policy shift is short sight pragmatic foreign policy sets. Since Turkey has priority to normalize relations with other emerging hegemons such as China and Russia as alternatives to US-NATO axis that will not be an easy task. Recent economic turmoil with high volatility in exchange rates has harsh impacts on macroeconomic indicators. Accordingly, it is not certain yet whether, Turkey achieves best V-shape economic growth performance or COVID-19 would affect the Turkish economy more than most people think (Turkish Heritage Organization 2021).

NATO is still the main security umbrella for Western countries with its own deficiencies and insufficiencies. Turkey as one of the pivotal partners of the organization has a long traditional history with special functions. Thus, even if US-Turkey relations have had problems in recent years, there are deep institutional roots that cannot be distorted by internal policy discourses. The short termism in those policies will not have any impediments and harsh outcomes due to the wise people who have corporate memories on both sides.

NOTE

1. For detailed explanation of this theory, Nicholas John Spykman's two books—*America's Strategy in World Politics* published in 1942 and *The Geography of the Peace* published in the year after Spykman's death—would be valuable assets.

REFERENCES

Aras, Bulent. *Guardian.* 4 4 2009. http://www.gab-bn.com/IMG/pdf/Tr2-_A_golden_era_for_US-Turkey_relations.pdf.

Aybar, Sedat. "Küresel İktisadi Dönüşümün Jeopolitik Yansımaları." *Ufuk Ulutaş* içinde, yazan Covid 19 Sonrası Küreel Sistem Eski Sorunlar Yeni Trandler, 102. Ankara: Ministry of Forgin Affairs Turkey, 2020.

Duran, Burhanettin. “Koronavirüs Sonrası Yeni Dünya Düzeni mi Düzensizliği mi.” *Covid 19 Sonrası Küresel Sistem: Eski Sorunlar Yeni Trendler* içinde, yazan Ufuk Ulutaş, 29. Ankara: Ministry of Foreign Affairs, 2020.

Friedman, George. *The Next 100 Years: A Forecast for the 21st Century Paperback.* Anchor, 2010.

Gordon, Philip, ve Ömer Taşpınar. *Winning Turkey: How America, Europe, and Turkey Can Revive a Fading Partnership.* Washington: Brookings Institute Press, 2008.

Gürdeniz, Cem. 18 8 2020. https://uwidata.com/13312-turkey-and-the-rimland-panic-of-the-us/?__cf_chl_captcha_tk__=f22c8e237306ed8f33cfd72a681ce7e029661788-1602415679-0-AY1FLuawSoGBqEsVSUHdf1SjZ6fbdvspGGlyDpZ31FCq_7Z5pXJoJW24RarZ7WSofkBFG65VzY9eDCPsVtnTjBvRZUorf-5hfFgvxgx7nZ87pdo4A.

Makovsky, Alan. *Problematic Prospects for US-Turkish Ties in the Biden Era.* Berlin: Centre for Applied Turkey Studies, 2020.

Pierini, Marc. *Emerging From the Pandemic, Turkey Rolls Out a More Assertive Foreign Policy.* June 3, 2020. https://carnegieeurope.eu/2020/06/03/emerging-from-pandemic-turkey-rolls-out-more-assertive-foreign-policy-pub-81963.

Pusane, Özlem Kayhan. *Turkey as a Middle Power in International Politics: Betwixt and Between a Militarized Foreign Policy and Active Diplomacy.* 18 2 2021. https://www.uikpanorama.com/blog/2021/02/18/turkey-as-a-middle-power-in-international-politics-betwixt-and-between-a-militarized-foreign-policy-and-active-diplomacy/.

Ricardione, Francis J. *How Will the Future of US Foreign Policy and Economic Engagement Affect Turkey?* 28 10 2020. https://www.atlanticcouncil.org/blogs/turkeysource/how-will-the-future-of-us-foreign-policy-and-economic-engagement-affect-turkey/.

Tan, Namık. *What Relationship Can the US and Turkey Have after 2020?* 15 10 2020. https://www.atlanticcouncil.org/blogs/turkeysource/what-relationship-can-the-us-and-turkey-have-after-2020/.

Taşhan, Seyfi. *Turkish-American Relations: A Conspectus.* 2016. http://foreignpolicy.org.tr/turkish-american-relations-a-conspectus-seyfi-tashan/#_edn1.

Turkish Heritage Organization. *Annual Review 2020 and Prospects for 2021.* Washington: Turkish Heritage Organization, 2021.

Ülgen, Sinan. *A Path for Joe Biden to Reset US Relations with Turkey.* 31 1 2021. https://www.ft.com/content/e4194007-b6be-4836-b936-cf0f2074df11?desktop=true&segmentId=d8d3e364-5197-20eb-17cf-2437841d178a.

Üstün, Kadir, ve Kılıç Buğra Kanat. *US-Turkey Relations in the AK.* January 2013. https://file.setav.org/Files/Pdf/20130131152815_seta_policy_brief_62_web.pdf.

Walker, Joshua W. *The United States and Turkey: Can They.* November 2010. https://www.brandeis.edu/crown/publications/middle-east-briefs/pdfs/1-100/meb46.pdf.

Chapter 7

Evolving Roles of China in the Middle East

Implications of COVID-19 Outbreak

Abdurrahim Sağir and Cengiz Mert Bulut

INTRODUCTION

China's economic and diplomatic activities across the Middle East have been increasing significantly in the last decade. The existing Chinese literature on the Middle East reveals that the Middle East is no longer a remote peripheral region to China, as it was earlier. Especially with President Xi Jinping's accession to leadership, as China has since been increasing its global governance efforts to play its role as a "responsible country" in the new era. As the region's significance increases for China, its chaotic nature forces Beijing to actively protect its interest. China, which has managed to protect and increase its interests without alienating both the United States and the Middle Eastern states, especially since the post–Cold War period, started to face some difficulties with the outbreak of the trade war and the COVID-19 pandemic. In the context of China and the Middle East, the challenges created by the pandemic will be closely tied to how altruist or self-interest they might be for the sake of their future interaction.

China's becoming more prominent on the international political scene as a global power has brought the need for a systematic analysis of its behavior and existence. But the large country complex imposes great responsibility. The world under the effect of COVID-19 has created several conditions that China no longer may remain studiously aloof from its responsibilities. So, the following questions are at the center of this study: What are China's roles in the Middle East within a historical context? What kind of activity and influence do these roles create for China in the Middle East? What kind of transformation should be expected in these roles of China after the

COVID-19 pandemic that broke out in 2019 and rapidly affected the whole world?

CHINA AS A RISING POWER IN THE MIDDLE EAST

The Chinese state has started to make its presence felt in the Middle East, which has become the chessboard of the great powers for most of the history. Positioning itself as the advocate of the third front between East and West right after its establishment, China has now begun to play a more assertive role in a spectrum that extends to the present day. Therefore, China's Middle East policies play a critical role in matters concerning global politics and the international community. A coherent and gradual historical context is essential to follow these roles of China.

Mao's "Intermediate Zone" and the Middle East

Wang Jisi, a prominent Chinese IR Scholar, describes China's international strategies under Mao's leadership as being "clearly dominated by political and military security interests" and "often being framed by ideological principles" (Wang 2011). China's Middle East strategy was no exception to this definition from 1949 to 1976. During this period, China's Middle East strategy was formulated under the framework of Mao's "intermediate zone" theory, which Mao put forward in 1946 and gradually evolved into the "two intermediate zones" and the "three worlds" theory. Driven from the Marxist doctrine of class struggle, the implementation of Mao's theory was suggesting solidarity among the Third World Countries. To put it differently, Mao's foreign policy practices were centered on organizing a "united front" against the imperialism of the West and revisionism of the USSR. For Mao, the strict control of this "front" would be crucial for the security of the regime in Beijing.

In the late 1950s, a number of developments, such as the threats to Syria, the hostile attitude toward the Iraqi revolution, and the direct Western intervention in Lebanon and Jordan, showed that the Middle East was the arena for Mao's intermediate zone (Shichor, 1979). China continued to support national liberation movements in the Middle East, although security concerns were the main focus in 1960 due to perceived threats from the United States and the Soviet Union.

China's objectives toward the region were firstly to gain diplomatic recognition as the sole representative of Chinese people and secondly to prevent the United States and the USSR from dominating the Middle East. In accordance with Holsti's description of the "bastion of revolution" role concept, under Mao's influence, Beijing assumed a responsibility to organize or support revolutionary movements abroad (Holsti 1970). Denying the dominance of any aggressive force for the maintenance of the region, China encouraged local governments or sometimes national liberation movements to defy foreign presence (Shichor 1979). Beijing's increased support for revolutionary movements in the region, such as Palestinian Liberation Organization, had been the main manifestation of this role concept. It can be said that the success of the communist revolution in China made it possible for Beijing to stand as a strong supporter of revolutions abroad. However, without any doubt, the most outstanding role adopted by China during the Mao era was "anti-imperialist agent." As Professor Niu Xinchun from CICIR highlights, China's policy toward the region appeared as support of anti-imperialist and anti-colonial national liberation movements under Mao's strong personal influence (Niu 2013). China's diplomatic and material support for Arab countries in their fight with Israel, which was perceived as a puppet of imperialism in the Middle East by Chinese leaders, could be regarded as a fulfillment of Beijing's anti-imperialist national role model. Mao's words are a clear reflection of Chinese leaders' mindsets:

> We must unite with the proletariat of all the capitalist countries, [. . .] for this is the only way to overthrow imperialism, to liberate our nation and people and to liberate the other nations and peoples of the world. This is our internationalism [. . .] (Mao Tse-Tung 1967)

China's Approach to the Middle East under Deng Xiaoping's Low-Profile Doctrine

At the end of 1978, the Third Plenary Session of the Eleventh Central Committee of the Chinese Communist Party made a historic decision to remove the mistaken theoretical and practical emphasis on "class struggle" and put the economy at the center of the Party and the governmental work. This decision marked China's entrance to the historical period of "reform and opening up," which resulted in various fundamental changes in the Chinese state, society, and economy. With the priorities of economic development, modernization, and domestic stability, China started to experience one of the most stupendous economic boom—catch up nearly 10 percent annual growth rate for the longest period in modern history (World Bank). In parallel with these developments, China's interest in the Middle East and correspondingly its approach to the region started to take a new form. In post-reform China, economic considerations started to overweight ideological factors as the driven factor of China's Middle East strategy. Similarly, while activities such as foreign aid with high political returns and low economic returns slowed down, areas such as trade with low political returns and high economic returns came to the fore.[1]

In parallel with these changing dynamics, Beijing's national role conception had experienced fundamental changes. Since the late 1970s, economic considerations started to outweigh the ideological factors in shaping the country's foreign policy. Beijing was no more interested in exporting revolution or supporting independence movements across the world. As economic development became the epicenter of the Party's agenda, a realm of foreign policy—as other realms—perceived as a tool serving countries' economic modernization. Deng Xiaoping's famous statement that "it doesn't matter a cat is black or white as long as it catches the mice" is one of the clearest manifestations of his pragmatist stance in foreign policy.

The significant shift from getting involved in world affairs to more concentration on economic modernization highly attributes to Holsti's "internal development" role concept that emphasizes the problem of internal development rather than dealing with the international agenda (Holsti 1970). Holsti's emphasis on "noninvolvement in international political matters" in his "internal development" role could be defined as the main pillar of Deng Xiaoping's well-known keeping a low-profile (Tāo guāng yang huì)[2] strategy. Deng realized that China could not canalize the entire capacity of the country toward internal development without providing a safe external environment. Therefore, his administration left aside especially the border problems and sea disputes with his neighbors, as well as the global anti-capitalist struggle in order to achieve internal development. To address this fundamental move, Professor Li Weijian underlines, Beijing adopted a "non-alignment" and "non-threatening" strategy under Deng Xiaoping's teaching of "keeping a low profile and remained solely concentrated on its economic and modernization goals" (Li 2018).

Interrelated with the internal development role, the second role conception defining China's role in the Middle East is "business seeker" notwithstanding the objections of Jin Liangxiang (Jin 2017).[3] The concept of a business seeker for China refers to a high level of commercial and financial interaction with the Middle East region determined to meet economic interests with a settled principle of "non-intervention" (Jin 2017). With the changes taking place in Beijing, the Middle East was re-emerging in the Chinese foreign policy agenda with two prominent features: an energy resource to fuel China's economic development and a growing market for Chinese products. Through the late 1990s, China's oil imports from the Middle East were averaging around half of its total oil imports while making the largest proportion of the trade between China and the Middle Eastern countries (see table 7.1). While acknowledging that since China emerged as an oil importer, energy cooperation has been the primary concern of Beijing in the Middle East, Professor Xiao Xian of Yunnan University reminds us that the significance of other dimensions of China's ties with the region should not

Table 7.1 China's Oil Imports between 1990 and 2002 (millions of barrels)

Years	*1990*	*1992*	*1994*	*1996*	*1998*	*2000*	*2002*
Imports from the ME	8.42	31.10	35.87	88.34	121.68	276.67	258.36
Total Imports	21.33	82.91	90.13	165.10	199.45	512.94	506.67
Proportion of the ME (%)	33.47	38.12	39.79	53.50	61.00	53.93	50.99

Source: *Jin Liangxiang, "China and the Middle East: Energy First," Middle East Quarterly, Spring 2005.*

be neglected, including commercial exports, military sales, labor exports, project contracting (Xiao 2018).

These roles that China continued in the Middle East during the Deng period formed the basis of pragmatist and constructive diplomacy. Over the years, China has succeeded in developing comprehensive relationships and several strategic partnerships with various Middle Eastern countries, as well as broadening the scope of commercial, energy, and military cooperation with the regional actors. One of the most remarkable achievements of Chinese diplomacy in the Middle East has been maintaining all-around diplomacy with all countries—including conflicting parties—in the region. Under the guidance of the non-intervention principle of Chinese diplomacy and Deng Xiaoping's low-profile doctrine, Beijing has kept its political involvement in the region at an extremely minimal level and followed diplomacy with a certain focus on economic matters. With regards to the regional crisis, Beijing refrained from taking clear-cut positions in the ongoing crises and regional controversies, which could antagonize one of the conflicting parties. In this regard, it can be said that during this period no intention of playing a mediatory role had been demonstrated by the Chinese leadership. Regarding regional conflicts, Beijing tended to go along with the United States and the international consensus on major issues and avoided any central or mediatory role in conflict resolution processes (Chaziza 2013).

Another distinctive feature of China's ME strategy was to avoid any confrontation with any great power in the region. Thus, China in light of its low-profile doctrine managed to elude a possible conflict especially with the United States, which has been the dominant power in the Middle East for decades. Despite its strong sentiments against external interference of sovereign states' internal affairs, Beijing has avoided direct confrontation with the United States over the latter's interventionist "adventures" (the Gulf War and Iraq Invasion) in the region. Despite the costs of US intervention to China's national interests (such as increasing oil prices and supply cuts), Beijing's reaction remained considerably weak due to the above-mentioned concerns.

However, the steady expansion of the global economic footprint of Chinese enterprises, especially after Hu Jintao's call for "going out," has been raised questions of the principle's sustainability in recent years. China's increasing economic footprint around the globe, including the world's most conflicted regions, has resulted in domestic discussions questioning the sustainability of China's non-interference policy (Zheng 2016). Together with domestic expectations, as China's capabilities increased dramatically, regional expectations for China to play a bigger role have increased as well.

Xi Jinping's "Chinese Dream" and Its Impacts on the Middle East

China's re-entrance to the Middle East after the opening-up policies was oriented to sustain its economic development rather than ideological reasons. Although Beijing's policies toward the region have caused some criticism among the global actors, within the regional context, Beijing has been able to create a positive image of China by its distinctive approach. In this regard, the focus of the study is also important because China has had to resort to intangible policies as well as material elements against the smear campaigns launched by the Western ruling powers against China. Therefore, the roles that China might develop in order to reflect its policies, influence, and presence in the Middle East in a more constructive way have gained importance.

Rooted in Hu Jintao's call for "going out" in 2001, China's gradual engagement with the Middle East has been accelerated significantly especially, under Xi Jinping's leadership. The relationship which was mostly limited to trade and energy flow has gained new dimensions in recent years. Several changing dynamics at the systemic and unit-level variables have paved the way for some transformative changes in China's ties with the Middle East. Along with investments covering, infrastructure construction, finance, (alternative) energy sources, nuclear power, agriculture, Chinese interests have been forcing Beijing to proactively engage in the Middle East's political and security affairs.

China's increasing presence in the Middle East from the economy to the security realm has enabled Beijing to pursue new roles. China tends to further consolidate these roles through the BRI announced in 2013 and recently with Beijing's vaccine and medical aid diplomacy during the COVID-19 pandemic. "Responsible stakeholder," a term for how successful states are in taking on a set of responsibilities for the common good, has been one of the most prominent roles for China especially after Xi Jinping's accession to power. Beijing's new foreign policy paradigm "major country diplomacy with Chinese characteristics" (*daguo waijiao*) introduced in the eighteenth Party Congress closely resembles the responsible stakeholder role of China. This role has been a turning point where the low-profile diplomacy has been left behind for a new proactive strategy that is designed to serve the "Chinese Dream." Under the new diplomatic framework, Beijing has increased its involvement in regional and global affairs and started to experience major power politics. This paradigm change has certain implications in China's approach to Middle Eastern political affairs as a "responsible major country."

The attempt to play a responsible stakeholder role is about the extent to which the interests of the other countries are also considered. While the growing and opening Chinese economy would be a huge market for other countries, China's experience of growth and development would serve as a model for them (Bijian 2005). Chinese economic activities and investments in the region are also in alignment with the Middle Eastern country's interests. Beijing's development-oriented approach is highly welcomed in most of the countries in the region, which are desperately seeking for restructuring their economies and ensuring social stability.

Another dimension of China's economic presence in the region has to do with its energy needs. China is one of the three largest oil importers in the region, primarily from Saudi Arabia, Iran, and Iraq (Grace, 2021). While signing a $65 billion bilateral agreement with Saudi Arabia in 2017, the "China-Oman Industrial City" was built for mega-ventures including oil extraction, petrochemical, e-commerce, and alternative energy sources worth $11 billion in Oman (Xinhua 2018). Moreover, China has been the biggest trading partner of Iran whose export to China soared to $18.9 billion after being economically troubled by the Trump administration's unilateral withdrawal from the nuclear deal with Iran and the subsequent imposition of sanctions (*Iran's Economic Overview* 2021).

In connection with this role, under Xi's leadership, China has increased the extension of its business seeker role model. In the last decade, bilateral trade between China and the Middle Eastern states has increased significantly, China becomes to be the largest trading partner of the region with investments worth $29.5 billion (Middle East Monitor, 2017). While industrial parks and ports are vital parts of China's investments in accordance with the BRI's action plan, China describes the association of these two areas as the "two-wheel and two-wings approach" (Lons et al. 2019). While projects such as Khalifa Port in the United Arab Emirates, Duqm Port in Oman, Jizan Port in Saudi Arabia, and Port Said in Egypt are some outcomes of this approach, in countries such as Iraq, Syria, and Yemen whose infrastructures are in ruins, the emphasis is on reconstruction projects (Lons et al. 2019).

CHINA DURING THE COVID-19 PANDEMIC: ADVERSITIES AND SOLIDARITY

As COVID-19 has become a global pandemic, the virus has not only become a threat to human health but has reached a size that causes profound problems for many states with its economic, sociological, and political effects, and may even cause changes in the structure of global politics. Loosening of collaborative networks due to essential needs such as masks and vaccines, declining trust in international institutions, and social and economic crashes brought about by excessive isolation are just some heralds of future changes. Moreover, concerning globalization, while the discussions about "the borders have lost their importance" continued, because of the isolationist policies caused by the pandemic threat, an environment where the borders between states were closed, the liberal economic order was paralyzed, and the political structure became dysfunctional. Developments in the process of combating the pandemic showed that international cooperation has a more fragile structure than anticipated.

Leading actors of the liberal global order, such as the United States and the United Kingdom, were incapable of dealing with the pandemic and suffered serious local opposition. On the other hand, China with a strong state authority has shown a more effective performance in the fight against the pandemic. These developments have led to heated debates that the distribution of power in global politics has changed and even this change will reveal a new global political order. The focus of the discussions is on the zone of influence between the United States, which tends to reduce its responsibility in the face of global problems, and China, which has assumed the role of providing global public benefit with the medical aid it provides during the pandemic process.

Looking at the developments in the context of global governance, it is obvious that the United States under the Trump administration continued to withdraw from global responsibilities during the pandemic process. While the international society was expecting the United States to contribute to the fight against the virus on a global scale, Washington came to the agenda with issues such as closing its borders with the EU unilaterally, competition with Germany over the vaccine patent, and cutting its financial support to the World Health Organization. On the other hand, China, which was able to deal with the pandemic, became the essential actor of activities of global public health. While this situation is generally interpreted in the West as China's effort to become a global leader, to Chinese analysts, the aid activities actually are moves to change the perception against China in the world public opinion (Sağır 2020).

With the spread of the disease globally China that took the pandemic under control in a relatively short period increased its assistance to other states to such an extent that it introduced the concept of "health diplomacy." Changing dynamics at the international level have set the stage for China to entrench its responsible stakeholder role on a global scale. The country's efficient control over the pandemic has enabled Beijing to appear as a global public good provider when the United States was preoccupied with its domestic situation. Under the banner of Xi's "global community of common destiny" slogan, these efforts have helped China to repair its image—at least at the regional level—that was badly damaged at the initial phases of the pandemic.

China, the Middle East, and the Pandemic

Previous chapters have endeavored to emphasize the importance of the Middle East for China since Mao's era, in the context of some of the roles China has played. The pandemic, which started in 2019 and affected the whole world in a short time, created some challenges and also areas of cooperation for both sides. This final part of the study aims to focus on the interactions between the Middle East, which is one of the geographies most affected by the adverse conditions of the pandemic, and China, which plays a leading role in the development of health diplomacy and vaccines in the pandemic.

Before getting into the details of China's active role in the pandemic process, it is worth a brief digression to explain why the Middle East is one of the regions most affected by the pandemic and the reasons behind it. Middle Eastern countries have long been facing serious problems such as political disorder, sectarian and ethnic conflict, and economic crises. In countries such as Yemen, Syria, and Libya, some hospitals have been destroyed due to prolonged wars; the health system has almost collapsed. Especially when the demonstrations stemming from corruption, cronyism, and lack of reform in the Arabian Peninsula and the economic protests in Iraq, Lebanon, and Algeria combined with the pandemic conditions, they became more severe and increased the risks. Iran, which has problems with both economic and medical equipment due to sanctions, has attracted attention not only in the Middle East but also globally with the number of cases and deaths in the early days of the pandemic.

There were also several profound reasons why the problems in the Middle East were worse than the rest of the world. These were massive migration waves, the authority gap and legitimacy crisis of governments, and limited healthcare systems and equipment. According to the IMF, relatively poor countries will suffer disproportionately from the global negative consequences of the pandemic as they have limited access to healthcare and low savings rates and budgets (Bloom et al. 2018). Another reason is originating from religious rituals. While tens of thousands of Muslims visit Saudi Arabia for their Hajj and Umrah pilgrimages, Shiites travel to Iran and Iraq for their holy duties. Also, a high level of international attractions to Turkey and Israel, which are foremost tourism centers, and Dubai and Abu Dhabi as the hub for the global financial market could be seen as another factor making things worse.

For these reasons aside, the pandemic has brought about disastrous economic circumstances for some Middle East countries. The extraordinary decline in oil revenues, which is by far one of the most important sources of income for some Middle Eastern countries, put these states in a difficult situation. While the price of Brent oil was $66 on December 1, 2019, it decreased to $22.74 on March 1, 2020 (Brent Crude Oil Price 2021). Moreover, a decline in energy demand of about 20 percent in China, the world's largest energy importer, stunned the largest shocks to oil exporters since the 2008–2009 crisis (Camp et al. 2020). Due to the worsening economic conditions caused by the pandemic, while the GDP level of the Middle East and North African countries in December of 2020 decreased by 7.5 percent compared to the averages of the previous year, the highest decrease was in the oil-exporting countries with 9.6 percent (Rivlin 2021).

China's Changing Role in the Middle East during Pandemic Period

The roles that China will play in the Middle East during the pandemic will be discussed within the framework of the projects and plans it has undertaken under BRI. In this context, China has significantly increased its physical presence through activities such as investments in many different fields and cultural exchange programs (Chaziza 2020). However, under stringent coronavirus measures, Chinese engineers and workers returned to their countries at the beginning of the pandemic, and the mobilization of employees among countries was significantly restricted. As long as this restricted situation continues, projects under BRI may be suspended or even terminated in the long term (Chaziza 2020).

It seems that the most important role China will play in the Middle East under the pandemic conditions might be related to its generosity. A significant portion of the loans distributed within the scope of BRI projects has been given to countries with the lowest credit ratings in the world. According to the OECD country risk classification, Middle Eastern countries such as Iraq, Iran, Sudan, Libya, Yemen, and Lebanon are among the riskiest countries with seven risk points (OECD 2021). According to the report of the *Financial Times*, Iran, Egypt, and the United Arab Emirates have requested debt relief, yet China's approach to this issue is highly negative. According to Mei Guanqun, a researcher at the China Center for International Economic Exchanges, Chinese commercial banks such as the Bank of China and ICBC do not lean toward debt forgiveness due to government pressure on financial stability (Yu and Kynge 2020). An adviser to the Beijing government rejecting to be identified stated that the number of requests for debt forgiveness or relief was high and that it is difficult to accept them; however, he stated that interest payments could be suspended after consideration (Yu and Kynge 2020).

However, China's presence and support in the global health sector is not as stable as it is in economic matters. China plays a critical role in some parts of the world in combating the pandemic. China has been acting as a global public goods supplier by providing a huge amount of health assistance and medical equipment. The medical aid it delivered to the countries at the beginning of the pandemic and the vaccine distribution it made with the discovery of the COVID vaccine come to the fore. As of early 2021, when this article was penned, according to the news of the official media agency of China, in this process, China provided masks, protective medical suits, and test kits to 127 countries and 4 organizations; 13 healthcare teams in 11 countries; and has conducted more than 70 video conferences to share its experiences with more than 150 countries and organizations (MoFA 2020).

Concerning the second dimension of Chinese aid serving as a global public goods supplier, China's pre-pandemic health diplomacy turned into vaccine diplomacy during the pandemic. China, which has carried out fast studies on vaccines, received the greatest support from the Middle Eastern states. The first countries to approve the Chinese vaccine, which started to be distributed in the last period of 2020, were the United Arab Emirates and Bahrain (Rudolf 2021). Immediately after, Egypt and Turkey also joined this bandwagon (Rudolf 2021). Over time, Chinese vaccines have become widespread across the Middle East as an implication of China's role as a regional public goods supplier. As Chinese state councilor and foreign minister Wang Yi stated after his visit to the region; "China had donated and exported nearly 38 million doses of COVID-19 vaccines to 17 Middle Eastern countries, fulfilling its commitment to make vaccines a global public good" (Yi 2021). In the global context, Airfinity's data on vaccine-producing countries illustrate China's distinctive position within the framework of "vaccine diplomacy." While the United States manufactured 164 million and UK 16 million vaccine doses up to March 2021 without exporting any of them, China on the other hand has been exporting nearly as much as its domestic usage. 114 million doses out of 229 million doses of the country's total vaccine production have been sent overseas (Airfinity 2021).

The "responsible country" role that China started to acquire with the Xi Jinping period was based on economic foundations. Over the time, China's prominent role in the global health industry during the pandemic has started to have a social impact on international politics. Chinese medical equipment and vaccines, which have been delivered with high media attention, were warmly welcomed by most of the Middle Eastern governments that were in need of such contributions during the pandemic. This exchange in return provided China with the approval of its new role across the Middle

East. In February of 2021, the Beijing government donated 250,000 doses of vaccine to Iran, which has been having a hard time in international trade due to US sanctions (Mehdi 2021). According to Kianoush Jahanpour, spokesman of the Food and Drug Administration, "this act and those similar to it by the government and nation of China are admirable and will, of course, remain in the historical memory of the Iranian nation" (Motamedi 2021). Similarly, China's donation of 300,000 COVID-19 vaccines to Egypt was described by the Chinese ambassador to Egypt as "a reflection of friendship" (AbuZaid 2021).

CONCLUSION

Sino-Middle East contemporary relations, which started with China's support for liberation movements during the Mao period, ceased to be ideology-based and settled on economic foundations since the opening-up reforms. After a long period of harvesting economic benefits without getting involved in regional affairs, China's approach to the Middle East in the Xi Era is shifting "towards a multi-dimensional engagement that covers all interests" as Professor Sun Degang writes (Lons et al. 2019, p. 18). As Middle East's peripheral position to China's national interest began to change in recent years, the country's increasing footprint in the region—in terms of Chinese citizens, investments, companies, various assets, and so on—required a rebalancing of Beijing's approach to the Middle East. Within this context, this chapter adopted Holsti's national role conceptions to trace China's changing roles in the region with a focus on the consequences of the COVID-19 pandemic.

While the outbreak triggered heated discussions on the efficiency of authoritarian governments vis-à-vis democratic ones in managing global health crises, highly strict measures taken by Beijing proved to be helpful in maintaining stability. Subsequently, built on China's success in controlling the pandemic, Chinese diplomacy has diversified its efforts by adding a social dimension to its economic and political network, concomitantly strategically targeted desperate middle- and low-income countries. Although China remained highly protective in the economic sense after the pandemic, it made serious efforts on the basis of the health sector and played a leading role regarding cooperation in such a global health crisis. Consequently, as this research suggests, China's better position has enabled Beijing to appear as a global public good provider in certain regions.

China has long been facing charges of free-riding in the rules-based liberal international order, especially in the Middle East. The COVID-19 pandemic has proposed China a significant opportunity to challenge this negative perception. And Beijing seems to be valuing this opportunity. While Chinese diplomats were busy giving interviews and writing opinion pieces to local media outlets about China's commitments to their countries, headlines of Chinese global media outlets were being occupied with phrases like "China's role in the global fight against COVID-19." While global discussions are still taking place over the country's responsibility for the outbreak of the pandemic, the Chinese efforts discussed in this chapter seems to have provided a positive and even a responsible image of China in most of the Middle Eastern countries.

NOTES

1. For example, the trade volume between China and Jordan, which was zero before, peaked in 1982, and Jordan became China's fourth largest export center thanks to imports from China of $1.3 billion. During the same period, trade gained momentum also with many Middle Eastern and Arab countries. Yitzhak Shichor, "China's Economic Relations with the Middle East: New Dimensions," *China Report* 34, no. 3–4 (August 1, 1998): 421–22, https://doi.org/10.1177/000944559803400310.

2. While the term "Tāo guāng yang huì" has widely translated as "hiding one's capabilities and biding one's time," Wang Jisi opposes the translation in his famous article "China's Search for a Grand Strategy," written for foreign affairs. For further reading: Jisi, "China's Search for a Grand Strategy."

3. In his study, Jin Liangxiang argues that China contributes to the stability and security of the region by performing the roles of important economic contributors, a low-profile mediator and a major provider of security public goods rather than business seeker or security free-rider roles. Liangxiang Jin, "China's Role in the Middle East: Current Debates and Future Trends," *China Quarterly of International Strategic Studies* 03, no. 01 (January 1, 2017): 39–55, https://doi.org/10.1142/S2377740017500014.

REFERENCES

Airfinity. "Airfinity – Predictive Science Intelligence." Accessed April 19, 2021. www.airfinity.com.

Bijian, Zheng. "China's 'Peaceful Rise' to Great-Power Status." February 15, 2019. https://www.foreignaffairs.com/articles/asia/2005-09-01/chinas-peaceful-rise-great-power-status.

Bloom, David E., Daniel Cadarette, and J.P. Sevilla. "The Economic Risks and Impacts of Epidemics." *Finance & Development, IMF* 55, no. 2 (2018). https://www.imf.org/external/pubs/ft/fandd/2018/06/economic-risks-and-impacts-of-epidemics/bloom.htm.

Chaziza, Mordechai. "China's Policy on the Middle East Peace Process after the Cold War." *China Report* 49, no. 1 (February 1, 2013): 161–75. https://doi.org/10.1177/0009445513479460.

———. "Coronavirus, China, and the Middle East." Research Report. Mideast Security and Policy Studies. Begin-Sadat Center for Strategic Studies, June 2020. https://www.jstor.org/stable/resrep26341?seq=1#metadata_info_tab_contents.

"China's Great Game in the Middle East." Policy Brief. European Council on Foreign Relations, October 2019.

Commodity.com. "Iran's Economic Overview - Top Commodity Exports & Imports Revealed." Accessed March 2, 2021. https://commodity.com/data/iran/.

"Coronavirus Stokes Middle East Boiling Points." BBC News, May 4, 2020, sec. Middle East. https://www.bbc.com/news/world-middle-east-52493608.

Holsti, K. J. "National Role Conceptions in the Study of Foreign Policy." *International Studies Quarterly* 14, no. 3 (1970): 233–309. https://doi.org/10.2307/3013584.

Investing.com. "Brent Crude Oil Price." Accessed March 4, 2021. https://www.investing.com/commodities/brent-oil.

Jin, Liangxiang. "China's Role in the Middle East: Current Debates and Future Trends." *China Quarterly of International Strategic Studies* 03, no. 01 (January 1, 2017): 39–55. https://doi.org/10.1142/S2377740017500014.

Jisi, Wang. "China's Search for a Grand Strategy: A Rising Great Power Finds Its Way." *Foreign Affairs* 90, no. 2 (2011): 68–79.

Kliman, Daniel, Abigail Grace. "China Smells Opportunity in the Middle East's Crisis." Foreign Policy (blog). Accessed March 2, 2021. https://foreignpolicy.com/2018/06/14/china-smells-opportunity-in-the-middle-easts-crisis/.

Liu Xi and Yang Yuanyong. "Spotlight: China, Oman Establish Industrial Park to Boost Bilateral Cooperation." Xinhua, 2018. http://www.xinhuanet.com/english/2018-12/19/c_137683272.htm.

Li Weijian. "From overall Detachment to Proactiveness: China's Middle East Diplomacy since Reform and Opening Up." *Arab World Studies* 178, no. 05 (2018): 3–13.

Mehdi, Syed Zafar. "Iran Receives First Batch of Chinese COVID-19 Vaccine." Anadolu Agency, February 28, 2021. https://www.aa.com.tr/en/latest-on-corona-virus-outbreak/iran-receives-first-batch-of-chinese-COVID-19-vaccine/2159898.

Middle East Monitor. "China Is Largest Foreign Investor in Middle East." 2017. https://www.middleeastmonitor.com/20170724-china-is-largest-foreign-investor-in-middle-east/.

Motamedi, Maziar. "Iran Receives China's Sinopharm Jabs as COVID Deaths Reach 60,000." Aljazeera, February 28, 2021. https://www.aljazeera.com/news/2021/2/28/iran-receives-chinas-sinopharm-jabs-as-COVID-deaths-reach-60000.

Niu Xinchun. "China and the Middle East: New Issues, New Perspectives, New Methods-Basic Features of China's Middle East Strategy." *Modern International Relations*, no. 12期 (2013): 1–3.

OECD. "Country Risk Classification." Accessed March 5, 2021. http://www.oecd.org/trade/topics/export-credits/arrangement-and-sector-understandings/financing-terms-and-conditions/country-risk-classification/.

Panorama. "Pandemi Sonrası Küresel Siyasetin Geleceğini Çin Nasıl Tartışıyor?-Abdurrahim Sağır." July 3, 2020. https://www.uikpanorama.com/blog/2020/07/03/pandemi-sonrasi-kuresel-siyasetin-gelecegini-cin-nasil-tartisiyor/.

Rudolf, Moritz. "China's Health Diplomacy during COVID-19." Stiftung Wissenschaft Und Politik. German Institute for International and Security Affairs, January 2021. https://www.swp-berlin.org/10.18449/2021C09/.

Shichor, Yitzhak. "China's Economic Relations with the Middle East: New Dimensions." *China Report* 34, no. 3–4 (August 1, 1998): 419–39. https://doi.org/10.1177/000944559803400310.

———. *The Middle East in China's Foreign Policy, 1949–1977*. LSE Monographs in International Studies. Cambridge: Cambridge University Press, 1979. https://doi.org/10.1017/CBO9780511598791.

Sitter, Christopher, Derek Wasilewski, Kevin M. Camp, David Mead, Stephen Reed. "From the Barrel to the Pump: The Impact of the COVID-19 Pandemic on Prices for Petroleum Products." *Monthly Labor Review*, U.S. Bureau of Labor Statistics, October 2020. https://doi.org/10.21916/mlr.2020.24.

"The Impact of COVID-19 and Conflict on Middle Eastern Economies." The Moshe Dayan Center for Middle Eastern and African Studies, January 2021. https://dayan.org/content/impact-COVID-19-and-conflict-middle-eastern-economies.

The Media Line. "Vaccines Offer China Increased Leverage in the Middle East." February 7, 2021. https://themedialine.org/by-region/vaccines-offer-china-increased-leverage-in-the-middle-east/.

The World Bank. "Overview of China." Text/HTML. Accessed December 30, 2020. https://www.worldbank.org/en/country/china/overview.

Tse-Tung, Mao. *Selected Works of Mao Tse-Tung: Volume II*. Second Printing edition. Foreign Languages Press, 1967.

"Wang Yi: China Is a Long-Term, Reliable Strategic Partner of Middle East Countries." CGTN, March 30, 2021. https://news.cgtn.com/news/2021-03-30/Wang-Yi-on-outcomes-of-his-Middle-East-tour-Z3GJ9ssbjW/index.html.

Xiao Xian. "Development of Economic and Trade Relations between China and Middle East Countries in the Early Period of Reform and Opening Up." *Arab World Studies* 178, no. 05 (2018): 46–59.

Yu, Sun, and James Kynge. "China Faces Wave of Calls for Debt Relief on 'Belt and Road' Projects." *Financial Times*, April 30, 2020. https://www.ft.com/content/5a3192be-27c6-4fe7-87e7-78d4158bd39b.

Zaid, Mohammed Abu. "Chinese Ambassador Says Vaccine Donation to Egypt 'Reflection of Friendship.'" Arab News, February 8, 2021. https://arab.news/535ts.

Zhao Lijian. Foreign Ministry Spokesperson Zhao Lijian's Regular Press Conference. Ministry of Foreign Affairs, the People's Republic of China, April 10, 2020. https://www.fmprc.gov.cn/mfa_eng/xwfw_665399/s2510_665401/t1768338.shtml.

Chapter 8

Soft Power Pursuit during the COVID-19 Pandemic

The Case of Turkish Foreign Policy

Göktuğ Sönmez and Murat Çemrek

The "soft power" concept erratically sounds paradoxical if not oxymoron for the ears hearing it firstly since power has never equated with softness neither ontologically nor epistemologically. After Joseph Nye's phenomenal article "Soft Power" had appeared in the *Foreign Policy* in 1990 (153–171), it had attracted a great deal of attention unexpectedly especially in the academic, policymaking, and to some extent media circles. One should keep in mind that Nye's piece has primarily focused on the ways and means to consolidate the American hegemony in the post-Cold War era. However, not only the very concept itself but also its applications by different actors through various cases challenging or supplementing it have been hotly discussed since then. Moreover, through either providing medical equipment or medical personnel, the COVID-19 era has offered some actors opportunities to be more active and influential at stages they already enjoy a certain level of involvement and further make a benign entrance to the theaters they strived but could not earlier succeed. Thus, as this pandemic seems to accompany us for the unforeseeable future even after the mass production of a vaccine or specific drugs in remedy, analyzing "soft power" seems quite a timely academic effort in response. In this context, a related and further important question is about which countries would be able to utilize opportunities provided by striking a wise balance between hard and soft power mechanisms and instruments, or achieve smart power simply. Without key hard power tools in the same or different stages at play, mere reliance on soft power tools such as medical aid in the form of facemasks, medical staff, and even vaccines would bear quite limited consequences since it is not sustainable as a cultural center at the last instance. However, the powers refraining and/or are not able to make use of any soft power tools via medical aid or provision of required expertise might experience questioning about their ultimate goals of power-maximizing behaviors. This might even turn to be judged as trivial selfishness rather than a pursuit of helping actors in need while improving their relative power positions.

The soft power has also been a clichéd concept in Turkish Foreign Policy (TFP) especially in the last decade through its zealous efforts increasing the number of diplomatic missions only in Africa from 12 in 2002 to 44 today and in total 239 globally making Turkey having the fifth largest diplomatic global network (*Anadolu Agency* 2018). Moreover, Turkey has also become the "most charitable nation in the globe," since Turkey's foreign aid—surpassing US$8 billion—per its GDP is higher than any other country including the expenses spent hosting about four million Syrian refugees according to the Global Humanitarian Assistance Report 2018 of the Development Initiatives located in the UK (Salcı 2018).

This article questions Turkey's COVID-19 policies with reference to the recent medical dimension of soft power and the concomitant foreign policy ambitions. Thus, we will firstly offer an insight into different conceptualizations of power, namely "hard power," "soft power," "smart power," and "sticky power." Secondly, we will briefly discuss American and Chinese soft power-driven policies to see how predominant players lead the game before touching upon some other actors' efforts in supplementing medical aid abroad for garnering soft power. This will bring us to the question of what tools and means Turkey's soft power pursuit has utilized so far and how the COVID-19 era has had an influence on this toolkit. This section will be followed by a conclusive discussion about the extent of soft power projection during the pandemic and what Turkey's case can provide us regarding this discussion whether or not we can talk about its hard, smart, and/or sticky dimensions.

POWER DIFFERENTIALS: HARD, SOFT, STICKY POWER, AND SMART ONE

Power, in short, is the ability to have the other/s behave in a way desirable for one's self or a state. One would not be wrong if s/he argues power is the essence of politics. That is why power has been traditionally one of the most intensively debated concepts of social sciences in general and Political Science (PS) and International Relations (IR) specifically through these disciplines' vast literature.

Here, then, the key question is how a state can achieve such a desirable outcome. Nye conceptualizes the "hard power" as "command power" focused on coercing or "pushing" others—so unwillingly—to behave in a certain way employing material items (Keohane and Nye 2011, 216–223). However "soft power" or "co-optive power" aims essentially at persuasion (Nye 1990, 166–167) resulting that particular state "may achieve the outcomes it prefers in world politics because the states want to follow it or have agreed to a situation that produces such efforts" (Nye 1990, 166). Nye, later on, in his *Political Science Quarterly* work, also defines soft power as "the ability to get what you want through attraction rather than coercion or payments" (2004, 256). In that case, a state would be exposed to less "resistance to its wishes" (Nye 1990, 167) as its power is perceived as legitimate. Such a privileged position would require several key components. They are composed of an attractive set of superior culture and ideology fostered by its development model, the ability to set and to propagate international norms in accordance with its societal ones and to sustain international institutions for desirable foreign policy choices in parallel with that particular "influencer" (Nye 1990, 167–168). The result would be to dodge the possible costs and backfires of hard power applications to some extent. Although successful assertion of soft power does not guarantee full abandonment of hard power moves, it rather needs them to have a comprehensive influence over others in a concerted way.

Nye delineates hard power deriving from the country's military and economic might whereas soft power is about "attractiveness of a country's culture, political ideals, and policies." However, Walter Russell Mead's (2009) piece in the *Foreign Policy* further contributes to the discussion and focuses on the sources of American power—as does Nye—arguing on the economic side. Indeed, it is neither hard nor soft power but rather sticky power which can attract "other countries to the US system and then trapping them in it." He further refers to military force as "sharp" and economic power as "sticky" lending another pair of binary lenses to the discussion. Having "stickiness" in the equation is important for any state either achieved through economic, cultural, or institutional means. Otherwise ad hoc alliances and vulnerable superiorities based on increases in "sharp" power might be short-lived. Moreover, only focusing on the "sticky" part without any coercive repertoire—even rarely spoken—would also fail equally in keeping permanent desirable power relations intact with others. Nye's other more popular conceptualization of "smart power"—appeared in *Foreign Affairs* (2009, 160)—highlights the importance of the combination of hard and soft powers. Thus any state would need combining both to have a comprehensive success in terms of presenting others' choices it desires. He further made this point in an eccentric example noting that "the fact that the North Korean dictator Kim Jong Il likes to watch Hollywood movies is unlikely to affect his country's nuclear weapons program" (Nye 2009, 161). Also according to Nye and Richard Armitage's report "A Smarter, More Secure America" published by Center for Strategic and International Studies (CSIS) on smart power, five points should be paid attention as alliances, partnerships, and institutions; global development; public diplomacy; economic integration; and technology and innovation (2007, 3).

Nevertheless, hard power has incrementally become more and more unacceptable since it has become further costly both politically and financially while especially economic interdependence in the international system has reached unprecedented levels (Keohane and Nye 2011, 216–223). Thus, soft power, over time, has proved to be as important as its hard counterpart. Giulio M. Gallarotti, in a similar vein, discusses the rise of the concept and notes that the impact of globalization has already diminished the utility of hard power due to the cited interdependence. He also pays attention to the rise of democracy since "modern populations" have a far more sensitive approach toward their economic fate in an era where sacrifice and "warrior ethic" have already been losing ground. Lastly, the growth of international organizations as the fundamental components of soft power makes sense in this context (2011, 37–38). It should also be added that the limits of hard power, even for the hegemon, are quite visible in various instances as well as indeed for others. Once a particular state following the hard path or not paying proper attention to other dimensions and forms of power, defying all the above-mentioned reasons and risks, it could frequently end up failing to achieve its desired outcomes. Reversely, to keep in mind, Gallarotti makes a clear case with respect to strike a wise balance presenting stress on soft power as a reaction to a long ritual of decision-making having disregarded profits of soft power and over-trusted on hard power. But it would also be shocking to national influence to become a paper tiger while bending too much on the soft power (Gallarotti 2011, 42).

The next section, in the light of the discussions above regarding the nature, extent, and forms of power and how to strike a balance between its different forms, we will briefly touch upon the use of soft power via different and sometimes common means and tools by hegemonic powers, great powers, or challengers.

HEGEMONIC AND RISING POWERS SOFT POWER PRACTICES: AMERICAN AND CHINESE CASES IN SHORT

Nye notes the soft power is as old as at least the *Alliance Française*, founded in 1883, to project French culture as a part of diplomacy imitated later by German and Italian counterparts. From radio broadcasts in several different languages as early as the 1920s to Soviet propaganda films of the same era could be other pioneering examples. However, the US Committee of

Public Information of World War I, despite being a short-lived project, was perfected later on with World War II and went beyond through the US Information Agency, USAID, Voice of America, and the Fulbright programs as further efforts were put in to increase American higher education attractiveness (Nye 2006, 70). Not only medical, social, and infrastructural aid but also provision of expertise went hand in hand while American soft power applications likened its French and British counterparts. This approach simply relied extensively on the export of cultural codes, artistic pieces, and language textbooks as the key pillars of public diplomacy acquiring consent to reinforce its soft power. However, the United States has kept enjoying its soft power more than anyone else since the end of World War II through different tools or common practices through extravagantly spending its tremendous resources and capabilities.

Cinema industry, video clips, and music have never been such an integral part of soft power projection earlier. Although the American case has highlighted their importance, it would be unrealistic to argue that other key actors in the system, France and the UK, had no chance to utilize them as effectively as the United States despite their zealous efforts for a strong presence in that realm. Higher education as a means of soft power projection has also been an indispensable part of the US soft power mechanism, especially with the Fulbright scheme. Since 1948 more than 380,000 people have benefited from this program not only in financial terms of the scholarship but also the prestige they enjoyed as recipients in their home countries.

Information production as the main aspect of consent production has quite close links with the increasing media activism of numerous crucial actors in the international system through official state TV channels and their multilingual have always been present in various countries. Thus, control over the flow of information and its strategic use, from the Voice of America to CNN's global offshoots, are significant players in this realm. This had widely discussed impacts covering a wide range from influence in the ex-Soviet area to current American initiatives abroad in particular ways.

It should not be forgotten that almost each and every piece of Nye's work on soft power basically aimed at not only conceptualizations but also—arguably even more primarily—how the United States performs in terms of soft power as already noted. Thus, he focuses on its strengths and weaknesses as well as prospects and risks for his country. So basically most of the discussion is revolving around the United States thus, needless to say, his work is absolutely American-centric. Considering the exceptional levels of American hard and soft power especially in the post-Cold War era, one might eventually evaluate this orientation fair enough. Yet, such an attitude would already narrow down the scope of conceptualization for further analysis. In that respect, especially extensive Chinese focus is well worth mentioning to give a bit of wider scope to the concept not provided by Nye deliberately.

In terms of the Chinese pursuit of soft power, several key components are worth mentioning such as Chinese cultural promotion through Confucius Institutes all over the world. These efforts are to persuade the globe about Chinese benevolent intentions of its peaceful rise referring to "harmony" extensively as they often do. While actively engaging in international and regional institutions and embracing considerably held norms and values, China sets financial ties and economic aid to promote the "Beijing consensus" coined by Joshua Cooper Ramo—an alternative to the famous "Washington Consensus" coined by John Williamson in 1990 as the embodiment of a broad agreement on neoliberal policies. The former, based on the "uniqueness of the Chinese development model" (Cho and Jeong 2008, 464; Wang 2008, 257–271) offers a development prospect for developing countries. This model prioritizes innovation and sustainability emphasizing independence as one of the most significant sources of the Chinese soft power to attract developing countries (Cho and Jeong 2008, 462–463). While asserting this soft power understanding, as a response to concerns about Chinese rise, the "peaceful rise" theory was coined by Zheng Bijian in 2003 and circulated by Chinese policymakers the very next year. This approach has even replaced the "peaceful development" rhetoric afterward to make it sound even more gentle and naïve as a major tool for China not to alert the United States and other rivals while consolidating its own power. Chinese foreign policy assumes hard and soft power typologies along with the expectation that such benevolence would also act as another element of soft power assertion by itself (Gill and Huang 2006, 17–36; Cho and Jeong 2008, 467; Mingjiang 2008, 293–294). As another component of the Chinese soft power projection, in line with Nye's focus on cultural values, the Confucius Institutes have functioned as the strategic basis for more than a decade since the first one opened in South Korea in 2004 (Cho and Jeong 2008, 469–471). As early as 2007, China had already invested remarkably sending more than 300 teachers as well as 300,000 sets of written and audio materials making up to an ambitious 26 million USD investments in three years considering the low number of institutes at that time (Paradise 2009, 653; Gill and Huang 2006, 25).

The Confucius Institutes and its various counterparts run by other nations are also particularly important. Nye, considering this fact in his piece "Soft Power and Higher Education," exclusively focused on the link between higher educational institutions and soft power projection quotes of the then US secretary of state Colin Powell: "I can think of no more valuable asset to our country than the friendship of future world leaders who have been educated here [United States]." Thus, with respect to the cultural exchanges between the USSR and the United States, Nye himself states that "American skeptics" at the time feared that visiting Soviet scientists and KGB agents would "steal us blind"; they failed to notice, however, that the visitors vacuumed up political ideas along with the scientific secrets "and thus these programs "played a significant role in enhancing American soft power" (2020). In a similar vein, within its closer neighborhood of Asia, as noted by Cho and Jeong (2008, 454), TV and radio broadcasting, use of ASEAN, and promoting China as a magnet for foreign students have been key elements of the Chinese soft power strategy (Wang 2008, 257–271).

Yet, it is quite debatable that the Chinese pursuit of soft power could bear the very desired results for several reasons. For example, China imported 4,068 book titles from the United States whereas exporting only 14 and that import/export ratio of China's intellectual property rights trade with the United States as 4000/24 highlights the weakness of its pursuit as a component of soft power (Mingjiang 2008, 297). However, the Chinese experience, overall, seems to mimic key dimensions of the hegemonic soft power projection while it seems more effective and advanced in some areas even baby steps in others. Thus, Chinese efforts to promote cultural and linguistic ties via Confucius Institutes reached the level of a more advanced mechanism with a high global outreach. This is in harmony with China's quite insisting mission of promoting itself as an economic alternative. However, especially Chinese totalitarian political regime stands before its economic success among societies in many countries. Besides, assuming that China is anywhere near to the French or British benefit of popular culture, let alone American exceptional and successful use would also be quite unrealistic. Moreover, this asymmetry would probably be the same more or less in the foreseeable future just because of the difficulties of the Chinese language, especially in its written form. Whether this drawback could be overcome by China through further economic involvements in other countries or frequent use of "harmony" and "reciprocity" is the fundamental question to assess China to be really regarded as a challenger to the hegemon.

Nevertheless, the Chinese case highlights that we can easily find common themes, tools, and measures regardless of who strives for it within the context of soft power. Thus, the Turkish case, similarly, shows us the importance of infrastructural aid, higher education exchange, establishing cultural and linguistic links and the use of popular culture especially soup operas.

TURKEY'S SOFT POWER TOOLS IN A NUTSHELL AND THE COVID-19 ERA

Turkey, starting with the end of the Cold War and specifically during the last two decades, strived for becoming a more active actor in terms of soft power applications. Within this context, several institutions and instruments played significant roles through Turkey's seek of soft power-related goals. Yunus Emre Institute (Yunus Emre Enstitüsü, YEE) and Yunus Emre Cultural Centers attached with the Institute, Turkish Cooperation and Coordination Agency (Türk İşbirliği ve Koordinasyon Ajansı Başkanlığı, TİKA), Presidency for Turks Abroad and Related Communities (Yurtdışı Türkler ve Akraba Topluluklar Başkanlığı, YTB) have all been such significant components of the Turkish soft power apparatus.

The Yunus Emre Foundation (YEF), formed with the Law 5653 on May 5, 2007, in Ankara, aims at "presenting Turkish cultural heritage, promoting cultural exchange, making information about Turkey available and providing educational services on Turkish language and culture and on the country's arts" (Kaya and Tecmen 2011). One may easily argue the YEF has almost identical goals and tools of the Alliance Française and the British Council formed much earlier, 1833 and 1934, respectively. The very first YEF cultural center was opened in 2009 in Sarajevo (Ekşi and Erol 2018, 30–31), a deliberate reminder of the Ottoman heritage and its Balkan component as well as the boundaries of Turkey's desired sphere of influence or layer of defense. Briefly, the YEF organizes cultural events and activities, Turkish proficiency tests, art exhibitions, and so on in order to convene people interested in Turkey and promote Turkish culture.

The TİKA as another key actor, similar to USAID, State Council & Eximbank of China, DFID of UK, AFD of France, and GIZ of Germany, was founded in 1992, earlier than any other organization of the Turkish soft power mechanism. The TİKA followed especially the fall of the USSR through the enactment of the Law 4668 with an eye on "providing aid to countries with mutual historical, political and cultural backgrounds" (Kaya and Tecmen 2011, 13). The primary goal, thus, was to promote Turkey's image in the ex-Soviet space or the Turkic world in brief and to some extent the Balkans and the Middle East. This scope has also widened to cover Africa and Latin America in the time since engagement in these regions has also significantly increased in parallel to Turkey's opening to both regions. In 2011, the TİKA's name has changed as "coordination" replacing "development" (Ekşi and Erol 2018, 37) highlighting Turkey's intention to promote soft power without alarming any audiences abroad. Besides the widened geographical scope, the TİKA's range of activities also amplified covering infrastructure, education and health services, and developmental support. Ekşi and Erol argue that the number of TİKA projects during the 1992–2002 period was around 2,000 executed in 28 countries climbing to 11,000 executed in 140 countries in the following 2002–2014 period (Ekşi and Erol 2018, 38; see also İpek 2015, 173–193). Even more importantly, the number of TİKA Coordination Offices abroad witnessed a significant rise from 12 in 2002 to more than 60 recently, while the organization is zealously involved in various social and cultural efforts in about 150 countries (TİKA 2020).

The YTB, founded in 2010 as a critical juncture in Turkey's diaspora politics, focuses on four key areas, namely Turkish citizens abroad, related communities, NGOs, and international students (Aydın 2014, 16.). One of the most important activities of the YTB is having combined earlier highly scattered various high education scholarships under the same roof named "Turkey Scholarships." Such educational activism has been one of the reasons behind "the number of international students studying in our higher education institutions has increased by 75%." This accounted for almost 110,000 students, a quarter of whom holding this scholarship, as proudly noted on the official website of the institution. Not only pure academic orientation but also social and cultural interaction as well as the development of political and diplomatic relations stand among the goals of this activism (YTB 2020). In order to coordinate these different soft power-related institutions, the Prime Ministry Public Diplomacy Coordination Office (KDK) was earlier established in 2010, further highlighting Turkey's desire toward soft power projection and also to accomplish it all in a more systematized way (Ekşi and Erol 2018, 29).

Turkey's another soft power tool of soap operas and TV series played a significant role in time. Nye has already mentioned the American film industry to "account for only 6–7 percent of all films" made globally but occupying "around 50 percent of world screen time." Even though neither as remarkable as Hollywood nor as Bollywood, Turkey's TV series have attracted quite large audiences especially in the Middle East, Balkans, Caucasus, Central Asia, and even in Latin America whose series has earlier dominated Turkish TV channels during the 1990s. Several soap operas especially attracted a vast interest in those regions such as *Gümüş* (known as Noor), *Ihlamurlar Altında* (Sanawat ad-Dayaa), *Kurtlar Vadisi* (Valley of Wolves), and possibly with the highest number of audience reaching as much as around 240 million, *Muhteşem Yüzyıl* (The Magnificent Century) (Kaya and Tecmen 2011, 16; see also Bal 2016, 390–400).

Turkey, as of August 2020, experienced the pandemic crisis with around 6.5 million tests, 260,000 patients, and 6,200 deaths. In terms of recovery rate, fatality rate, and test per person figures, Turkey's performance has been quite effective so far (Bakir 2020, 426). At a time when the capabilities and promptness of the United States, the EU, and the WHO have been questioned widely, bilateral aid and support from specific countries have attracted even more attention in a much more welcoming attitude and a higher public diplomacy "point." Turkey has been one of the most active countries providing many countries free medical kits in return helping Turkey further strengthen its soft power profile established over decades thanks to the efforts put by the above-mentioned actors.

Turkish foreign minister in late April stated that the country received requests from more than 100 countries and delivered aid to 57 countries (*Anadolu Ajansı*, April 27, 2020) climbing to around 80 in mid-May, including Germany, United States, Albania, Bulgaria, Kosovo, Georgia, Moldova, Libya, Lebanon, Algeria, Israel, Pakistan, Afghanistan, Guinea, Somalia, Uganda, China, and Indonesia (*Daily Sabah*, May 15, 2020). Turkey's aid and medical supply deliveries were appreciated by the WHO, of which European Regional Director Hans Kluge thanked specifically Turkey for this display of "international solidarity" (WHO, July 22, 2020).

Turkey's aid to the NATO allies in Europe including Spain, Italy, and the UK was channeled through Euro-Atlantic Disaster Response Coordination Centre (EADRCC). This was evaluated as a further sign of Turkey's commitment to keep the momentum of its relations with the NATO and Europe whereas Turkish supplies to the United States were seen as a move to lower tensions in several key issues including the American position regarding the YPG and Turkey's acquisition of the Russian S-400 air defense systems (Tol and Bechev, 2020). As of late April, Turkey sent Italy and Spain a military plane carrying 450,000 facemasks and 116 ventilators sold to Spain with exceptional permission due to the ban on these tools' export in many countries including Turkey. One should also keep in mind that while the Syrian civil war heated up to the extent that Turkey's involvement in Northern Syria became a security necessity, Spain was the only country that did not call for the withdrawal of its Patriot systems operating under the NATO, stationed in Adana, south of Turkey (*Takvim*, April 28, 2020). The UK has also received not only aid from Turkey but also bought medical equipment, as did the United States. Iran received around 1,000 test kits, more than 25,000 medical clothes, and 80,000 facemasks of which 4,000 were N95 whereas Erbil Province in Northern Iraq received 30,000 facemasks (*BBC Türkçe*, April 28, 2020). Turkey's aid and provision of medical supplies were also applauded officially in Twitter accounts from the Red Crescent organizations of various countries to the NATO, the US, and UK leaderships. With respect to diaspora politics, too, Turkey has been quite active during the first two months of the pandemic when the country transferred more than its 70,000 citizens abroad from more than 110 countries (*NTV*, May 19, 2020).

CONCLUSION

The actors according to their capacities and instruments in their hands have utilized various forms of power depending on opportunities in changing periods of political history. In this context, especially in the last several centuries, the use of soft power, at least as important as hard power tools, has been an indivisible part of power projections and the effort to gain influence in different regions and geographies. Culture, art, historical ties, and language have been at the forefront of such zealous efforts in soft power politics. Superpowers and middle-range powers notably utilize distinctive tools and methods putting serious efforts to win hearts and souls shadowing their coercion or hard power with consent or soft power. Striking a balance between hard and soft power has also been a key challenge to achieve the desired end of increasing influence abroad. Relying too much on either form of power risks failing in this ultimate goal or being labeled as a quite coercive actor or a glass cannon.

Turkey's decades-old strive for a higher soft power capability covers its several institutions' different facades of such an effort from higher education scholarships to language promotion as well as infrastructure works and architectural restorations for the sake of highlighting historical and cultural links. The recent pandemic, amid all the difficulties and tragedies surrounding it, provided Turkey, among many other actors, a new window of opportunity to further project its soft power with a new set of instruments and measures. Benefiting this opportunity went hand in hand with its discourse of helping others reinforced Turkey's significantly rising levels of humanitarian aid in the last two decades. Turkey provided free medical aid to many countries while supplying the ones in need with either scarce or prohibited to export goods also in return for due payments.

Consequently, the sustainability of such mechanisms and instruments is uttered important in this context. Trade links, educational exchange, cultural and linguistic camps, and artistic activities, infrastructural work, and so on can act as more sustainable and visible tools of soft power. Its impact would last beyond generations in most cases whereas context-dependent aid, in case it is not sustained in the long run and reinforced with other tools and mechanisms, might not bear the same results. Furthermore, without the hard power component, the impact of soft power projection is always questionable if not totally useless. Nevertheless, Turkey's increasingly more visible hard power in Libya and Syria as well as its engagement in the Eastern Mediterranean should also be kept in mind in this context. Thus, one could easily question that whether hard power can reinforce soft power efforts as mentioned regarding the recipients of Turkey's pandemic era support and aid. So, while Turkey's support abroad seems quite valuable and is being applauded by many international actors, once it is assessed as a soft power tool, its "stickiness" and "smartness" can be moderate since it is not sustainable.

REFERENCES

"About Us." TİKA Website. https://www.tika.gov.tr/tr/sayfa/hakkimizda-14649 (accessed August 1, 2020).

"Çavuşoğlu: 135 ülke bizden tıbbi malzeme talebinde bulundu." *NTV*, May 19, 2020.

"International Student Mobility." YTB Website. https://www.ytb.gov.tr/en/international-students/international-student-mobility (accessed August 5, 2020).

"Koronavirüs: Türkiye hangi ülkeye ne kadar yardım gönderdi?" *BBC Türkçe*, April 28, 2020.

"Turkey boasts no. 5 diplomatic network in the world." *Anadolu Agency*, February 9, 2018.

"Turkey delivers medical aid to 80 countries amid pandemic." *Daily Sabah*, May 15, 2020.

"Turkey sent aid to at least 57 countries to fight virus." *Anadolu Ajansı*, April 27, 2020.

"Türkiye hangi ülkelere yardım gönderdi?" *Takvim*, April 28, 2020.

"WHO Regional Director for Europe signs agreement for new centre of excellence and visits Gaziantep, marking 60 years of cooperation with Turkey." World Health Organization Europe Website, July 22, 2020, https://www.euro.who.int/en/health-topics/health-emergencies/coronavirus-COVID-19/news/news/2020/7/who-regional-director-for-europe-signs-agreement-for-new-centre-of-excellence-and-visits-gaziantep,-marking-60-years-of-cooperation-with-turkey (accessed August 6, 2020).

"Yunus Emre Vakfı Kanunu." Law No. 5653, adopted May 5, 2007, Art. 1.

Aydın, Yaşar. "The New Turkish Diaspora Policy: Its Aims, Their Limits and the Challenges for Associations of People of Turkish Origin and Decision-makers in Germany." *SWP Research Paper* 10, October 2014, 16.

Bakir, Caner. "The Turkish State's Responses to Existential COVID-19 Crisis." *Policy and Society*, vol. 39, no. 3 (2020): 424–441.

Bal, Özlem. "Muhteşem Yüzyıl Dizisinin Türkiye İmajına Etkisi." In *Türkiye'nin Uluslararası İmajı*, eds. by Elif Yıldız and Tuba Gültekin. Konya: Atlas Akademi, 2016: 390–400.

Cho, Young Nam and Jong Ho Jeong. "China's Soft Power: Discussions, Resources, and Prospects." *Asian Survey*, vol. 48, no. 3 (May/June 2008): 453–472.

Ekşi, Muharrem and Mehmet Seyfettin Erol. "The Rise and Fall of Turkish Soft Power and Public Diplomacy." *Akademik Bakış*, vol. 11, no. 23 (2018): 15–45, 30–31.

Gallarotti, Giulio M. "Soft Power: What It Is, Why It's Important, and the Conditions for Its Effective Use." *Journal of Political Power*, vol. 4, no. 1 (2011): 25–47.

Gill, Bates and Yanzhong Huang. "Sources and Limits of Chinese 'Soft Power'." *Survival*, vol. 48, no. 2 (2006): 17–36.

İpek, Pınar. "Ideas and Change in Foreign Policy Instruments: Soft Power and the Case of the Turkish International Cooperation and Development Agency." *Foreign Policy Analysis*, no. 11 (2015): 173–193.

Kaya, Ayhan and Ayşe Tecmen. "The Role of Common Cultural Heritage in Extrenal Promotion of Modern Turkey: Yunus Emre Cultural Centres." *Istanbul Bilgi University European Institute*, Working Paper 4 (2011).

Keohane, Robert O. and Joseph S. Nye Jr. *Power and Interdependence*. London: Pearson, 2011: 216–223.

Mead, Walter Russell. "America's Sticky Power." *Foreign Policy*. October 29, 2009. https://foreignpolicy.com/2009/10/29/americas-sticky-power/ (accessed August 4, 2020).

Mingjiang, Li. "China Debates Soft Power." *Chinese Journal of International Politics*, no. 2 (2008): 287–308.

Nye, Joseph and Richard L. Armitage. *A Smarter, More Secure America, CSIS* (2007): 1–83.

Nye, Joseph. "Get Smart: Combining Hard and Soft Power." *Foreign Affairs*, vol. 88, no. 4 (July/August 2009): 160–163.

Nye, Joseph. "Soft Power and American Foreign Policy." *Political Science Quarterly*, vol. 119, no. 2 (2004): 255–270.

Nye, Joseph. "Soft Power and Higher Education." MIT Forum, http://forum.mit.edu/articles/soft-power-and-higher-education/ (accessed July 5, 2020).

Nye, Joseph. "Soft Power." *Foreign Policy*, no. 80 (Autumn 1990): 153–171.

Nye, Joseph. "The Information Revolution and American Soft Power." *Asia Pacific Review*, vol. 9, no.1 (2006): 60–76.

Paradise, James F. "China and International Harmony: The Role of Confucius Institutes in Bolstering Beijing's Soft Power." *Asian Survey*, vol. 49, no. 4 (July/August 2009): 647–669.

Salcı, Tayfun. "Küresel İnsani Yardım Raporu: 'Dünyanın En Cömert Ülkesi' Türkiye." https://www.aa.com.tr/tr/dunya/kuresel-insani-yardim-raporu-dunyanin-en-comert-ulkesi-turkiye/1180618 (accessed February 5, 2020).

Tol, Gönül and Dimitar Bechev. "Can Corona Diplomacy Cure Turkey's Foreign Policy Isolation?" *Middle East Institute*, April 29, 2020.

Wang, Yiwei. "Public Diplomacy and the Rise of Chinese Soft Power." *The ANNALS of the American Academy of Political and Social Science*, no. 616 (2008): 257–271.

Chapter 9

COVID-19 Impact on Turkish Foreign Policy

Hüseyin Bağci and Ali Serdar Erdurmaz

The world that we must live in has experienced a very sensitive pandemic as Coronavirus that would affect every aspect of standard of living with a wide spectrum globally. And Coronavirus scourge put its all impact on the one hand in the health of society and economics of the countries and foreign affairs on the other hand. It seems globalization gets huge harm since every country should deal with this pandemic with its own potentials and powers without paying any attention to any other countries to get in cooperation to defeat this disease at all.

While the obligation of wearing a mask and keeping social distance and working from home would be standard of daily living, all countries try to enforce all opportunities to continue their economic welfare and social lives by adapting themselves to new normal conditions dictated by pandemics.

Even though the pandemic is prevailing in every aspect of the life of the states, there is no change in the problems of the foreign policy of every country.

US president Donald Trump's motto "America First" indicates its conservative foreign policy that Mr. Trump does not intend to continue US traditional superpower foreign policy either in the Middle East, Asia, or Northern Africa; instead, he wants to focus on internal affairs especially with the new world order of Coronavirus pandemic (Talad 2020). In the wake of Coronavirus, President Trump should deal with the foreseen new presidential election in November 2020 and recover the US economy that crashed because of the pandemic. That means, President Trump will turn his face to domestic issues primarily, and current foreign policy will be in second priority.

It seems that there is a consensus between Russia and China against the United States to contain Washington's global superpower leadership all over the world. Russia uses its military power to exist even in the Middle East and

Libya by establishing some naval and air bases in the region. While China builds up great infrastructure project "The New Silk Road-Belt and Road Initiative" (DW 2020d; Chatzky and McBride 2020) in Asia and penetrates the other regions of the world with its economic power (Harriet and Wim 2019), it makes the massive foreign investment all over the world (Falk 2013). That means either Russia uses its military power or China uses its economic power to contain and put pressure on the United States as a superpower and the one actor leadership globally to exert both kinds of hard power tools against it.

In Syria, Washington decided to withdraw its troops from Syria saying that the conflict with ISIS is over and ISIS has taken under control by the leadership of the United States (AL-Jazeera News 2018; Idrees and Phil 2018; Haass 2020). However, Washington is following new strategies to confirm its place in Syria by making some petroleum agreements with local invaders (PYD) and leaving some amount of troops to protect and control the petroleum regions in Syria against the Russian efforts to capture reserve areas by Russian Wagner Group mercenaries. The US secretary of state Mike Pompeo announced that the US military will remain to protect petroleum in Syria together with Syrian Democratic Forces (PYD) (DW 2020b). Immediately afterward the agreement both Ankara and Assad regime declared that this agreement was against the sovereignty of unified Syria (MFA 2020a; DW 2020a). In any case, leaving US diplomacy and forces from Syria pave the way for strengthening of Russia and China in the region to support Assad regimes that would secure his position much more than ever. And, Ankara feels alone itself to act free from the pressure of Russia and China. The future of Assad and Syria will be depending on Russian and Chinese influences and decisions anymore. For that reason, Ankara enforced to choose a political alternative to act in cooperation with Russia to prevent any attempt to build up a terrorist corridor by PYD/PKK just down the Turkish Syrian border. Thus, the Astana initiative has been born by tripartite (Turkey, Russia, and Iran) to deal with the Syrian problem in a peaceful way.

Russian economy most likely is being shrunk because of the Coronavirus and even before that pandemic, it was not sufficiently good because of the western countries' economic sanctions (Forolovski 2020). Deteriorating economic struggle probably will make Russia more cautious on Syria and Libya conflict in regard to military expenditures and economic aids. Despite the pandemic, Russia sent its fighter jets to establish two air bases in eastern Libya strengthening the growing Russian presence around the Mediterranean just like done in Syria to put its military expanding in Northern Africa using government-supported mercenaries of Wagner group (Dixon 2020).

Russia would like to have two different aims for been in Libya.

1) To obtain regional existence just in the southern side of the European Union and Mediterranean in respect to geographically with its military power by establishing bases in Libya.
2) To have diplomatic privileges as an arbiter superpower on regional issues and others such as Ukraine, conflict and military sanctions applied by the United States and Western countries as well (Ramani 2020).

Presumably that these two powers would not leave Syria in the short run.

Naturally, Coronavirus put a great impact on either economy or social life in Turkey. Nevertheless, all major foreign issue engagements shown below continue with all gravity despite the Coronavirus pandemic prevailing heavily all over the world and Turkey as well.

- Syria civil war has been going on with changing aspects regarding Turkey's involvement initially.
- Eastern Mediterranean natural gas reserves took all attractions and anxiety of littoral states of the Middle East, Cyprus, Greece, and Turkey, and even the European Union. In this context, Ankara has the determination to protect its International Maritime Rights.
- In compliance with the Eastern Mediterranean issue, Turkey involved in Libya Civil War to support UN-backed government in Tripoli.
- Political tension between Ankara and Washington keeps its gravity and needs to reset to improve again. The United States administration needs Turkey both in Syria and Libya to curb Russia.

TURKEY IN SYRIA

At the beginning of the Syrian crisis, Turkey's initial policy to topple down Bashar Assad changed later to prevent PYD/YPG to establish a "terror corridor" just below the Turkish border in Syria. However, these policies have been changed radically after the involvement of Russia in 2015 to bolster the Assad regime together with Iran.

Washington's failed strategy to fight against ISIS altered to support PYD/YPG as a proxy force made Ankara distance with Washington since Turkey considers that organization as a terrorist fraction affiliated with the PKK. This would be the main reason to enforce Ankara to get close to Russia (DW Türkçe 2018). The downing of the Russian fighter jet in November 2015 and the assassination of Russian ambassador Andrey Karlov in Ankara in December 2016 could not preclude the partnership of both countries.

Meanwhile, Turkey, Russia, and Iran held a meeting in Moscow amid this disturbance and announced a joint declaration. Consequently, series of meetings of the Astana peace process would be initiated, establishing in Moscow meeting, under the guarantors of Turkey, Russia, and Iran in January 2017. The main mission of the Astana peace process aiming at ending the Syrian civil war rather than to determine the future of the Bashar Assad regime as a complementary gathering of Geneva negotiations by the leadership of Russia. However, Ankara put reservation against the solution could include Assad in this process (DW Türkçe 2017). Meanwhile, in January 2018, Turkey executed Operation Olive Branch against PKK/PYD-YPG in Afrin region successfully (Cavusoglu 2018).

Eventually, Astana peace process declined when Russian-backed Syrian government air forces shelling on Turkish troops and killed thirty-five in İdlib region on February 27, 2020. Turkey set up and maintains twelve observations that were targeted by regime forces. In March 2020, President Recep Tayyip Erdogan and Russian president Vladimir Putin held a meeting to establish a reconciliation to provide stability in the Idlib region. According to the protocol annexed to the memorandum announced by both countries, first, a demilitarized zone will be established in 15–20 km deep. Second, a joint military patrol comprising Turkish and Russian military forces will be contacted both on M4 route connecting Aleppo-Latakia and on M5 route connecting Aleppo-Latakia. As a result, Ankara enforced to leave the control of both routes to Russia and squeezed the region west of the M5 route and North of the M4 route (Voltairenet 2018).

The problem of Syria now seems freezing because of the Coronavirus pandemic. However, Turkey preserves its current position in the Idlib area and western region of the Euphrates river. As a matter of fact, the Turkish primary target initially to topple down the head of Syrian regime Bashar Assad has changed later, when ISIS emerged, to fight against ISIS, and PYD/YPG. In this phase, especially Ankara achieved to prevent the terrorist corridor just near the Turkish-Syria border extending from the west of Euphrates river to İdlib.

Turkey's primary aims in Syria are shown below:

- To fight PYD/YPG terrorist organizations to secure Turkish sovereignty and national interests.
- To fight ISIS together with coalition forces.
- To topple down Bashar Assad and contribute to establishing a new government in unified and sovereign Syria.

At the point reached, Ankara achieved the first two targets and now tries to keep its current position in partnership with Russia and coordination with the United States.

While Coronavirus prevailing all over the world, President Putin determined to continue its Syria strategy and wanted to expand its military bases in Syria and ordered to begin negotiation on this issue (DW 2020c). These facilities make an opportunity, for the first time since World War II, to exist on literal of Eastern Mediterranean Sea to control air and maritime region free from depending on its motherland (Mercouris 2017).

Even though President Donald Trump has withdrawn all troops from Syria, he located certain number of soldiers to protect the petroleum reserve areas in the eastern side of the country. Additionally, the US government announced that it would support the oil agreement made by one of the US private oil company and PYD/YPG administration (Snell 2020). Turkey immediately condemned, but weakly, US governmental support saying that it is against the international law, illegal, and a violation of territorial integrity.

It seems very complicated when we look at the current map of Syria. The United States will keep its presence in the eastern and northern part of Syria and by going on to bolster PYD/YPG terrorist organization, while Russia has the intention to expand its military bases all along the Mediterranean Sea in the west of Syria together with Assad regimes. Turkey has its own troops in Jarablus, Afrin, and Idlib region. Iran has Hezbollah together with regime forces, nevertheless, after the death of Kasim Soleimani could not find sufficient ground to strengthen its position anymore.

Meanwhile, despite Coronavirus, Ankara has shown its resoluteness also in Iraq and on May 27, 2020, Operation Claw-Eagle air assault has been launched in Qandil Mountains, the Sinjar District, and Makhmur in the northern Iraq region by Turkish Air Forces, followed by Operation Tiger Pawn carried out by Land Forces in order to destroy terrorist bases to prevent infiltration of PKK and PYD terrorist groups over Turkey (Anadolu Ajansı 2020).

Nothing new in the Syrian front for Turkey in the era of Coronavirus pandemic, Ankara should keep its strategy within the determination to protect its national interest and actions of Kurdish terrorist groups coming from beyond the border. Actually, after withdrawing of the US forces, the aggressive action of PYD/YPG significantly decreased since retaliation is highly probable and would be put in action by Turkey immediately (CNBC 2019). But, in Idlib province, Turkey must maintain peace and stability with its dignity and cooperation with Russia.

Turkey in Libya

We have been witnessed with anxiety that peace and stability could not be established there after the death of Qadhafi. As a result, the United States withdrew over Libya, but Russia is still there. Today there is an endless conflict and civil war in this country also with foreign forces involved according to their own national interests.

As is known, there are two sides who claim the governance of the country now. The Government of National Accord (GNA) which was installed in Tripoli in March 2016 under Fayez al-Sarraj as Prime Minister is the only legitimate government recognized by the UN and supported by Italy, Britain, and Turkey. On the other hand, the government of Tobruk, also known as the Provisional Government, is backed by regional power-Egypt, the UAE and Saudi Arabia, Russia, and France as EU member states. In May 2014, former general Khalifa Haftar, a prominent figure who participated in the civil war since 2011, established Libyan National Army (LNA) and launched "Operation Dignity" that claimed to aim primarily to restore security in the east of the country-Benghazi region against the so-called terrorist groups indicating a wide range of Islamist groups.

In June 2014, a new election was held aiming to create a Council of Deputies, which GNC was supposed to turn over to it. But Islamist party rejected to accept the victory of the secular side and left away from GNC and coerced the newly elected House of Representatives to flee from Tripoli and it moved to Tobruk allying with the Khalifa Haftar's LNA. As a result, the House of Representatives that fled to Tobruk established its own financial institutions to control the oil revenues of the National Oil Company and Central Bank of Libya. In this wain, some of the Islamist militias launched "Operation Libya Dawn" to capture Tripoli International Airport against the militia group which had announced to ally with general Khalifa Haftar.

In 2016, the UN has taken an initiative to form an interim government for Libya, a new government established under Fayez al-Sarraj, Prime Minister, as the GNA. Nevertheless, the House of Representatives previously promised to recognize but later refrained to recognize the GNA, requesting to new election to take place in 2018.

In May 2019, LNA launched a military operation against GNA and local militants aimed to capture and control Tripoli. This attack coincided with just before the National Dialog Conference to set up a map for security, economics, and political issues of Libya under the umbrella of the UN.

In November 2019, Ankara has signed a maritime agreement with GNA, which was also a mutual security cooperation between two nations. Air defense system, UAV, and official supervisors and counselors, arms and equipment support have been provided by Turkey to strengthen GNA in the framework of this agreement.

In January 2020, multilateral diplomatic initiatives put endeavors to realize political dialog and ceasefire agreement however, a temporary truce attempt failed made by Turkey and Russia on January 12, 2020. On January 19, Germany and UN Security Council Permanent Members in participation with Turkey held a conference in Berlin to ensure durable solution to end hostilities and bring lasting peace. Nevertheless, both leaders of GNA and LNA did not commit to a ceasefire and sign the 55-point Berlin Communique (United Nations Security Council 2020). But, at the end of the conference, all participants announced that they are against solving problems using military forces but the peaceful process (Blanchard 2020).

Later UN developed a draft ceasefire agreement for conflicting parties but upon the achievement of GNA backed by Turkish military experts and unmanned combat aerial vehicles forced the LNA to withdraw from Tripoli region in April. By June, the frontline has shifted toward the western outskirts of Sirte and Al Jufra airbase, where Russian aircraft were located to operate from (Blanchard 2020). Even though Egypt had proposed the removal of all foreign mercenaries from Libya and lay down all sides arms to solve the current situation, GNA did not comply with the offer and continued to advance toward Sirte.

In June, Turkish foreign minister Mevlut Cavusoglu came up with a plan that would be discussed with GNA officials to establish two military bases, for future use of Turkish forces in Libya (Coskun and Gumrukcu 2020). Al Watiya airbase and Misrata naval base were on the agenda for Turkey. Using the naval base particularly would strengthen Turkey's presence in the Eastern Mediterranean Sea on the issue of natural gas resources conflict against Arab and European adversaries.

On June 20, Egyptian president Abdel Fattah el Sisi ordered his army to be ready to carry out mission either inside or outside of borders, saying that intervention is a legitimate right to Libyan territory by Egypt, highly possible if Sirte and Al Juffra would be under attack which is our red line (Mourad 2020). Right after that Saudi Arabia, United Arab Emirates, and other Arab League members announced their supports for Egypt, but Russia warned all parties to solve this issue only in peaceful ways and negotiations in line with the declaration of the Berlin Conference (Teslova 2020).

In late June, both the United Nation Support Mission in Libya (UNSMIL) and the Arab League and also the US authorities expressed their peaceful settlement approaches saying that "*External actors stop fuelling conflict, cease all hostilities and military movements and uphold commitments to reaching a formal, comprehensive and permanent truce agreement under UN auspices.*" Later, Germany, France, and Italy participated in this good intend (Blanchard 2020). Whereas France has bolstered LNA under the leadership of Haftar to facilitate Paris policies on former colonies in North and West Africa (Demirtas 2020). In June 2020, a French frigate was trying to stop a Turkish vessel on the allegation that Turkey was smuggling arms to GNA illegally and Turkish warships did not allow the investigation of the French frigate. Consequently, a crisis arose between both countries and France took this matter to NATO (Rettman 2020). Eventually, France withdrew from the NATO operation.

David Schenker, assistant secretary for Near East Affairs at the State Department, said to Reuther about the European maritime mission in the Mediterranean Sea, implementing UN arms embargo to Libya is not sufficient since it is limited to the interdiction of Turkish military materials but not that of Russian's, UAE's, and Egypt's aircraft and military equipment send to Libya (Pamuk 2020). If they are serious enough, they must apply this process (arms embargo) to all sides without making any difference, he said. That means Europe and especially France has the hypocrisy to deal with its mission within NATO naval operation to enforce UN embargo without taking any sound action against countries that supported Khalifa Hafter.

The roots of French-Turkish disagreements mainly lay down on the below issues (Abdullah 2020):

- Growing Turkish influence in areas has worn out the traditional strength of French influence in North Africa.
- At the political level, Turkish support to GNA enhancing the military capacity and capability of them to defense Tripoli against Haftar led LNA backed by France lost an opportunity to control the capital of Libya.
- At the military level, Ankara's request to establish military bases particularly in al Watiya is a strategic loss for France because this base was under the use of France since the post-Gaddafi era for a long time (Abdullah 2020).
- At economic level, France was scared that Ankara would have control over the oil crescent in Libya.

Since France supports Haftar's LNA together with Russia contradicts the US vision which aims to keep away Russian permanent military presence in Libya as a priority, if Russia accomplishes to have bases just southern shores of Mediterranean Sea constitutes a sound new non-traditional threat to NATO and the interests of all allies as well.

On May 11, 2020, Egypt, Greece, Greek Cypriot Administration (GCA), France, and the UAE Minister of Foreign Affairs made a joint declaration on the Eastern Mediterranean and Libya, but Italy did not join the statement, denounced Turkey to break the stability and peace in the Eastern Mediterranean Sea region and Libya as well (Antonopoulos 2020) (Fr24news 2020). But Ankara, immediately, respond to this blame with the announcement made by Turkish Foreign Affairs spoke person Hami Aksoy, saying that this declaration has shown the hypocrisy of a group of countries who are seeking chaos and instability through the policy pretending that Turkey and Turkish Cyprus have no rights in the Eastern Mediterranean (*hurriyetdailynews* 2020).

On August 12, 2020, the spoke person of the Minister of Foreign Affairs announced that France should follow a more reasonable and discreet policy in order not to lose its neutral position and opportunity to contribute to stability (*hurriyetdailynews* 2020).

On the other hand, Turkey sees an opportunity to re-improve or reset relations with the United States. On June 9, 2020, Turkish president Recep Tayyip Erdogan said, after telephone diplomacy with his US counterpart Donald Trump, "*A new period may begin between the US and Turkey regarding the [Libya] process, and we had some agreements during our conversation, and such a step could be taken*" (Yackley 2020). Ankara is ready to turn its face again to Washington using the position in Libya to support UN-approved GNA (Jones 2020). In June, US ambassador to Libya, Richard Norland, explained the US positions emphasizing the importance of the LNA withdrawal from northwest Libya for durable arms truce and commencing political negotiations to end the conflict. And in his speech, it seems he underlined covered support in favor of Ankara as shown below:

> *It's time for all mercenaries and every one foreign forces to start to de-escalate and depart Libya. If there's one motto we're applying to the situation now, it's "Libya for the Libyans." Now, when you talk about Turkey, we have to recall that the real escalation in this conflict began with the intervention by Wagner forces from Russia in October, and the Turkish intervention was in reaction to that.* (Blanchard 2020)

That means Turkey contains the expanding of Russian role in Moscow, which eventually serves the interest of both NATO and EU either in Syria or in Libya (Yinanç 2020).

Libya is very important for Europe for three main points: security, immigration, and energy resources. Regarding security, Libya is considering a major safe haven for al Qaeda in the Islamic Maghreb (AQIM). Libya is an essential route for the massive African immigration to European countries. And Libya has great oil reserves called "sugar petrol" to indicate its quality operated by European energy companies; however, it could be changed if Russia strengthens its position as a dominant power in the country (Yildiz 2020). Despite these facts that will have a great impact on the EU did not interested in Libya crisis as an organization accept for Germany, Italy, and France individually. As a matter of fact, Turkey also implicitly covers and protects the interest of the EU by keeping its presence against Russia and France.

As it is easily seen, Turkey curbed Russia either in Syria or Libya since the United States is reluctant to involve and interfere with both issues directly and EU remains indifferent.

THE EASTERN MEDITERRANEAN NATURAL GAS RESERVES MULTILATERAL CONFLICT

The main reason for Ankara to involve in Libya issue seems geostrategic. According to the US Geostrategic Survey, the Eastern Mediterranean Sea basin contains natural gas worth approximately 1.7 billion barrels of oil (Shama 2019). Hydrocarbon discoveries in the Eastern Mediterranean basin have brought before main conflicting results in the region. Maritime boundaries and Exclusive Economic Zones (EEZ) in the Eastern Mediterranean have become subjects of disputes between Turkey and the EU and Turkey-Israel and Egypt. Meanwhile, Turkey has dissented gas discoveries by Greek Cyprus, EU member, until the Cyprus problem will be solved, since the Turkish side must have equal rights on it and must not be violated.

In February 2003, Greece, Israel, Greek Cyprus, and Egypt signed an agreement to establish an alliance that has left Turkey outside, even it has the longest border with the Eastern Mediterranean Sea, in its own backyard (Aydinbas and Dacey 2020). In 2004, Greek Cyprus adopted a law limiting its EEZ by twelve nautical miles. The EEZ is in compliance with bilateral agreements with Israel, Lebanon, and Egypt. Greek Cyprus delimited its maritime jurisdiction with Lebanon.

In this context, Greek Cyprus administration put in the agenda to the determination of the EEZ boundaries seen as a sovereignty problem by littoral states in respect to the international law, nonetheless, the EU has been forced to take part in the process as one of the sides, due to its member-Greek Cyprus maritime jurisdiction is acknowledged under the EU sovereignty region. As a matter of fact, European Union aims to create a common maritime jurisdiction for it and supports whole efforts to the delimitation of EEZ process and maritime border demarcation of its member states within the union or nonmember countries. In this process, obviously, member states have a great deal of advantages against the nonmember states. This privilege paves the way that the Greek Cyprus and Greece apparently follow to protect their national interests in harmony while establishing the European Union maritime jurisdiction and EEZ, the main reason that Turkey and the EU, together with Greece and the Greek Cyprus, stand out against one another, This confrontation seems much more political rather than international maritime law (Başeren 2013).

Thus, maritime boundaries and EEZ in the Eastern Mediterranean have become subjects of dispute between the European Union and Turkey. Since the perceptions of the EEZ either for Turkey or Greek Cyprus-UE are not matched, however, Turkey did not declare its EEZ delimitation yet (Turk Deniz Araştırmaları Vakfı 2019). Even though, Turkey and Greek Cypriot have overlapping claims of EEZ for offshore oil and gas against Turkey's reaction in the Eastern Mediterranean, Israel signed a military cooperation agreement with Greece in 2015 (Korzun 2018) while improving a strong defense and military relations with Cyprus (ekathimerini 2018). Three nations declared a commitment to develop deep military ties and the leaders of tripartite paid a joint visit to Washington in May 2018 (Korzun 2018). And, the US senate ratified a bill to promote security and energy partnerships with Greece, Israel, and Greek Cyprus. This bill obviously pointed out that the United States has given unquestionable support to the Greek Cypriot as well as Greece and Israel (Government of the US 2019). Meanwhile, the bill has an item about Turkey's S-400 purchase from Russia:

> It is the policy of the USA to strongly oppose any actions that would trigger mandatory sanctions pursuant to section 231 of the Countering America's Adversaries Through Sanctions Act (CAATSA) (Public Law 115–44), to include the purchase by Turkey of an S–400 system from the Russian Federation. (Government of the US 2019)

This bill banned F-35 fighter jets' sale to Turkey formally.

That is why the United States' political support of the Tripartite agreement is to impose pressure on Ankara by political sanction exploiting this issue due to the fact that Turkey has close relations with Russia on Syrian civil war and it is the determination to purchase S-400 ballistic missile defense system from Russia against the strong objection of the United States that Turkey as a NATO member must not go in such an agreement with potential hostile of NATO.

Meanwhile, the EU high representative/vice-president Federica Mogherini expressed union concern about Turkey's initiatives to carry out drilling activities within the EEZ of Cyprus, saying that:

> *In March 2018, the European Council strongly condemned Turkey's continued illegal actions in the Eastern Mediterranean. In this context, we urgently call on Turkey to show restraint, respect the sovereign rights of Cyprus in its exclusive economic zone and refrain from any such illegal action to which the European Union will respond appropriately and in full solidarity with Cyprus.* (European Union 2019)

In this vein, Turkey is against the effort of Greek Cyprus exploitation of gas reserves just around the island until the Cyprus issue is resolved, endeavoring that the rights of Turkish Cypriot are being violated and the Turkish navy shows its determination to block the drilling was made by foreign companies in the region. Since 2011, various confrontations between Turkey and Greek Cyprus have occurred in response to the exploration and development of hydrocarbon resources off the island's southern coast because the Greek Cyprus did not take Turkish view into considerations either on conflicting EEZ or TRNC must have equal right to share the discoveries. As a result, Turkey has deployed warships, to show its determination, to conflicting EEZ areas where international companies have conducted drilling and sent research vessels to the island's disputed EEZ to protect Ankara's maritime jurisdiction interests (BBC Türkçe 2019).

Meanwhile, transportation of natural gas by pipeline is another issue that ignores Turkish rights in the region. Trilateral Summit in Jerusalem composed of Greek Cyprus, Greece, and Israel with the participation of the secretary of state Mike Pompeo, on March 20, 2019, reached an agreement to realize East-Med pipeline (EuroAsia 2019). In their joint declaration, it is stressed that they affirm their shared commitment to promoting peace, stability, security, and prosperity in the region and the US support for the trilateral mechanism established by Israel, Greece, and Greek Cyprus. Expressing "*The leaders agreed to increase regional cooperation; to support energy independence and security; and to defend against external malign influences in the Eastern Mediterranean and the broader Middle East*" that they demonstrate a sort of solidarity against external malign influences highly probably remarking Turkey during this vein (Release 2019). (In the Senate of the US, 2019). And undoubtedly, they formed an alliance against Turkey backed by the United States.

Up on those actions against Turkey, Ankara made very wise action to take sound respond and strengthened its positions to protect maritime rights and interests. On November 27, 2019, Ankara made an agreement on Maritime Boundary Delimitation deal with Tripoli UN-recognized government (GNA) in Libya and informed the UN after approval of both countries. Thus, Ankara has given clear massages to coastal states in the region that she is able to block East-West pipeline routes by this deal and any project can be realized by ignoring Turkey from now on (TRT World 2019).

At the end of July, Ankara has announced to send drilling vessels under the protection of Turkish Maritime Forces warlords to conflicting sea regions to make research emerged crises both in Greece and the EU. However, Chancellor Merkel made a phone call to either Recep Tayyip Erdogan or Greece prime minister Michotakis to prevent potential conflict in the sea region (DW Türkçe 2020).

On August 6, 2020, Greece and Egypt signed an agreement designating an economic exclusive zone in the Eastern Mediterranean between two countries and Ankara denounced right away, saying that

> a maritime boundary between Greece and Egypt does not exist. With reference to Turkey, the so-called maritime delimitation agreement signed today is null

> and void. This understanding will reflect on the bottom and at the table. The supposedly delimited area lies within the Turkish continental shelf as declared to the United Nations. . . . It is without a doubt that Turkey won't allow any activity at the area in question and can resolutely still defend its legitimate rights and interests as well as those of the Turkish Cypriots within the Eastern Mediterranean. (MFA 2020b)

Eventually, on August 7, 2020, Turkish president Recep Tayyip Erdogan announced Turkey would resume carrying out a seismic survey in the designated area in the south of Karpathos, Rodos, and Kastellorizo/Meis in the middle of the Greek-Egyptian maritime deal (SHOD 2020).

Greece and Greek Cypriot immediately called the EU to denounce Turkey right after Ankara declared Navtex to make drill in a certain region in the sea basin considered continental shelf after Egypt and Greece signed a controversial maritime demarcation agreement (Guler n.d.). Nevertheless, they did not get any sound support from the EU member states, especially Germany, and by the administration of EU since Germany was head of the council for six months (EU Affairs 2020).

CONCLUSIONS

Even though Coronavirus pandemic has been continuing its impact gradually increasing all over the world, foreign affairs of the countries have been going on without interruption. Moreover, states spend all efforts to get benefits and to convert this disease as an advantage or opportunity to overcome in the face of their rivals. However, we have witnessed while governments on the one side spend their utmost effort vanquishing the Coronavirus pandemic and its social and economic effects on the other side, they pursue obstinately their foreign policy in compliance with their national interests and goals.

In this framework, the United States proceeds its trade wars with China outside and prepares itself for the presidential election held in November 2020 with all its mighty. Along with those troubles Washington has other problems in Iran, Syrian regime and Russia and in Libya even Washington is reluctant to engage. However, sanctions applied upon Iran and Russia in addition to Coronavirus huge impact on social and economic lives in both countries. Meanwhile, Washington deployed a number of troops to secure the oil reserve areas in Iraq and Syria as well and will keep its presence in low profile.

Russia even has a great negative influence of Coronavirus in its continent and focused all efforts to find a vaccine for the disease. In foreign policy, it continues its determination according to its "Russia superpower again" policy either in its neighborhood like Belarus and Ukraine and the Middle East or

Libya. Putin does not refrain to interfere in the domestic politics of Belarus and Ukraine covertly and pursue its support to Bashar Assad together with Iran. Moreover, Putin wants to be a prime game changer in Libya playing a bilateral game with both GNA and LNA. But, sending fighting aircraft to Al Juffra airport revealed his real intention against the US policy. In any case, Russia insistently follows its foreign policy strategy in harmony with its national interests despite the Coronavirus pandemic. Russia's ambition as a superpower was sustained stubbornly all in all.

China is a central source of the Coronavirus pandemic that seems to get control of the spreading of disease in the country. Xi Jinping using its economic mighty to maintain a trade war with the United States and improve its infiltration to Asian and North African cities gradually.

Ankara is aware of the pandemic and mobilizes all resources to take control of the pandemic effects of social life, economics, and health domestically. Besides, Turkey pursues a foreign policy in all troubled areas with decisiveness. In Syria, security and stability measures in Idlip region have been continually coordinated actions with Russia. In Astana's cooperation with Russia and Iran, Ankara controls both countries intend in Syria may get benefit to the United States. On the other hand, Ankara has been executing military operations against PKK, PYD/YPG terrorist organizations in Syria and Iraq. Ankara maintains its back to GNA and constrains Russian greed in Libya should contribute to the US and EU policies in the region indirectly.

The states which have sound diplomatic traditions may be affected by such pandemics and natural disasters temporarily. However, recovering in a short time, they continue and maintain their foreign policy to cope with all troubles in coordination with their national interests and strategy. And, Turkey is in the same position as a state has sound diplomatic tradition coming from its deep history.

REFERENCES

Abdullah, Bilal. 2020. "French-Turkish-Disagreements-in-Libya-Dynamics-and-Prospects." Emirates Policy Center. https://epc.ae/brief/french-turkish-disagreements-in-libya-dynamics-and-prospects.

AL- Jazeera News. 2018. "US Plans Complete Withdrawal of Troops from Syria: Officials." Al Jazeera. https://www.aljazeera.com/news/2018/12/weighs-complete-withdrawal-troops-syria-media-181219143708576.html.

Anadolu Ajansı. 2020. "Turkey Launches Operation Claw-Eagle." Ankara: Anadolu Ajansı. https://www.aa.com.tr/en/turkey/turkey-launches-operation-claw-eagle/1877001.

Antonopoulos, Paul. 2020. "Greece, Egypt, Cyprus, France and the United Arab Emirates Denounce Turkey in Joint Statement." Greek City Times. https://

greekcitytimes.com/2020/05/12/greece-egypt-cyprus-france-uae-denounce-turkey-in-joint-statement/.

Aydinbas, Asli, and Julian Barnes Dacey. 2020. "Eastern_med @ Www.Ecfr.Eu." Ecfr.Eu. 2020. https://www.ecfr.eu/specials/eastern_med.

Başeren, Sertaç Hami. 2013. "Doğu Akdeniz Deniz Yetki Alanlarında Hukuk ve Siyaset." In *Doğu Akdeniz Deniz Yetki Alanlarında Hukuk ve Siyaset*, edited by Sertaç Hami Başeren, 1st ed. Ankara: A. Ü. Siyasal Bilgiler Fakultesi. http://politics.ankara.edu.tr/dergi/kitap/2013/Dogu-Akdenizde-Hukuk-ve-Siyaset.compressed.pdf.

Blanchard, M. Christopher. 2020. "Libya: Conflict, Transition, and U.S. Policy." Washington, DC. www.crs.gov.

Cavusoglu, Mevlut. 2018. "The Meaning of Operation Olive Branch." Foreign Policy. 2018. https://foreignpolicy.com/2018/04/05/the-meaning-of-operation-olive-branch/.

Chatzky, Andrew, and James McBride. 2020. "Chinas-Massive-Belt-and-Road-Initiative @ Www.Cfr.Org." https://www.cfr.org/backgrounder/chinas-massive-belt-and-road-initiative.

CNBC. 2019. "Kurds Mobilize in Syria as Turkey Poised for Imminent Attack." CNBC. https://www.cnbc.com/2019/10/09/syria-kurds-mobilize-as-turkey-poised-for-imminent-attack.html.

Coskun, Orhan, and Tuvan Gumrukcu. 2020. "Turkey Eyes Libya Bases for Lasting Military Foothold: Source." https://www.reuters.com/article/us-libya-security-turkey-russia-idUSKBN23M1D9.

Demirtas, Ali. 2020. "How Turkey Sees COVID-19 as a Foreign Policy Opportunity." responsiblestatecraft. https://responsiblestatecraft.org/2020/04/29/how-turkey-sees-covid-19-as-a-foreign-policy-opportunity/.

Dixon, Robyn. 2020. "Russia's Ally in Libya Is Battered by Defeats. But Moscow Has Wider Goals to Expand Its Influence." *The Washington Post*. https://www.washingtonpost.com/world/europe/russia-libya-war-putin/2020/06/05/c3956bf4-a109-11ea-be06-af5514ee0385_story.html.

DW. 2020a. "Ankara'dan SDG'nin Petrol Anlaşmasına Tepki." DW. https://www.dw.com/tr/ankaradan-sdgnin-petrol-anlaşmasına-tepki/a-54416481.

———. 2020b. "Pompeo: ABD Askerleri Petrol Için Kalacak." DW. https://www.dw.com/tr/pompeo-abd-askerleri-petrol-için-kalacak/a-51257041.

———. 2020c. "Russia Aims to Boost Military Facilities in Syria." DW. https://www.dw.com/en/russia-aims-to-boost-military-facilities-in-syria/a-53624765.

———. 2020d. "What Is China's World Order for the 21st Century?" DW. 2020. https://www.dw.com/en/what-is-chinas-world-order-for-the-21st-century/a-54368354.

DW Türkçe. 2017. "Dört Soruda Astana Görüşmeleri." DW üirkçe. https://www.dw.com/tr/dört-soruda-astana-görüşmeleri/a-38672495.

———. 2018. "Türkiye'nin 7 Yıllık Suriye Politikası." DW üirkçe. https://www.dw.com/tr/türkiyenin-7-yıllık-suriye-politikası/a-42980399.

———. 2020. "Merkel Kıta Sahanlığı Gerginliğinde Devreye Girdi." DW üirkçe. https://www.dw.com/tr/merkel-kıta-sahanlığı-gerginliğinde-devreye-girdi/a-54268852.

EU Affairs. 2020. "Together-for-Europe-s-Recovery-Germany-Takes-over-Council-Presidency @ Www.Europarl.Europa.Eu." EU News. https://www.europarl.europa.eu/news/en/headlines/eu-affairs/20200624STO81905/together-for-europe-s-recovery-germany-takes-over-council-presidency.

Falk, Taylor. 2013. "Chna's Massive Foreign Nvestment, in One Map." ZDnet. https://www.zdnet.com/article/chinas-massive-foreign-investment-in-one-map/.

Forolovski, Dmitriy. 2020. "The Pandemic May Change Russia's Calculus in the Middle East." Al Jazeera. https://www.aljazeera.com/indepth/opinion/pandemic-change-russia-calculus-middle-east-200413135440728.html.

Fr24news. 2020. "Greece-Egypt-Cyprus-France-and-the-United-Arab-Emirates-Denounce-Turkey-in-a-Joint-Declaration." Fr24news. https://www.fr24news.com/a/2020/05/greece-egypt-cyprus-france-and-the-united-arab-emirates-denounce-turkey-in-a-joint-declaration.html.

Guler, Sena. n.d. "Greece, Greek Cypriot Adm Empty-Handed from EU Meeting." Anadolu Ajansı. Accessed August 15, 2020. https://www.aa.com.tr/en/europe/greece-greek-cypriot-adm-empty-handed-from-eu-meeting/1942432.

Haass, Richard. 2020. "Present at the Disruption @ Www.Foreignaffairs.Com." *Foreign Affairs*, 2020. https://www.foreignaffairs.com/articles/united-states/2020-08-11/present-disruption?utm_medium=newsletters&utm_source=twofa&utm_campaign=Present at the Disruption&utm_content=20200814&utm_term=FA This Week - 112017.

Harriet, Moynihan, and Wim Wim. 2019. "China's Growing Global Role and the Impact of International Law." World Economic Forum. https://www.weforum.org/agenda/2019/02/chinas-growing-global-role-and-the-impact-of-international-law/.

hurriyetdailynews. 2020. "Turkey-Slams-Joint-Statement-by-Five-Nations-on-East-Med-Sea-Libya-154679 @ Www.Hurriyetdailynews.Com." Hurriyetdailynews. https://www.hurriyetdailynews.com/turkey-slams-joint-statement-by-five-nations-on-east-med-sea-libya-154679.

Idrees, Ali, and Steward Phil. 2018. "Trump Starts Withdrawal of U.S. Forces from Syria, Claims Victory." Reuters. https://www.reuters.com/article/us-usa-trump-syria-idUSKBN1OI1JC.

Jones, Dorian. 2020. "Analysts See Thaw in US-Turkish Relations." VOA. https://www.voanews.com/usa/analysts-see-thaw-us-turkish-relations.

Mercouris, Alexander. 2017. "Russia's Military Bases in Syria." DW. https://theduran.com/russias-bases-syria/.

MFA, Turkey. 2020a. "No: 159, 3 August 2020, Press Release Regarding the Announcement of the Oil Contract Signed by the 'Syrian Democratic Forces', Which Is Led by the PKK/YPG Terrorist Organization." Ankara: MFA. http://www.mfa.gov.tr/no_-159_-pkk-teror-orgutu-gudumundeki-suriye-demokratik-guclerinin-yaptigi-duyurulan-petrol-anlasmasi-hk.en.mfa.

———. 2020b. "No: 165, 6 August 2020, Press Release Regarding the Signing of a So-Called Maritime Delimitation Agreement between Greece and Egypt." Ankara: MFA, Turkey. http://www.mfa.gov.tr/no_-165_-yunanistan-ile-misir-arasinda-sozde-deniz-yetki-alanlari-anlasmasi-imzalanmasi-hk.en.mfa.

Mourad, Mahmoud. 2020. "Egypt Has a Legitimate Right to Intervene in Libya, Sisi Says." Cairo: Reuters. https://www.reuters.com/article/us-libya-security-egypt-idUSKBN23R0W1.

Pamuk, Humeyra. 2020. "Libya-Security-Usa-IdUKL5N2EN60K @ Uk.Reuters.Com." Reuters. https://uk.reuters.com/article/libya-security-usa-idUKL5N2EN60K.

Ramani, Samuel. 2020. "Russia's Strategy in Libya." RUSI. https://rusi.org/commentary/russias-strategy-libya.

Rettman, Andrew. 2020. "France and Turkey Fracture Nato on Libya." Brussels: euobserver. https://euobserver.com/foreign/148704.

Shama, N. Nael. 2019. "The Geopolitics of a Latent International Conflict in Eastern Mediterranean." El Jezeera. 2019. https://studies.aljazeera.net/en/reports/2019/12/geopolitics-latent-international-conflict-eastern-mediterranean-191223074025635.html.

SHOD. 2020. "Antalya-Navtex-Station @ 212.174.0.150." SHOD. Antalya. 2020. http://212.174.0.150/shodb_esas/index.php/en/safety-of-navigation/navigational-warnings/antalya-navtex-station.

Snell, Joe. 2020. "Turkey Joins Syria in Slamming Oil Agreement between US Firm, Syrian Kurds." Al Monitor. https://www.al-monitor.com/pulse/originals/2020/08/intel-turkey-syria-slam-oil-agreement-kurds-sdf-kobani.html.

Talad, Khalid. 2020. "China's Economic Revolution & World Power Politics." The Prodesi. 2020. https://theprodesi.com/china-economic-revolution-world-politics/.

Teslova, Elena. 2020. "Russia Urges Libyan Warring Sides to Declare Cease-Fire." Ana. https://www.aa.com.tr/en/middle-east/russia-urges-libyan-warring-sides-to-declare-cease-fire/1887168.

TRT World. 2019. "Why-Did-Turkey-Sign-a-Maritime-Deal-with-Libya-32064 @ Www.Trtworld.Com." TRT World. 2019. https://www.trtworld.com/turkey/why-did-turkey-sign-a-maritime-deal-with-libya-32064.

United Nations Security Council. 2020. "Letter Dated 22 January 2020 from the Permanent Representative of Germany to the United Nations Addressed to the President of the Security Council." New York: UN Security Council. https://www.securitycouncilreport.org/un-documents/document/s-2020-63.php.

Voltairenet. 2018. "Memorandum on Stabilization of the Situation in the Idlib De-Escalation Area." Voltairenet. https://www.voltairenet.org/article203066.html.

Yackley, Ayla Jean. 2020. "Turkey Sees Success in Libya Shaping Relations with US." Al Monitor. https://www.al-monitor.com/pulse/originals/2020/06/turkey-libya-war-us-relations.html.

Yildiz, Guney. 2020. "How-Russia-and-Turkey-Sidelined-Europe-on Libya." Middle East Institute. 2020. https://mei.edu/publications/how-russia-and-turkey-sidelined-europe-libya.

Yinanç, Barcin. 2020. "The Contrast in Turkey's Relations with France and Russia." Istanbul: Hurriyetdailynews. https://www.hurriyetdailynews.com/opinion/barcin-yinanc/the-contrast-in-turkeys-relations-with-france-and-russia-156921.

Chapter 10

New World Order in Post-Pandemic Process and Turkey

Hüsamettin İnaç

INTRODUCTION: A GENERAL OVERVIEW OF THE CONCEPT "WORLD ORDER" WITH THE THEORETICAL AND HISTORICAL BACKGROUND

Global security, the international system, the distribution of national powers, and the concept of world order itself are controversial and interchangeable words in the international relations discipline. The elements and capacities of national powers and capacities owned by the states since the period when the modern states have emerged, and the relations initiated among them determine the distribution of powers within the state system. Depending on this distribution, while a coercive peace term shaped by one hegemon state, all global conditions determined by this dominant actor were experienced, it was possible to witness a chaotic period in which no state had a capacity to dominate over the international system alone. Even though the concept "world order" has been frequently used together with or substituted by the term "international system," both of them represent different meanings and evocations. As a matter of fact, the international system refers to the organic functioning mechanism resembling the human body depending upon the roles played by each state over the relations established among the actors within the framework of internationally accepted norms and rules. On the other hand, the "world system" is the name of a system of structures which has been shaped by the international economic and political coalitions and cooperation. The structure here describes the modalities of thought and action constituted by the people, states, corporations, NGOs, and multilateral institutions.

The world order and its structures have been shaped by the short- and long-term security interests of the preponderant actors as well as the value and belief system of the dominant powers (Cox 1987, 43). The modern structural framework of the world order and the international relations that have been formed by this order are positioned in line with the Westphalian nation-building project and strategies. The Westphalian period which has been referred to here begins with the settlement of the European peace negotiated in Westphalia as a result of the Thirty-Year Wars in 1648. Together with the peace agreement, the internal competition among the Christian sects has ended, the regnancy of the king has been consolidated, and the division of Catholic and Protestant has been removed to a great extent.

This situation has accelerated the necessity of land control and made the creation of the independent nation-state system easier. Consequently, the world order within the framework of these developments can be comprehended as the "equilibrium" among the interests of the concerned parties over the long-term core referential values of social actors such as liberty, order, and justice along with the Westphalian period and their short-term interests of national security (Hettne 2007, 74–77). Gramcsi who involved in the political dynamics holding their effectiveness within the society and the discussions about the "hegemony" points out that the dominant narrative is greatly shaped by the historical block, which has sufficient political power in order to have hegemonic power (Dural 2012, 310) such that this block is an essential actor which established the newly emerged world order. Nevertheless, the historical block formed by the political alliance among the different social powers is possible to be overthrown by other hegemonic power with alternative narratives and oppositions.

The Hungarian historian and anthropologist Karl Polanyi who has a different approach toward the world order defines the political dialectics which has been shaped along with the industrial revolutions in Britain during the eighteenth and nineteenth centuries as a "double movement" (Campbell 1992, 199). The extensification of the market, the fragmentation of the social security networks, and the narrative of the equilibrium among liberty, order, and justice create the first movement. On the other hand, the self-defense and the reaction of the society against the first movement create another narrative of equilibrium among the liberty, order, and justice that appeared as the second movement. As a result of the ideological struggle holding among the historical blocks, the final and ultimate equilibrium has been formed. The weakness of the civil society makes the conflict among the rival narratives inevitable. According to the Westphalian nation-state project, progress and modernization is one of the essential parameters for the sake of the survival of the state within the antagonistic atmosphere. Poverty and being underdeveloped is the outcome of backwardness. The security narrative has been categorized within the high politics is the basis of the contract signed between the state and citizens.

In fact, the narrative of security is so significant that any narrative cannot be prevalent because it is generally assumed that the citizen can sacrifice his freedom for the sake of protection from the dangerous and harmful. However, the state takes his legitimacy from his protection capacity for citizens. In addition, the national security is explained by the connection between the external interest of the state and his defense of internal priorities (Campbell 1998, 66–69). In this context, the welfare and justice are essential elements and parameters directly relevant to the security of state and internal stability as well as the use of forces against the attacks directed toward the sovereignty rights and the territorial integrity of the state-owned lands.

The international anarchy arisen from the perception of threat and danger in the Westphalian period creates a security dilemma which destroys the hopes for the favor of keeping the peace. In order to tackle this dilemma, it is inevitable to establish a balance of power among the concerned parties (Fierke 2007, 44). Every world order develops identity by shaping a balance of power among the prominent states, by inventing a way of legitimizing method reflecting the political entities and by implementing a sui generis mode of governance. The world order considered necessary for the international economic cooperation needs a prevailing actor who has the capacity to enforce and execute the internationally accepted norms and standards and to put and impose the sanctions when required. The world order leadership, historically, establishes a balance between the hegemony grounded by the soft power and the hegemony grounded by the hard power that applies coercive actions and measures the precautions.

PANDEMIC AND NEW WORLD ORDER

Following the spread of Coronavirus and the transformation of the epidemic into a pandemic, the world public opinion has precipitated a great debate about the forming of a new world order over the new positioning of global actors in line with the current world politics. Nevertheless, the world order brought along the Cold War and its institutions and organizations had the tendency to collapse before that time when the COVID-19 came to the fore because of many reasons. Essentially it is apparent that the bipolar world order formed by the United States as the triumphant state from World War II had critical discrepancies and these discrepancies turned into deadlocks. Actually, by exacerbating and pushing the USRR into another polar, the artificial ideological cleavages have been forged by exaggerating the communist threat and all Cold War institutions and organizations were designed merely for the sake of American interests. It was the initial weak part of this bipolar world system in respect of shaping the globally functioning mechanism.

American occupation of Iraq and Afghanistan as trundling out 9/11 terrorist attacks and being overwhelmed by its increasing strategic ambitions, a gross violation of human rights, and systematic torture exercised over the Muslim prisoners in Abu Gurayb jail in Iraq triggered the hostility and anger against American politics and world order. Moreover, the fabrication of the term Islamic terror by the NATO as the American-led organization to pave way for the clash of civilizations vitiated the prestige of the existing world system to a large extent. Correspondingly, the ideological and unfair attitudes of the international organizations to international conflicts as the outcomes of the Cold War period such as IMF, WB, UN, NATO, and European Council made the existing world order open to debate radically. However, globalization and neoliberalism as the ideology of globalization were far away from developing a fair and impartial commercial regime, it could not bring the conflicts and wars to a close and it could not produce the global solutions for the global problems. At the end of the day, a kind of global governance model could not be developed to solve the deep-rooted troubles such as poverty, unemployment, inequality of income, authoritarian bodies, terror, conflicts, uncertainties, and threats against the human health. As if that were not enough, the universal consents of the existing world order lost their persuasive characters in the course of time.

Primarily it became apparent that Russia, as the other of the United States, is not a strong state, as the United States claimed, and can find the realm of existence in as much as the United States allows. Evidentially, the United States demonstrated to weaken the Russian economy by manipulating the oil prices by force of Bretton Woods arrangement. On the other hand, it is evident that the United States is no longer a hegemon power as it is so far and the American adversary has strengthened and different trajectories and alternative polarities formed over this hostility against the American hegemony. As a matter of fact, it was widely seen that any American military intervention didn't reach its political targets anymore since the First Gulf War of 1991. In addition, the 2008 global financial crisis declared to world public opinion that globalization is not a security blanket as it was claimed previously and the intervention of nation-state is essential to tackle the economic crises as contrary to the past assumptions. Ultimately, it was started to put into words that the existing American-led world order formed over the conventional weapons, blackmails, and out of date perception of threat has a tendency to collapse.

In the midst of all this turmoil, the humanity encountered a Coronavirus surprisingly. This virus has accelerated the changing of the existing structure as a catalyst which has already slummed with its institutions, organizations, and working mechanisms. In other words, COVID-19 indicated this transformation apparently and demonstrated the weakness and desperation of the United States as well its losing hegemonic position and narrative.

Firstly, it is certain that the newly formed world cannot be constructed over the Russian and American disputes. Even it is gradually understood that the Russia and the United States act in concert in various scopes of the international issues from the beginning. From now onward it is time to mention about the China and United States as the two hegemon actors of the newly established world order. As a matter of fact, it was clarified that the rivalry between two states appeared as the division of digital realm into two distinct categories and this cleavage will trigger the outbreak of a new technological Cold War. The new order will be designated as "second edition Cold War" or "Cold War 2.0" (Rasmussen 2001, 217). In this futuristic perspective, the military tension will be replaced by financial and technological competition as a distinctive feature of the new era.

The story starts with an approach called as "Kissenger Doctrine" (Roham 2016, 41) which was developed approximately twenty years ago and envisages the direction of American and European private sectors' factories and the centers of production toward China as the low-cost labor, probably independently of the state. By means of the rapidly growing economic transactions, China became the inevitable primary actor in supply chain and production within the world by producing and processing the raw materials. In fact, China possessing 1.2 billion dollars of US bonds and bills gradually gained the wealth and capacity to impoverish the position of dollar as the global reserve currency. In addition to this singular and unexpected reality, the Chinese claim and declaration of having global leadership triggered the ruthless trade wars and led to erupt the cyber warfare and technology combats by opening new fronts for the fatal blows as the latest version of the combat. In this context, the main motif and concern which forces Trump's hands to fight with China is the idea that China achieved dominance over almost all global scopes such as technology, ecology, geopolitics, economic, and security issues as well as its economic performance as the leader of the production upset the balances in Chinese favor to a great extent. To make matters worse, China transferred the technologic competition into the international system and had an alternative infrastructure to US-led security, geopolitics, and ideology, particularly in 5G technology.

However, China lent credence to Trump's apprehensions by initiating some provocative actions starting from 2008 when the Olympiads had been held in Pekin. In this period of time, Chia was very silent, moderate, and precautious and confined itself with the policies limited with its region. However, China didn't refrain himself declaring "Belt and Road Project" which was known as "Silk Road" and "One Belt and One Road" at the early stage of the constitution period of the initiative, especially during 2013 (Köksoy 2017, 38). As a matter of fact, this declaration was a signal flare of the China's challenging appearance as a global actor and it demonstrated its policy to curb the control in seas and ports and implement preemptive attacks against the United States in various sectors for the sake of establishing global superiority.

In this period of time, it was witnessed that China gave notably African states a loan of money together with the backward, underdeveloped, and developing countries as exorbitant sum credits knowingly they are debts impossible to be paid intentionally in order to confiscate the debtor countries strategically important lands, islands, and harbors. As a logical extension of these policies, the issuing of the China Defense Policy Paper in 2019 expressing the statement that "China is decisive to build his own global security architecture by referring his own modality of value and cooperation" (Seibert 2019) became the final straw for the China-US relations. Above all, the president of China Xi Jinping's flamboyant pageant of seventieth establishment anniversary of China and its challenging and defying remarks against the United States during the ceremony was rather obtrusive:

> The Chinese nation made considerable progress by struggling together in past 70 years. In this day and age the socialist China has endured solid and survived within the east part of the world. None of the powers can unsettle status of our great homeland and any state can be obstacle on the almighty development of Chinese people and nation. (Çetin 2019)

On the contrary to severe hostility displayed by China, the United States had announced China as a "threat risk" in US Security Strategy Paper declared in 2017. In a similar way, that is the first time in history, in a declaration issued after the leaders' summit held in December 2019 in order to celebrate the seventieth foundation anniversary ceremony of NATO, China included into the top level in risk classification. However, Jens Stoltenberg, the secretary general of NATO, explained the Chinese policy of the alliance in this meeting with these words:

> We witness China while he makes an infrastructure investment in North Polar Region, in Africa, in cyberspace and Europe. We must comprehend the rise of China better. We must determine what kind of challenges and opportunities this situation brings to our security. (Bakıcı 2019)

Highlighting that they do not have the intention to create a new enemy such as China, Stoltenberg drew attention that the Beijing administration made progress to an extent to change the global balance of power and took the second place in defense expenditure within the world and invested substantially to develop new abilities. He pointed out that the Chinese army included approximately eighty ships and submarines together with shipbuilding and marine structures and developed long-range nuclear missiles threatening the United States and Europe.

Unfortunately, one of the most disturbing troubles for US-China relations is the seventh article of the China Intelligence Act declaring that "all Chinese citizens are obligated to support the intelligence activities of the state and responsible to cooperate and contribute to the central authority" (Köksoy 2020, 359). This article comprises so expansive and broad content that includes starting from 5G technology to Huawei extends over espionage, sabotage, biological weapons, artificial intelligence, biotechnology, and big data by containing evocations to unsettle the existing ideological order completely (Griffiths 2019, 47–49). In this context, the competing interests of China and the United States will dichotomize the world over digital technology and the new version of the Cold War will be redefined mostly by communication technologies on the basis of bipolarity.

The United States as the other pole of the newly formed world order was too weak to play a hegemon power in tackling the pandemics and could not behave becoming to peculiarities of the world leadership indisputably. In line with this comprehension, Trump administration preferred becoming introverted and struggling with the crisis on account of pandemics at national level. From the very beginning, the United States foregone conclusion became apparent since 9/11 2001 terrorist effects in consequence of its culture-bound separatist reactions instead of behaving moderately and prudentially. In the initial stage of the pandemics, the US authorities couldn't realize the peril of the situation which pandemics gave rise outrightly. Notably, Trump and his working team underestimated and ignored to cope with the COVID-19 rather focused on the approaches to be adopted and the trajectories to be followed during the presidential elections held imminently. Moreover, Trump attempted to trespass the destruction originating from the Coronavirus for the favor of himself during the election process and regarded it as a part of his competition with China by calling it "Chinese virus" within the daily press conference whose main theme was teasing with the medical authorities dealing with the pandemic. On the other hand, the autonomous character of the healthcare system and deprivation of many American citizens from access to social services and social security made tackling the pandemic difficult. Besides that the adequacy of the medical materials, protecting tools, test kits, ventilators are another problem together with the medical demands of the American provinces from different countries independent from each other as well as the inability of the federal government to the requests of help turned the crises into unmanageable dimension. In addition to this, Trump who goes to any extreme for the sake of winning the elections was rather quick in moving to the normalization process and revitalizes the economic situation which was on the verge of recession as much as possible.

However, another deadlock for Trump was China's way of struggling with the United States over the existing commercial relations. That is, the United States which has 16 trillion dollars gross national product and 24 trillion dollars debt had sold China 1.2 trillion dollars governmental bonds and bills in exchange for ordered production cost per year. Greatness of the amounts and its reflection into the political sphere felt the United States under the threat of China which will be expected to be the biggest economic actor within a decade by the prominent think tank institutions. Moreover, the China's declared public/health diplomacy to world public opinion over its glorious achievement in dealing with the Coronavirus fight disturbed the Trump administration extremely. Likewise, China sent health reliefs and tolls such as medical materials, protecting tools, test kits, ventilators to the European Union member states, especially Italy, Spain and used this help for the sake of hegemonic superiority as well as transformed its practice into the success story and exposed its greed and ambition in playing to global leadership.

In sharp contrast to the public diplomacy narratives and global leadership claims of the Chinese government, Trump administration accused China of reproducing the human-made virus snidely in laboratories and publicizing the pandemic late intentionally and killing or curbing the doctors and experts who concentrated on removing the illness as well as calling the COVID-19 as Chinese virus or Wuhan virus and the popularizing the usage of the Chinese Communist Party instead of the Chinese government.

These allegations which were perceived as the conspiracy theories at the initial term were turned into the propaganda process by consolidating with the concrete evidences and arguments such as China was not willing in sharing their data with World Health Organization (WHO), the shared data was distorted for the favor of proving the Chinese early success and the denial of collaboration request of the Europe and the United States by China. As it is easily understood the United States focused on putting into words the China's responsibility for the spread of virus on a global scale and requiring the payment of compensation for the damage arisen from the loss of lives and economic costs underwent all over the world. In this way, the diplomatic attacks of China became reversed surprisingly together with the escalating the crisis caused by the worthless and poor quality medical tools as aid materials sent to Europe. In fact, China taught a painful lesson by bringing out the truth that as a supply chain China rendered the United States and Europe helpless and desperate. It was nearly the end of cooperation among them in respect of losing confidence and trust mutually. In addition, the revision in death toll in Wuhan by adding 1297 more because of the Coronavirus on April 17, 2019, increased the suspicions felt to China vehemently.

In response to these developments, Trump took concrete steps without delay by turning the situation into an advantage by repudiating the accumulated foreign debts to China and recovering damages in substantial amount as redemption of the crisis. Moreover, as a contraty to the past American governments, the Trump administration accused the WHO of being a diplomatic mission of China and declared he will of pay anymore for the WHO as the specialized institution the UN. All these precautions served the huge damage that emerged from the pandemic regarded with severe economic results worse than 1929 Great Depression chalked China's negligence and malevolence. Actually, expected utility from these allegations and accusations to reduce the emerging acceleration of China and keep the United States as unique global hegemon power by winning the trade war and by getting rid of the Chinese threat.

From this point of view, the United States attempted to exercise influence over China by exploiting some sensitivities such as environmental awareness, opposition of consumption, injustice of the globalization, and excessive urbanization and biological weapons as did communist Russia during the establishment of the bipolar world order in post–Cold War period by abusing the universally accepted norms and values such as human rights, supremacy of law, and multiculturalism. As a logical extension of this approach, the United States supported the pro-democracy protestors opposing the proposed law of "restitution of the suspects to China" in Hong Kong initiated on July 20, 2019, persisted up to now. On the other hand, the United States provided financial and political support to an opponent wing against the existing Communist Party under the pledge of secrecy to change the regime in China. Consequently, it was ensued that the United States got off the ground to reconstruct China as "Other" replaced by the previous China that manipulated the WHO, produced the bioterrorism by spreading virus and jeopardized the whole world by reporting the pandemic too late and the rejected the cooperation with the "civilized world."

The possibly formed world order dependent upon goings-on related with positioning in challenging Coronavirus and methods and narratives referred during this process resembles the disputes and controversies which were exposed between Russia and the United States in Cold War period in many respects. As we mentioned above, the existing world order before the pandemic was in a tendency to collapse because of the various reasons because the controversies and contradictions arising from the distribution of power have become apparent since two decades especially from 9/11, 2001, terrorist attacks, the United States lost its hegemonic capacity because of the internal problems such as poverty, unemployment, injustice in the distribution of income, apartheid implemented for the black people, the violence of the police, the unclear election system, and lack of persuasive and plausible ideology and vision to be presented for the world public opinion. Therefore, the search of forming a new world order become inevitable and COVID-19 became an accelerative catalyst for this process to promote new values and systems preponderantly.

The main characteristics of the newly emerged world order have been shaped in accordance with the challenges with the pandemic and the troubles suffered all over the world for two decades. One of these characteristics to be expected is to get the globalization slower and each state will try to solve their problems brought about pandemic within their national frontiers as solitary, single-handed, and isolated from the global environment. Especially the rescue operations, the state interventions, and Keynesian precautions will be interceded, respectively, against the increasing unemployment and the serious poverty issues. Nevertheless, the opening up for the sake of promoting globalization some steps will be taken gradually in order to sustain the reconstruction of supply chain, agricultural products, food security, and human health and biological threats. In addition, putting the revolutionary developments in digital space in order within the political level will be the primary priority for the newly reformed system. The artificial intelligence, big data, internet of things, nanotechnology, and following the people with face reading systems and chips will become widespread and prevalent within the foreseeable future.

In this process, the subject of the transformation of state will be necessarily the main matter because of the changing character of the state activities and of citizen-state relations and of the realm of authority. From a first impression, the strength of the nation-state seems increased and enhanced by newly extended scopes of authority such as imposing restrictions on the individual freedom and widening the area of governmental disposal inevitably. However, the individuals are bound to renounce from some rights willingly and voluntarily if he/she feels his/her health and security is under the threat and tolerates the formation of more authoritative structures temporarily, especially during the pandemic period. Nevertheless, after getting over the pandemic completely the individual will find a way to confront and settle accounts mutually with his/her state in order to investigate or interrogate the incomplete and wrong implementations and take his/her rights back immediately. It is to bear in mind that the success story of China as an authoritative state and its propaganda made on the health diplomacy will change by reversal in a short span of time. Unfortunately, the authoritarian states of the Middle East will be objects of regime changes, military interventions, and migration waves resulted from the chaotic and anarchical environment.

In this new era, neither China nor the United States will lead the global issues because they lost their ability and reliability to have domination. Precisely because of that different global cooperation models and various power combinations will be essential during the establishment of new world order in order to deal with the global problems by filling a huge gap in the balance of power. As it was witnessed from the progress of the pandemic, it is impossible to solve a global problem like Coronavirus by means of isolation, protectionism, and most particularly within the national borders. The pandemic must be brought under control as a global problem, development of the vaccine and global remedy and the maintenance of the global stance against the probable new biological threats are directly relevant issues with the shaping of global leadership and hegemony.

Certainly, after this point the United States' allegation of global hegemony is not persuasive and plausible because of its great failure in managing the pandemic, the irrational policies it implemented on global scale, and its internal unsolvable problems that destabilize the country as we mentioned before. However, especially Trump administration has destroyed respectively almost all pillars deemed necessary to dominate politically. As a matter of fact, the main parameters to make America hegemon power has been eroded gradually: firstly, dollar as international reserve currency related to oil in Bretton Woods has faded away because of mostly preferring national currencies; secondly, military bases pervasive to almost all strategic regions have been withdrawn progressively; thirdly, the globalization and the neoliberalism as its ideology has lapsed from grace a considerable extent. In addition, the United States didn't hesitate to discriminate against its provinces and different segments of society and its fanatical patriotism in the economy with the discourses of "America First" and "Make America Great Again" (MAGA). Under these circumstances, asking the question is rather plausible: Is it possible for the United States to create a commonly shared wisdom in the public interests?

As regards to China, as it has been mentioned earlier, which has unreliable and untrusty production, worked behind closed doors, uninspiring with manipulative data drastically distorted the brand image of the country. On the other hand, the United States and EU seem decisive to perceive China as a threat and stop making Chinese production but it seems that China gets the United States and the EU closer and conduce toward creating a collective vision between them as common Other. In this case, China conceivably will lose out its privileged position it acquired in the global supply chain within the very near future. The United States and the EU agonizingly understood during the pandemic period that transferring all production to China cost them a lot such that they could not mask, ventilator, medical materials, protecting tools, and test kits. Even Russia who was surrendered by the United States holding the oil pricing power is bound to act against China in coordination with the United States and the EU.

China's inferring from being a production center will change all global balance drastically. By the China's exclusion from the production cycle, this production will be substituted by the Southeastern Asian countries neighboring China, India being in the first place. In this context, the states that manage the crisis well, protect their citizens, and have strong and solid health infrastructure, and have prudence in supervising the process will receive their shares during the redistribution of roles in global production significantly. Turkey as one of these countries for many respects such as its geopolitical position, its agricultural and industrial potential, its cheap, flexible, and qualified labor force, and working culture with the Europe as the negotiatory state with the EU will perform a significant role at the edge of constructing a new world order.

As a consequence, this world order which will be slated was characterized by these peculiarities: defined as Cold War 2.0 or new version of Cold War separate the world into two parts over the digitalization and technology, does not allow for the political domination of a single country, prevail the multiple leadership mechanism without any single superiority relations, and replaced the regional predominance and regionalism instead of universal hegemony and universalism. In this context, Turkey as a middle-size state will determine the Middle East, the Northern Africa, the Caucasia, and Balkan Peninsula as a sphere of influence and change its attitude and mentality in the Cold War period and not prefer to take sides with one hegemon power.

PANDEMICS FROM PAST TO PRESENT AND THE DISCUSSIONS ON NEW WORLD ORDER

The discussions on new world order are topical issues immemorially concerned with the global political analysis. Especially plagues, black deaths, epidemics have been perceived as the sociopolitical trends of change that triggered such kind of discussions during the history. However, Coronavirus became a harbinger of such a kind of transformation that will lead to the emergence of a new world order. For whom those argue this idea, nothing will be as before and the word economic and political system will drastically change, the number and the effectiveness of the authoritarian regimes will increase for a short time, and the globalization and neoliberalism will end and the serious power shifts will emerge in international relations.

However, we witnessed many times that nothing has been changed following the great events in spite of the contradicted ideas. Nevertheless, it can be argued that the correlation established between the pandemic and world order is rather significant. As a matter of fact, the same as it was today, the Italy-centered Black Plague suffered in 1337 rapidly and radically transformed the European fate and history by causing the loss of Church its prestige as a result of the sequence of events such as Reformation, Renaissance, Enlightenment, humanism, rationalism, and eventually modernism (İnaç 2016, 164). Immediately after this pandemic, the naval powers such as Spain, the Netherlands, and Portugal occupied and colonized new territories by moving toward the west called as the "westernization of west" and constituted a phenomena of "civilization" by universalizing their own national cultures (İnaç 2004, 36).

Another pandemic was lived in Britain where Newton invented the famous findings called Newton laws of motion during the self-quarantine period. Yet another one was the Spanish flu suffered in 1918–1920 which was effective in all Europe and United States became a very prominent factor in breaking out World War I by upsetting and disturbing the existing balance among the states (İnaç 2007, 27). Under these circumstances, the damages caused by the COVID-19 appeared gradually especially some new approaches and attitudes such as searching for national solutions against the global problem, leaving each country to their own fate, fortifying the national borders, and becoming the societies withdrawn strictly. In addition to this, according to the famous economists, the existing pandemic crisis creates more negative influence than the Great Depression of 1929 on global scale.

Essentially the discussions on the new world order were triggered by three main parameters. One of them was the distortion of the coherence and consistency among the global actors where the distribution of the roles was not functional anymore and each country felt threatened by another one and eventually the international order was disturbed. The second one is the inertia and stagnancy within the working of the system related to the lack of the hegemon power which has a capacity to regulate the operational mechanism as the last and third factor. In this context, these three parameters are reasons why we are looking for a new world order in recent years. Moreover, the UK as the empire on which the sun never sets was powerful and mighty incomparably in today's United States in which almost all institutions lost their prestige and inequality of income reached boiling point and the discrimination within the different segments of society more apparent as the Achilles' heels for sake of the alternative actors attempting to power grabbing. Therefore, the European Union, Russia, and the China became global actors because of the weakness of the United States in many respects. It is true that the United States is still superpower but not a hegemon power because it is deprived of the consent of the international community. For instance, the UK achieved to give an impression for the colonized societies that they are dignified and respectful to share alike and as if they are equal entities during the nineteenth century.

In fact, because the UK saw that the United States couldn't play its hegemon role conveniently, it desired to take back its previous position which was taken over by the United States in the aftermath of World War II as a result of the five-day bargaining process between Roosevelt and Churchill. Nevertheless, it was clear that the United States preferred to exploit its hegemonic position by applying economic nationalism and by satisfying its extreme strategic ambitions. Actually, who can argue that the United States dispenses justice and contributes the international peace and solidarity? Vehemently the United States refused the Russian offer a hand of friendship, escalated the disputes and cleavages, and triggered the ideological polarity intentionally in order to construct an "Other" required for bipolarity and build the institutions of the Cold War suspiciously as Roosevelt admitted to his immediate surroundings that

> We will establish a United Nations (UN) which we manipulate in order to serve for just the sole interests of the United States but we will reflect as if the UN works for the sake of protecting interests of the whole world. (Lukacs 2018, 57)

In line with this idea, the UN left almost all international issues delegated itself unsettled during its long history and that all issues were manipulated by the American interests turned the UN into the waste of the history. As a matter of fact, other fundamental institutions of the Cold War closely resembled the UN in many respects because they were formed by the same logic such as NATO, European Council, World Trade Organization, World Bank served under the global empire shaped by the United States.

As a concrete product of the NATO alliance, three mechanisms have been established in order to secure the US hegemony in newly established world order after the completion of the institutional architecture. One of them was the Bretton Woods system that established a correlation between the US dollar and the oil production (petro-dollar) and imposed it as the global currency (Dedeoğlu 2018, 57). Another important parameter that made America a hegemon power was its military bases launched in almost all strategic points of the world where the United States interfered these points by the excuse of appeasing the crisis or arise a crisis available to intervene (Dedeoğlu 2008, 97). During this military occupation process, the United States was abusing the NATO umbrella as the security and defense organization so that it was impossible to separate which one belongs to the United States or NATO powers. In this ambiguous and anarchical order, the United States made a military coup in a country desired to occupy and exploit, took over the regimes governed by the collaborators and mostly terrorist groups, toppled the regimes resisting the American system of exploitation, and exercised influence and power over the regimes by hybrid wars waged by the US-made terrorist groups. The third and last parameter used by the United States for being a hegemon power was globalization which made the circulation of the goods, services, workers, and capital all over the world without having an obstacle and neoliberalism which focused on the erosion of nation-state and induced the foreign direct investments, joint ventures, and multinational corporations instead of the strong states as the ideology of globalization. Moreover, the ideology of neoliberalism argued that these commercial institutions could replace the modern states in respect of giving identity, belongingness, and loyalty or having potential and capacity to wage a war or stop it.

This economic settlement was accompanied by so strong sociological pillars to form a perception of civilization and worldview that neoliberalism, for Fukuyama, corresponded to the "End of History" (Berting 2018, 77–79). In other words, as long as the phenomenon of globalization and the United States as its master exists, any alternative history, ideology, or mode of civilization no longer gets out into the realm of existence within the globe. As a member of this way of thinking Daniel Bell put forward a thesis of "End of Ideologies" during the 1960s and Francis Fukuyama asserted his thesis known as "End of History" at the beginning of the 1990s. Nevertheless, surprisingly, these argumentations which attempted to emphasize the superiority of the United States as well as its preponderant cultural and political system was started to investigate and criticize as a result of the American military intervention of Iraq against Saddam's aggression for Kuwait (Örs 2009, 10–11). During this period, the United States developed an attitude toward the Islamic values and all Muslims without any exceptions on behalf of tackling the brutality of Saddam. This assault damaged the reliability and the prestige of globalization which includes all people under commonly shared ideals without any ethnic, religious, and national discrimination (İnaç 2020, 39). This period passed into history together with being the normative values of globalization interrogated radically because the common values and collective interest were slough off and the clash of civilizations tended to rise as Samuel Huntington proved (Berting 2018, 95–96).

On the other hand, the fall of Berlin wall in 1989, the outbreak of the resistance movements against communism in Eastern Europe in 1990, and the declaration of the USSR (Union of Soviet Socialist Republics) its ideological collapse and economic bankruptcy as a result of dissolving the Communist Party in Moscow inflamed the initiation of a discussion on a new world order further (İnaç 2020, 41). Until the beginning of the 2000s, Clinton Administration adhered to the basic values and principles of globalization a considerable extent and sought after taking precautions to minimize the disputes and conflicts within the world. However, the United States brought peace and tranquility extended to the whole world and if this administrative mentality was kept, the United States would remain sole hegemon power long time when the USSR fades from the international scene.

Unfortunately, the geopolitical ambition of the United States and the war cabinet composed of the neo-cons and the appearance of 9/11 terrorist attacks dubiously made a new world order inevitable. Actually, this time human beings were confronted with a ruthless and brutal world and prognosticated the end of the American century by means of the sequence of events such as the American invasion of Iraq and Afghanistan (İnaç and Aktaş 2013, 8–12).

The remarks of Paul Wolfowitz displayed the prevailing visibility of the period apparently: "We are crusading not only for the invasion of Iraq but also the annihilation of the UN as a drawback of our expeditions" (Üstünel 2015, 76). It was the admittance of declaring their ambitions to change the world forcibly by snubbing the internal law, precedents, particular customs, and global balances.

In this respect, proceeding to the next step was possible with the financial crisis of 2008 in searching for new world order. Within this time period, the mortgage crisis arisen from the over credit facility, stock manipulations, and bad loans canceled out the market confidence and global security and triggered the social movements against Wall Street (Attali 2015, 124). Excessive state interventions, rescue operations, and monopolistic corporations shaped the economic structure of the period, nevertheless, thereafter overcoming the crisis the international community rejected and refused the corporative state model virulently. Even though it was expected that global financial crisis of 2008 paved the way to new world order in line with the Arab Spring of 2010 which was supposed to bring democracy, welfare, human rights, and tranquility for the Middle East and resume to proceed the sociological time repeatedly. In consequence of two important turning points anticipated and prospected world order in no way realized because the human being is enslaved by his regular practices, habits, and customs and conservative in maintaining the existing social and political order (İnaç 2018, 309). However, merely epidemics, pandemics, and black deaths had a capacity to change the world order and conduce toward a new world order without any exceptions.

CHANGING TURKISH FOREIGN POLICY IN POST-PANDEMIC PERIOD

The remarkable changes within the main trajectories of foreign policies followed by states became unavoidable as long as the economic and sociopolitical outcomes of the pandemic were more visible. It is early days yet in order to evaluate the cost of damage the pandemic left behind but it seems that new modality of relationships within the different levels established by the states will shape the global politics, power shifts, and alliances for the sake of determining the new world order. Moreover, while some states declared that they gained a victory to overcome the pandemic prematurely, on the other hand some states which could not expose the expected performance were completely defeated, failed, and crashed by the heavy burden of the Coronavirus. As a matter of fact, the fighting against the disease was the most important determinant in designating the brand value of the states as well as their ways of crisis management, health infrastructures, their relations with the external world, and the importance given for their citizens during this process.

At the first glance, regarding these parameters, it can be witnessed that the states having the administrative structure depends upon the pluralist, transparent, democratic, and open market economy-oriented values came to nothing from the process, while the authoritarian and even totalitarian states came through and made a strong impression on tackling the crisis in general terms. Nevertheless, for a short term it was understood that this perception of success couldn't sustain forever and it was not commonly held assumption indeed. In addition to this, the China as an authoritative and even totalitarian state announced that she entered into the process of normalization in the short run and implemented a public policy by propagandizing that she has a precious experience to share, qualified med kits to be donated, and proficient and wise experts ready to support all people. Nevertheless, contrary to expectations, the official pronouncement of the WHO became a very hot issue and frustrated the world public opinion on several counts. Firstly, the China deceived the WHO by hiding information about the number of case, mortality rate, and the exact time of appearance of Coronavirus and its speed of propagation as well as caused the rising of death tolls and financial losses within the world. Most importantly China rejected to take joint action with the international community and institutions and share their actual data about the latest situation, to crown it all; it turned the aid material sent into the means of propaganda despite the fact that the aid material is under the counter and out of standard production.

These realities were articulated with its leadership clash with the United States, its entrance into the hard discussion with the WHO, and going to the relentless trade wars with the global authorities drastically deteriorated the positive image of China on a vast scale. This situation made the US-EU relations closer around the common vision created by the perception of the common threat the first time in the near future. It should be pinpointed that the reapproachment of two sides of the Atlantic (EU-United States) will end up with the deactivation the China from being the center of production and supply chain of the world which provides China approximately to be economically hegemon power in twenty years.

The China's exclusion from the supply chain will change the global balance radically and the production will shift to its neighboring states notably India toward the Southeastern countries to great extent. In this context, Turkey is a very remarkable state with its capacity to manage the crisis, strong health infrastructure, and prudential policies and precautions to overcome the epidemic. Definitely, thanks to its positive peculiarities as mentioned below and the contribution of its unique geopolitical positioning, Turkey will receive its share from this redistribution of income and shifting the supply chain duly.

Indeed, in addition to its decisive advantage in the geopolitical position which will facilitate the logistic needs, its agricultural and industrial potential and qualified and skilled labor force and background of relations with the Europe extended to five centuries notably as a negotiator candidate with the EU will upgrade Turkey into the high-level position in configuration and hierarchy of states during the forming process of the new world order.

As mentioned before, newly established or prospective world order defined as new version of Cold War or Cold War 2.0 categorize the world over the digitalization and technology into two parts, and never allow having a mighty state's hegemony and create multiple leadership mechanisms depend upon a dominant power for each region. In this context, Turkey as a medium-size regional state will have influence over the Middle East, Balkans, Caucasia, and North Africa but will not prefer to take sides with mere one of the great powers by reorienting its mentality, attitudes, and views in post–Cold War period.

Although it is really hard to sit on the fence for a moderate-sized country like Turkey in spite of the pressures applied by the great powers, it is obvious that Turkey will not single out China or the United States by rejecting to be engaged. However, Turkey neither resigns from the membership of NATO nor desists from the Belt and Road Project. Especially its eyeful achievement in tackling the pandemic will differentiate it from the rest of the world in a positive meaning. It will give an additional new positive image to Turkey has never had before and at the same time this acquisition will reshape its relations with the world entirely.

In addition to its decisive advantage in geopolitical position which will facilitate the logistic needs, its agricultural and industrial potential and qualified and skilled labor force and its background of relations with the Europe extended to five centuries beside its recent relations within the extent of the Customs Union and the EU membership process. Turkey is a unique country which is secular, democratic within a great harmony and equipped with western/modern values, combined Islam and democracy together with the working open market economy, internalizing and adopting a rational legal judicial system will be cut out for cooperating with the European working culture by regarding the commonly shared past history. Besides that, the mostly repeated geopolitical importance of Turkey will become concrete in filling a gap made by China as its close-range with the Central Asia and Caucasia and passageway or transition country between East and the West. If we take into account all of these, it is easily understood why Turkey invests some mega projects to transform itself into a logistic center and an epicenter of global trade such as third bridge, third airport, Channel Istanbul, Marmaray (undersea connection with railway between two continents), and at least one airport project for every city.

INTERNATIONAL ORGANIZATIONS AND TURKEY IN POST-PANDEMIC PERIOD

Despite the fact that the USSR as a pole of the Cold War was removed in 1991, the outdated and constant existence and appearance of the Cold War period institutions is an impenetrably controversial issue to lead the global system to a stalemate. As a matter of fact, it can be easily and perfectly understood why the recent world deprived of having a working effective and influential order in case of analyzing the international organizations which were formed by the Cold War conditions.

NATO, as a leading and primary institution which was created in post–Cold War era, carried out to redefine itself within the period when it was believed that its reason of being was removed synchronically with the economic and ideological collapse of the Soviet Union (Aydın 2005, 251). Adopting a strategy known as Harmel Doctrine, NATO pointed the Islamic terror as a target in order to protract its length of time by exploiting the outcomes of 9/11 terrorist attacks. Eventually, NATO kept its positive image by refunctioning by means of "out of area operations" (Çomak 2010, 74) during the partition period of Yugoslavia.

In the Lisbon Summit of October 2010, NATO redefined itself as an evolving entity from being a regional defense actor into a global security organization in accordance with the new conditions of the changing conjuncture. However, in accordance with the strategic concept "Active Engagement and Modern Defense" (Akçadağ 2010, 89) NATO commits the alliance to prevent crises, manage conflicts, and stabilize post-conflict situations including by working more closely with international partners, most importantly the UN and the EU. It was the commitment to fight against new threats by means of new assets and new capabilities in a changing world. It was also determined that the essential values of NATO would not change even though the world has drastically changed by the phrase: "While the world is changing, NATO's essential mission will remain the same: to ensure that the alliance remains an unparalleled community of freedom, peace, security and shared values." Thus, the freedom, peace, and shared values would sustain the society always keep alive. New security risks were cyber-attacks, the proliferation of nuclear weapons, terrorism, instability, and conflict beyond the NATO borders including by fostering extremism, terrorism, and transnational illegal activities such as trafficking in arms, narcotics, and people. NATO member states form a unique community of values, committed to the principles of individual liberty, democracy, human rights, and the rule of law.

Unfortunately, NATO didn't conform to these ideals and norms stated in official papers, especially in areas related to Turkey. On contrary, NATO member states had good relations with some terrorist organizations such as FETO (Gulenist Terrorist Organization), YPG, and PKK which threaten Turkey and prefer to cooperate with them in solving the regional problems instead of Turkey as a confidential alliance. The reason behind this choice was the differences of the member states about evaluating the violence, marginalization, and terror, the proliferation of weapons of mass destruction and instability as well as the security matters caused by the failure state. Therefore, the mostly failed scope of the NATO is to struggle with terrorism and migration because that member states could not reach a compromise and settlement on these issues in their ways of definitions and solutions. Due to the fact that the NATO is bound to decide unanimously and prioritize the sovereignty of the member states by giving them the possession of the right of veto, it is not able to take the joint position against the asymmetric threats and accomplish to compound the different approaches in its structure.

Unfortunately, the NATO is caught unaware to confront some new challenges such as unemployment, breaking down the food supplying chain, dramatical decrease in the global growth caused by the pandemic. NATO is deprived of having an eligible mechanism to tackle the internal instabilities of world states, conflicts, and turmoil expected as a result of the collapse accompanying the COVID-19 pandemic. Moreover, it will be possible to witness that NATO gives its way to the multiple administration systems because of its inertia and stagnancy against the racist, chauvinist, marginal, and ideological movements that increasingly become visible over all Europe by losing its ever-decreasing prestige completely. If this international organization does not develop a model embracing to strive with the new troubles including the pandemic and global warming, contrary to its existing position that behaves as if there is no pandemic in the world, and new security architecture appropriate to the current situation, the NATO will probably lose its distinguished position within the foreseeable future.

As a transnational structuring model, the EU delivers an underwhelming performance in a similar vein with the NATO in respect of its struggle with the pandemic because of its dilapidated and old-fashioned structure together with its never-ending internal conflicts and clumsy bureaucracy. In the first stage, its tardiness in response to the pandemic, lack of particular mechanisms to deal with such a kind of threats, and prioritizing the member states their own interests by setting the ethos and common spirit of the Union aside are some of the reasons behind the complete defeat of the Europeans against the pandemic. On the other hand, the European value system and neoliberalism which promise to solve the global problems with global solutions and remedies suffered from the crisis seriously from the moment the first death knell was announced caused by Corona because all European countries closed their borders rapidly and disregarded the ideal of "Single Europe" (Berting 2017, 66) and even stole the medical supplies of each other by grasping them over the sea.

Germany, as a leading figure of the EU, seems to overcome the pandemic crisis by having a great success while France, Spain, and Italy slog on weathering the storm triggered by the COVID-19. It can be said that the EU didn't suffer from such a kind of weakness in its history in respect of clumsy decision-making mechanism, hapless trauma, and shock caused by the Brexit, as the first exit from the Union. In addition, the weak and narrow-minded EU leaders left the member states with their own fate, spoiled the richness and sources in bureaucratic labyrinths, and inexperienced and novice who have been newly elected and appointed to the new positions at the initial point of the Coronavirus.

It won't be easy normalizing the Turkey-EU relations in post-pandemic period because of many reasons. Firstly, the existing voting system in EU enables the small member states to have overrepresentation such as Greece and Greek Cypriot community willing to disrupt and poison the ongoing relations and prevent to set up positive agenda to improve them (İnaç 2016, 185–186). Above all, Turley-EU relations seem to be reduced on updating the customs union and the matter of readmission agreements. Regrettably, the EU keeps away from confessing the reality that Turkey was left alone to its own resources to manage with troubles related with the immigration caused by the turmoil within the region and Turkey again stands to host the maximum immigrants all over the world in proportion to its national income (Açıkgöz 2015, 44–46). In response to this, Turkey is bound to prefer to develop bilateral relations with Germany, Poland, Spain, Portugal, and Italy apart from the union level.

On the other hand, the UN holds in the pledge of five members of Security Council as the United States, Russia, China, the UK, and France that President Erdogan criticized this situation with the warning of "the world is bigger than five." The exclusive veto right and the balance established among these states put the system out of commission. It is surprising that the representation of the EU has been allocated to France as the weakest and poorest member of the Union in respect of strategic wisdom and experience after Brexit. It proves that it is not possible to mention about the fair representation mechanism in proportion to the economic and political powers of the states. For instance, Germany as the pushing power in the UN is not representable while the developing countries such as Turkey and Japan in post–Cold War period have been overlooked with the mentality of the bipolar period. In this respect, the UN does not have the intention, capability, and capacity to come up with the problems transferred to it with a final settlement.

The burning question nowadays is the specialized institutions as the parts of the UN associated with the pandemic. In particular, these institutions have been accused of being transformed into bureaucratic, firm, uncompromising, and self-feeding entities in the course of time. Undoubtedly the WHO has been taken into account as foremost among them because of its confusion in identifying and determining the ways of tackling the pandemic since the initial point of the crisis and this indecisive attitude led to perturb the world public opinion. Especially the United States and the United Kingdom accused the WHO of casting doubt on determining a policy depend on the distorted and manipulative data of China and behaving as if the Chinese representative and diplomatic mission. Above all this institution which was expected to develop vaccines and remedies for the pandemic still hesitated over using the mask as a precaution to the Coronavirus tragically. Surprisingly, WHO exhibits behavior like a figure under the pressure of China and a spokesman for the incomprehensible policies implemented by China.

By the way, Trump took the specialized institutions of the UN under review since the first day of coming into power, especially WHO. While China gives support to such a kind of institutions in order to balance against the threat perceived by the outside world, the Trump administration gave preference to resign from the UNESCO, withdrawn the support from the WHO because of making bad business and dirty cooperation with China, and cut off relations with WTO because of its destabilizing thrusts to the detriment of the United States. In response to this, China attempted to expand its alliance with new and alternative institutions such as Asia Infrastructure Financing Initiative (AIFI) and New Development Bank (NDB) as the founder and holding the right of veto strongly together with Russia, Brazil, India, and South Africa.

Under these circumstances, it is possible to come to the conclusion that the international organizations and institutions have been formed in post–World War II and with the mentality of Cold War and established just for protecting US benefits merely but disguised ambitions were well-hidden in the foundation phase as if they serve for the international community. Therefore, their contributions to global peace, security, and collective welfare remain limited as Roosevelt advised in the establishment process of the UN: "We should forge an international organization just for the sake of American interests and pretended as if serve for humanity" (Hargrove 2000, 68). Above all when the intends of the founding fathers of such organizations like EU, UN, and NATO have been analyzed, it can be easily comprehended that their primary objective is to establish a global empire under the leadership of the United States as the unique state. In line with this, so many times international media organizations declared that all states must deliver their sovereignty rights into the UN outrightly in order to fight against the pandemic by implying paving ways to the global US empire to rule all over the world as a unique state.

As a matter of fact, the most important priority for these organizations is supposed to analyze the newly emerging world order prudentially in line with the changings, transformations, and waving which Coronavirus accelerated in post–Cold War period, to diagnose the problem and find global solutions for global problem with collective conscience by getting rid of US influence, and to reform the system by depending upon reliable, logical, fair, comprehensive, and transparent mechanism. For instance, in accordance with these assumptions, the EU will be open to debate with its inappropriate policies to the human rights, democracy, supremacy of law, and multiculturalism which made it legitimate in front of the world public opinion (Budak 2019, 43). Some implementations related to the fight against the pandemic are contrary to the EU value system such as the declaration of stats of emergency, curfew, lockdown, restriction on individual freedoms by means of the speaking drones, warning applications in case of exceeding the certain limit, and mobile telephone tracking systems. In addition, the problems caused by the pandemic may transform the states more authoritarian, more nationalist, and more protectionist, even the members of the EU. Above all biological threats will be the preeminent perception of security in foreseeable future. Does the EU have any idea and plan for all problems of recent vintage? Who knows?

On the other hand, the revolutionary developments in digital scope must be considered at global level and the international organizations are required to be reorganized themselves in accordance with the wide spreading technologies such as artificial intelligence, big data, internet of things, nanotechnology, and the control of people with face recognition/reading cameras and chips embedded to the brain in order to sustain their existence to provide the global security.

CONCLUSION

Turkish foreign policy is bound to confront local, national, and global challenges in recent years. These confrontations are directly relevant with the emerging new world order which can be described as the multiple administration systems which does not allow emerging an almighty hegemon power and becoming the regional policies prominent and losing the international organizations their legitimacy as the remnants of the Cold War political conditions. This new political atmosphere led to revitalize the frozen conflicts as the inheritance remaining from the last century and leave every state to own destiny and prevail the chaotic and anarchical international system over the world politics. In many respects, this era and conjuncture give Turkey the opportunity to be raising power in the region with its geopolitical horizon and its cultural heritage within the Mediterranean, Balkan, Caucasia, Middle East, and Europe because Turkey includes the identities of these regions in its structure since the past history. The decisive advantage and the geopolitical superiority of Turkey derived from its elements of national power and its fight against the pandemic with great success as well as health infrastructure and protecting national interests especially in Eastern Mediterranean, Syria, and Southern Caucasia thanks to the nationalized defense industry. The imperial past, recent legal but aggressive policy, and unique strategical superiority associated with the glorious achievement against the pandemic lead Turkey to be a global power in the newly established world order.

In fact, the United States desiring to penetrate into the Black Sea and Caucasia is compelled to cooperate and coordinate with Turkey while consolidating the international organizations such as NATO and the EU being in the first place need the moral and material support of Turkey to attain its goal. As expected that the United States will clash against the China professing to be hegemon power over the Central Asian geography which Turkey has a great influence on ethnic, religious, and historical reasons. The Mediterranean admitted as the geopolitical center of the newly emerged world order is a sea along with which Turkey has the longest fronts and maritime boundaries as well as has right to guarantee in Cyprus together with has sponsorship right of the Tripoli government recognized as the only legitimate government in Libya. Lastly, its decisive advantage in the geopolitical position will facilitate the logistic needs, its agricultural and industrial potential and qualified and skilled labor force, and its background of relations with Europe extended to five centuries beside its recent relations within the extent of the Customs Union and the EU membership process, Turkey is a unique country which is secular, democratic within a great harmony, and equipped with western/ modern values, combined Islam and democracy together with the working open market economy, internalizing and adopting a rational legal judicial system will be cut out for cooperating with the European working culture by regarding the commonly shared past history.

REFERENCES

Açıkgöz, Meral. 2015. "Turkey's Visa Policy: A Migration- Mobility Nexus, Summer 2015." *Turkish Policy Quarterly* 14(2): 97–107. Accessed December 12, 2015. http://turkishpolicy.com/article/762/ turkeys-visa-policy-a-migration-mobility-nexus-summer-2015.

Akçadağ, Emine. 2010. "NATO'nun Yeni Stratejik Konsepti: Aktif Angajman, Modern Savunma." Accessed December 27, 2020. http://www.bilgesam.org/tr/index.php?option=com_content&view=article&id=884:natonun-yeni-stratejik-konsepti-aktif-angajman-modern-savunma&catid=122:analizler-guvenlik&Itemid=147.

Arı, Tayyar. 2013. *Uluslararası İlişkilere Giriş*. Bursa: Marmara Kitap Merkezi (MKM) Yayınları.

Attali, Jacquez. 2015. Kriz ve Sonrası: 2008 Krizinin Üzerinden Ufka Bakarken, İstanbul: Ekslibris Yayıncılık. Yayın No: 9.

Aydın, M. 2005. "Geçiş Sürecinde Kimlikler: Orta Asya'da Milliyetçilik, Din ve Bölgesel Güvenlik." In *Küresel Politikada Orta Asya – Avrasya Üçlemesi 1*, edited by Mustafa Aydın, 245–266. Ankara: Nobel Akademik Yayıncılık.

Bakıcı, Fuat. 2019. "Çin Halk Cumhuriyeti, Kuruluşunun 70'inci Yılını Kutluyor." Accessed December 11, 2020. https://www.aa.com.tr/tr/dunya/cin-halk-cumhuriy-eti-kurulusunun-70-inci-yil-donumu-kutluyor/1598509.

Berting, Jan. 2017. *Avrupa: Miras, Meydan Okuma, Vaat*. Translated by Hüsamettin İnaç. Ankara: Adres Yayınları.

Berting, Jan. 2018. *Mağara Duvarından Yansımalar*. Translated by Hüsamettin İnaç. İstanbul: Bilge Kültür Sanat Yayınları.

Budak, Ali. 2019. *Osmanlı Modernleşmesi, Gazetecilik ve Edebiyat*. İstanbul: Bilge Kültür Sanat Yayınları.

Campbell, David. 1992. *Writing Security: United States Foreign Policy and the Politics of Identity*. Minneapolis: University of Minnesota Press.

Campbell, David. 1998. *Writing Security- United States Foreign Policy and the Politics of Identity*. Minneapolis: University of Minnesota Press.

Çetin, Şerife. 2019. "Nato'nun 70. Yıl Kutlamalarında Stoltenberg Çalışanlara Yermek Servis Etti." Accessed December 12, 2020. https://www.aa.com.tr/tr /dunya/natonun-70-yil-kutlamalarinda-stoltenberg-calisanlara-yemek-servis-etti /1673178.

Çomak, Hasret. 2010. "Güvenliğin Yeni Boyutlari, Nato Ve Türkiye." Accessed September 27, 2020. http://www.tasam.org/tr-TR/Ic guvenligin_yeni_boyutlari _nato_ve_turkiye.

Cox, Robert. 1987. *Production, Power and World Order- Social Forces in the Making of History*. New York: Columbia University Press.

Dedeoğlu, Beril. 2008. *Uluslararası Güvenlik ve Strateji*. Second Edition. İstanbul: Yeniyüzyıl Yayınları.

Dedeoğlu, Beril. 2018. *Uluslararası Strateji ve Güvenlik*. Fourth Edition. İstanbul: Yeniyüzyıl Yayınları.

Dural, A. Baran. 2012. "Antonio Gramsci ve Hegemonya, Elektronik." Sosyal Bilimler Dergisi. Kış-2012 Cilt:11, Sayı: 39: 309–321.

Fierke, Karin M. 2007. *Critical Approaches to International Security*. Cambridge: Polity.

Griffiths, James. 2019. *The Great Firewall of China: How to Build and Control an Alternative Version of Internet*. London: Zed Books.

Hargrove, Julia. 2000. *Franklin D. Roosevelt's Four Freedoms Speech*. Dayton: Teaching and Learning Company.

Inac, Hüsamettin, and Fatih Aktaş. 2013. "11 Eylül 2001 Terör Saldırılarının Amerikan Güvenlik Bürokrasisine Etkileri." Akademik Bakış Dergisi, Sayı. 34: 1–19.

İnaç, Hüsamettin, and Selami Erdoğan. 2012. "The Historical Dynamics of Modernizm: A Critical Perspective." 3rd International Symposium on Sustainable Development, May 31 - June 1, 2012. Sarajevo: 661–669.

İnaç, Hüsamettin. 2007. "Rethinking Democracy and Governance in the EU." *Journal of Academic Studies* 9(32), February–April: 1–31.

İnaç, Hüsamettin. 2004. "Identity Problems of Turkey during the European Union Integration Process." *Journal of Economic and Social Research*, 6(2): 33–62.

İnaç, Hüsamettin. 2020. "Yeni Dünya Düzeni Bağlamında Azerbaycan-Ermenistan Çatışması ve Kafkas Baharı." M5 Ulusal Güvenlik, Savunma ve Strateji Dergisi, Yıl: 46, Sayı: 352: 34–44.

İnaç, Hüsamettin. 2016. Türkiye'nin Kimlik Problemleri. Adres Yayınları.

İnaç, Hüsamettin. 2018. "The Possibility of Multicultural Practice During the Age of Collective Identities in Line With Arab Spring." Akademik Bakış Dergisi, Ocak-Şubat, Sayı 65: 306–315.

Köksay, Fulya. 2017. ABD-Çin İlişkileri (2001-2008). DER Yayınları.

Köksay, Fulya. 2020. "Kopenhag Ekolü Bağlamında Siber Güvenlik: Kavramsal ve Teoretik Bir Analiz." In *Güvenlik, Teknoloji ve Yeni Tehditler*, editted by Ali Burak Darıcılı, 355–382. Ankara: Nobel Akademik Yayıncılık.

Lukacs, John. 2018. *Yirminci Yüzyılın Sonu.* Translated by Mehmet Harmancı. Ketebe Yayınları.

Örs, H. Birsen. 2009. "Postmodern Dünyada İdeolojinin Dönüşümü." İstanbul Üniversitesi Siyasal Bilgiler Fakültesi Dergisi, No:40: 1–12.

Rasmussen, Greg. 2001. "Great Power Concerts in Historical Perspectives." In *The New Great Power Coalition Toward a World Concert of Nations*, edited by Richard Rosecrance, 203–220. Maryland: Rowman&Littlefield Publishers.

Roham, Alvandi. 2016. *Nixon, Kissinger, and the Shah: The United States and Iran in the Cold War.* New York: Oxford University Press.

Seibert, Thomas. 2019. Turkey's ties with EU, US under pressure as Ankara pulls away from traditional allies. Accessed December 27, 2020. https://thearabweekly.com/turkeys-ties-eu-us-under-pressure-ankara-pulls-away-traditional-allies.

UNCTAD. 2000. World Invest Report 2020. Accessed November 12, 2020 https://unctad.org/webflyer/world-investment-report-2020.

Üstünel, Rüstem. 2015. "2003 Yılı Sonrası Irak'taki Gelişmelerin Türkiye'nin Güvenliğine Etkilerinin İncelenmesi." Unpublished Master Thesis, Ankara Kara Harp Okulu.

About the Contributors

Ahmet Salih İkiz works as faculty in Political Science and International Relations at Muğla Sıtkı Koçman University, Turkey. He holds MSc degrees in International Financial Management from Istanbul University and International Trade and Finance from Lancaster University. He completed his PhD on the shadow economy and economic growth in Turkey at Dokuz Eylül University, Turkey. He has published on EU studies, the shadow economy, and the Turkish economy. He had research trips to Russia, Kazakhstan, and abroad.

Emre Alkin was born in 1969 in Istanbul. He graduated from Saint-Michel French High School in Istanbul and B.A. from Istanbul University Faculty of Economics English Economics in 1991. The same year he was accepted as a research assistant to the Istanbul University Faculty of Economics. He received the title of associate professor in the theory of economics when he was doing his military services in 1997, as a project officer in F-16 Tactical Aircraft Systems. Prof. Dr. Emre Alkin wrote books about risk management and financial institutions and he was on the board of management and worked as a consultant for several investment companies. He became a professor in 2002. He participated in the business development of Cukurova Holding, Anadolu Industry Holding, Dogan Holding, and Altınbaş Holding in various sectors. Emre Alkin worked as an economy commentator for TV Channels such as TV8, FOX, CNNTURK, and CNBC-E and wrote columns for newspapers. Between 2000 and 2014, he was on duty as secretary general of the Turkish Exporters Assembly, member of the National Tax Council, secretary general of Federation of Captive Finance Companies, secretary general of Turkish Football Federation, and member of UEFA Marketing Committee. Today he is a non-executive board member of Galatasaray Inc. Prof. Alkin gives lectures and also there are books written by himself in Turkish and English. He held various positions in GSM and Telecommunication, International Financial İnstitutions, Payment Systems, Energy, and Iron-Steel Industry. Furthermore, he gives economy classes at the Altınbaş University and continues its mission as vice president. He still takes part in international projects about payment systems and financial management. Today, Prof. Alkin is Columnist in the business newspaper *DUNYA* and have two best-seller novel in Turkish about socio-economics and writes about new dimensions in the business life in the various magazines. He has two sons and speaks French and English. He is currently Rector of Ayvansaray University in İstanbul.

Hüseyin Bağcı is a professor of International Relations at the Middle East Technical University in Ankara and the chair of the department since October 2011. In 1988, he received his PhD in Political Science from the Rheinische Friedrich-Wilhelms-University in Bonn. He was a guest researcher at the German Society for Foreign Affairs (DGAP) in Bonn, and Senior Fellow at the Center for European Integration Studies (ZEI) in Bonn and at the Landesverteidigungsakademie und Militarwissenshaftliches Büro des Bundesministeriums für Landesverteidigung in Vienna. He has published several books and a large number of articles on Turkish Foreign Policy and Turkish-German relations. Prof. Bağcı is a famous TV and Radio Commentator in Turkey. Prof. Bağcı is a member of IISS in London and Center for European Policy Studies (CEPS), Brussels, Belgium. He is also deputy director of Foreign Policy Institute in Ankara. Prof. Bağcı has been visiting professor at the University of Bonn as Anna Maria Schimmel Professor, 2007, University of Rome "La Sapienza," 2007 (Italy), and University of Lublin, 2008 (Poland), and 2010–2011 Humboldt University Berlin (Germany). Prof. Bağcı is also widely quoted by the national and international press. Prof. Bagci is the Chair of the International Relations Department since 2001.

Ayşe Aylin Bayar is Associate Professor of Economics at Istanbul Technical University. Her main areas of research are Labor Economics and Macroeconomics, in particular inequalities in the labor market, poverty and income distribution. Aylin holds MA in Economics and a MA in Management and a PhD degree in Management Engineering from ITU. She has had the opportunity to serve as researcher in EU Project Increasing the Institutional Capacity of the Ministry of Family and Social Policies in the Field of Social Inclusion Policies (ICMoFSP)_and several Erasmus+ Programme projects. In addition to the skills developed in her research experiences at ITU, she also strengthened her research skills through two visiting scholarship positions at University of Laval, Canada and University of Sussex, United Kingdom.

Cengiz Mert Bulut currently pursues his PhD studies in the Department of Global Studies at Shanghai University as a sponsored scholarship student affiliated with the Ministry of National Education of Turkey. After completing his bachelor's degree at Ege University, he received his master's degree in International Relations from Dokuz Eylül University in 2017. Bulut coauthored a book chapter from an international publisher. During his doctorate studies at Shanghai University, Bulut has been awarded the Chinese Government Outstanding International Student Scholarship in the year 2019 by China Scholarship Council. Bulut continues to work on foreign aid provided by China in the African continent.

Murat Çemrek is instructor and chair in the Department of International Relations at Necmettin Erbakan University, Konya, Turkey. He graduated from the Department of Political Science and Public Administration at Middle East Technical University (1996) and completed his MA (1997, Thesis; "Özal's Politics with Special Reference to Religion") and PhD (2003, Thesis; "Formation and Representation of Interests in Turkish Political Economy: The Case of MÜSİAD [Independent Industrialists' and Businessmen's Association]"), respectively. Çemrek had his post-doc research in "Turkey-EU Relations: The Question of Human Rights in the Collegium Budapest," Institute for Advanced Studies, Hungary (2004). He taught in several universities: Necmettin Erbakan, Selcuk (Konya, Turkey), Police Academy (Ankara, Turkey), Ataturk Alatoo (Bishkek, Kyrgyzstan), Al Farabi (Almaty, Kazakhstan), and gave several seminars in numerous universities: Karamanoglu Mehmet Bey (Karaman, Turkey), International Hoca Ahmet Yesevi Turkish-Kazakh University (Turkistan, Kazakhstan), Oslo University (Norway), University of Szczecin (Poland), Central European University (Budapest, Hungary), Oradea University (Romania). He is a member of various international academic organizations and journals as well as an organization committee member and attendant to varied conferences, summer schools, and workshops in thirty countries. Çemrek also worked at different administrative layers as vice-chair, chair, and Department Erasmus coordinator in the Department of International Relations at Selcuk University from 2004 September to 2012 September as well as the founding director of the Eurasian Research Institute in Almaty (International Hoca Ahmet Yesevi Turkish-Kazakh University) from 2012 September to June 2014. He has also been the Erasmus+ coordinator and the director of Erol Güngör Turkic Diaspora Research Center at Necmettin Erbakan University from 2014 July and November, respectively, till February 2018. He has also been the academic representative for Turkish Scholarships interviews in Iran, Georgia, Russia, Kazakhstan, Kyrgyztsan, Tajikistan, and Mongolia during 2012–2017. His research interests include globalization, Turkish Foreign Policy, Middle East, Central Asia, as well as Islam and politics.

Emre Erdoğan is the head of the Department of International Relations at Istanbul Bilgi University. With a doctoral degree in Political Science from Boğaziçi University, he has served as a researcher and senior consultant in various projects in academia and civil society. His research focuses on political participation, foreign policy, and public opinion, child and youth well-being, methodology, and statistics. He extensively studies and publishes about youth in Turkey, integration of Syrian refugee youth in Turkey, othering, polarization, and populism.

Ali Serdar Erdurmaz had MA on "International Relations" in "Université Libre de Brussels/Belgium" during his external duty as "Military Attaché and NATO Officer" (1987–1990). In 2003, He got his PhD on the same subject in "Gazi University/Ankara." He has written the book "Weapons of Mass Destruction in The Middle East, Arms Control and Turkey" and published various studies and articles in Turkish, English, German, and Russian languages. He wrote three different books on Libya, Arab Spring, and disarmament. Dr. Ali Serdar Erdurmaz was awarded as the associated professor in October 2013 and a full professor in 2020. He was the chairman of the political sciences and international department in Hasan Kalyoncu University between 2011 and 2019. In 2019–2021, he has been in Istanbul Gelişim University as a full professor. Now, prof. Dr. Erdurmaz is a Security Studies director in Foreign Policy Institute in Ankara, working with prof. Dr. Hüseyin Bağci. Prof. Erdurmaz study on Libya, Eastern Mediterranean issues, NATO, Middle East security problems, Terrorism and Weapons of Mass Destructions.

Öner Günçavdi is professor of Economic Development at the Faculty of Management, Istanbul Technical University (ITU). He holds a BSc degree from *ITU*, MSc degrees from *ITU* and the *University of Warwick*, and finally PhD degree from the *University of Nottingham*. He is the author of two books: *From Dream to Reality: Elginkan Holding Group in the Process of Turkish Industrialisation* (2009, Istanbul: Turkish History Foundation) and *The End of the Road: Growth, Interest Rate, Distribution and Discourse of New Turkey* (2015, Ankara: Efil Publishing Company). He published various research papers in domestic and international academic journals such as the *Journal of Development Economics*, the *Journal of International Development*, *Applied Economics*, *the Journal of Policy Modelling*, *Turkish Studies*, and *Empirical Economics*. He is also the author of various chapters in international book projects. He widely writes about the different aspects (such as international trade, the business history of the Turkish corporate sector, income distribution, and poverty) of the Turkish economy and development economics.

Hüsamettin İnaç was born in Uşak (located very close to İzmir) and has graduated from Marmara University International Relations Department in 1997. After completing his master in Sociology and Anthropology Department of the same university with the thesis "Sociological Comparison of Marx and Pareto," he wrote a PhD thesis titled "Identity Problems of Turkey during the EU Integration Process" and graduated from Marmara University European Community Institute in 2002. Prof. Dr. İnaç who studied at the Dumlupinar University in the Faculty of Economics and Administrative Sciences between 1998 and 2009 left when he was appointed as the secretary general for Zafer (Northern Aegean as former name) Regional Development Agency covering Kütahya, Afyon, Manisa, and Uşak cities in order to use his theoretical knowledge on the practical scope of economic development and regional growth for a year. Professor Hüsamettin İnaç is still working in Dumlupinar University Political Science and International Relations Department since 2010 by focusing on the theory of International Relations, foreign policy, Turkey-EU relations, political sociology, national/ethnic identity issues, and international organizations. Prof. İnaç is the author of eleven books. Prof. Dr. İnaç has been appointed as the professor and the chairman of the Political Sciences and International Relations department in August 2013.

Bahadır Kaleağasi is president of the Paris Bosphorus Institute, lecturer at the Galatasaray University in Istanbul, Brussels Energy Club's honorary chairperson, and board member of or adviser to several companies, think tanks, and nongovernmental organizations. He was formerly an academic at Université Libre de Bruxelles, a researcher for the European Commission's Forward Studies Unit, successively EU representative, international coordinator, and CEO of Turkey's main business association, TUSIAD, and executive board member of BusinessEurope (The Confederation of European Business). He is the author of several books on international affairs, sustainable development, and Turkey.

Pinar Kaynak graduated from the Department of Economics at Middle East Technical University (METU) in 2009. She received her master's (2012) degree from Lausanne University Hautes Etudes Commerciales (HEC) Department of Economics. She worked as a researcher in the Policy Integration and Employment departments at the International Labor Organization (ILO) Geneva headquarters between 2012 and 2013, and at TEPAV between 2013 and 2014. Kaynak, who received a full scholarship from the Swiss National Science Foundation, completed her doctoral studies in 2020 in Applied Economics at ETH Zurich. Since 2014, she has been contributing to the Social Policies Application and Research Center (SPM) with the "Industry Developments and Employment Bulletin," which is regularly published every month and involves labor market forecasts. Her main areas of interest are international trade, labor markets, and panel econometrics. Languages she speaks include Turkish, English, German, and French.

Hasan Kazdağli received his PhD in economics from Hacettepe University in Ankara. Later, he worked as a lecturer and professor in the Department of Economics of the same university for more than thirty years. His main areas of expertise are public economics, international economics, education economics, and digital economics. He progressed in his professional career as an academic and practitioner. Dr. Kazdağli worked as a senior consultant at the Turkish Higher Education Council and the Ministry of National Education and played critical roles in higher education planning in Turkey. He also served as vice-rector for four years at Hacettepe University and contributed to various universities in Turkey. Professor Kazdağlı took part in the establishment of Pamukkale University and manage the university as a rector for more than eight years. Pamukkale University, today, is one of the leading higher education institutes in the country, with some 50,000 students in Denizli, an industrial city in western Turkey. He produced numerous reports for the Turkish Government on international economic relations and investment incentives, and human capital development in Turkey. He held some senior management positions in the Government—Deputy Undersecretary for Defense Industries of Turkey; a member of the board of directors of the Turkish Aerospace Industries (TAI); and Chairman of the board of the General Directorate of Student Loans and Dormitories. He acted as the Chief Economic Advisor to the Minister of Economy between 2013 and 2016. In this role, he actively participated in the policymaking process and bilateral meetings with some countries and trade negotiations with the EU and the United States. He participated in some projects sponsored by the World Bank, the European Union, and UNICEF. He served as a Senior Consultant for Price Waterhouse Coopers in Turkey. He is currently the president of the Turkish Economic Association, a ninety-two-year-old nongovernmental organization.

Abdurrahim Sağir is a PhD student in the field of International Relations at Ankara Social Science University. After earning a bachelor's degree in Chinese Law from Wuhan University, he received his master's degree in International Relations and Diplomacy from Shanghai University in 2019.

His research focuses on China-Middle East relations, Chinese Diplomacy, and Chinese think tanks. He has published a journal article and a book chapter on the development of Chinese think tanks.

Göktuğ Sönmez got his bachelor's degree in International Relations from Bilkent University, his master's degree in International Relations from London School of Economic (LSE), and his PhD in Politics and International Studies from the School of Oriental and African Studies (SOAS), University of London. His research areas are Radicalization and Violent Extremism, Non-State Armed Actors, Turkish Foreign Policy, and Energy Politics. He conducted research on these areas at several institutions and think tanks including the Center for Strategic Research of the Ministry of Foreign Affairs of the Republic of Turkey, BOTAŞ, and the Global Strategy Institute. He is the director of Security Studies at ORSAM and teaches at Necmettin Erbakan University, International Relations Department. He published many pieces in national and international journals, comments on radicalization and terrorism topics, as well as Turkish foreign policy on several media outlets, attended many international meetings and conferences primarily on Radicalization and Violent Extremism, and occasionally wrote op-eds for newspapers.

www.ingramcontent.com/pod-product-compliance
Ingram Content Group UK Ltd.
Pitfield, Milton Keynes, MK11 3LW, UK
UKHW020840290926
15470UKWH00004B/1467

9 781793 638502